DAY HIKING
South
Cascades

East Fork Lewis River

Wildflower masses on Silver Star Mountain

Previous page: Meadows of wildflowers on the hike to Goat Lake

Next page: Mount St. Helens and Spirit Lake from Norway Pass

Mount Rainier from the summit of Hamilton Buttes

View of Indian Racetrack from Red Mountain

Previous page: Lupines and balsamroot on Dalles Mountain

Mount Adams as seen from the summit of Snagtooth Mountain

Beargrass on ridgeline near the summit of Silver Star Mountain

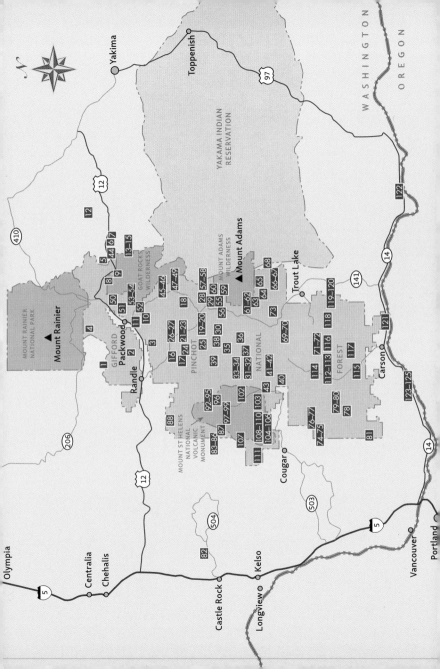

DAY HIKING
South
Cascades

mt. st. helens / mt. adams / columbia gorge

Dan A. Nelson
photography by
Alan L. Bauer

THE MOUNTAINEERS BOOKS

THE MOUNTAINEERS BOOKS
*is the nonprofit publishing arm of The Mountaineers Club, an
organization founded in 1906 and dedicated to the exploration,
preservation, and enjoyment of outdoor and wilderness areas.*

1001 SW Klickitat Way, Suite 201, Seattle, WA 98134

© 2007 by Dan A. Nelson

First edition, 2007

Manufactured in the United States of America

Copy Editor: Jane Crosen
Cover and Book Design: The Mountaineers Books
Layout: Jennifer Shontz, Red Shoe Design
Cartographers: Marge Mueller, Gray Mouse Graphics; Jennifer Shontz, Red Shoe Design
Photographer: Alan L. Bauer

Cover photograph: *Wildflower explosion near the summit of Silver Star Mountain looking toward
Mount Adams*
Frontispiece: *Lupine meadows around Killen Creek, looking toward Mount Adams*

Maps shown in this book were produced using National Geographic's *TOPO!*
software. For more information, go to *www.nationalgeographic.com/topo.*

Library of Congress Cataloging-in-Publication Data
Nelson, Dan A.
    Day hiking South Cascades / Dan A. Nelson ; photos by Alan L. Bauer.
        p.   cm.
    ISBN 978-1-59485-045-5 (pbk. : alk. paper) 1. Hiking—Washington (State)—Cascade Range
Region—Guidebooks. 2. Cascade Range Region (Wash.)—Guidebooks. 3. Washington (State)—
Guidebooks. I. Title.
GV199.42.W22C375 2007
796.5109797'5—dc22
                                                                                    2007004060

 Printed on recycled paper

Table of Contents

LEWIS RIVER REGION

GOAT ROCKS REGION

MOUNT ADAMS AREA

INDIAN HEAVEN / TRAPPER CREEK REGION

SIOUXON / SILVER STAR AREA

MOUNT ST. HELENS AREA

THE COLUMBIA RIVER GORGE AREA

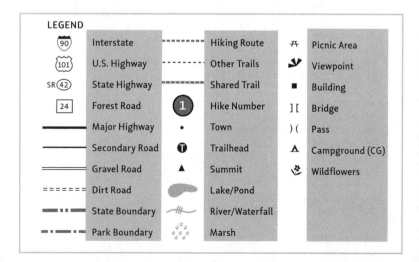

A Quick Guide to the Hikes

Use this guide to quickly find a hike you'll like. These hike listings are organized according to popular features, followed by a summary of additional information. To pick a hike:

- Glance over the categories to find the one you want.
- Narrow your choices to those close to where you are or where you're going: WP means White Pass Corridor / Cowlitz River Valley; DD means Dark Divide / Cispus Area; LR means Lewis River Region; GR means Goat Rocks Region; MA means Mount Adams Area; IH means Indian Heaven / Trapper Creek Region; SS means Siouxon / Silver Star Area; MSH means Mount St. Helens Area; CG means The Columbia River Gorge Area.
- Find a hike with a distance and difficulty level that will work well for you.

Note that mileage for some hikes is one-way and for others is round-trip; refer to the full description for these and other details and driving directions.

No.	Hike Name	Area	Miles	Difficulty	Highlights
MOST FAMILY-FRIENDLY HIKES					
5	Sand Lake	WP	6.0	easy to moderate	swimming, huckleberries
8	Clear Fork-Lily Lake	WP	3.0	easy	river, fishing
43	Cedar Flats Nature Trail	LR	1.0	easy	picturesque river, lush plant life
56	Council Bluff	MA	3.0	easy to moderate	cool lake, views from summit
91	Ryan Lake	MSH	1.0	easy	interpretive loop, views of Mount St. Helens
BEST HIKES TO LAKES FOR WADING OR SWIMMING					
29	High Lakes Ramble	DD	5.4	easy to moderate	series of mountain lakes
44	Shoe Lake	GR	14.0	moderate	alpine lake surrounded by wildflowers
51	Packwood Lake	GR	10.0	easy to moderate	mile-long lake with campground
55	Takhlakh Lake Loop	MA	3.0	easy to moderate	lakeshore trail leads through lava field
70	Blue Lake	IH	13.0	moderate	trout-filled lake, berry-filled meadows
96	Meta Lake	MSH	1.3	easy	lake in forest that survived 1980 eruption
BEST HIKES ALONG CREEKS AND RIVERS					
37	Quartz Creek	LR	8.0	moderate	mountain creek, canyon walls
38	French Creek	LR	7.0	moderate to strenuous	creek through dense forest
40	Curly Creek	LR	1.0	easy	creek, Lewis River, waterfalls

No.	Hike Name	Area	Miles	Difficulty	Highlights
BEST HIKES ALONG CREEKS AND RIVERS					
42	Speed onto Lewis River	LR	2.0	easy to moderate	beautiful river with steelhead runs
75	Lower Siouxon Creek	SS	6.5	easy to moderate	forest hike, evidence of past fires
111	Kalama River	MSH	4.0	moderate	beautiful river valley, forest
BEST HIKES FOR VIEWING WATERFALLS					
41	Big Creek Falls	LR	1.5	easy	ancient forest, awe-inspiring waterfall
76	Upper Siouxon–Horseshoe Falls	SS	4.5	moderate	waterfall on wild river
95	Harmony Falls	MSH	2.0	easy to moderate	waterfall altered by eruption of Mount St. Helens
112	Lower Falls Creek Trail	CG	5.0	moderate	100-foot waterfall in thick forest
124	Hardy and Rodney Falls	CG	3.5	moderate to strenuous	two waterfalls
BEST HIKES FOR FINDING SOLITUDE					
15	North Fork Tieton-Tieton Pass	WP	11.7	strenuous	deep pine forests, view of Tieton Peak
49	Coleman Weedpatch	GR	9.0	moderate to strenuous	wildflower meadows, ridge views
52	Glacier Lake	GR	4.0	easy to moderate	alpine lake, ancient forest
77	Horseshoe Ridge	SS	8.0	strenuous	wildlife, dense forests
109	Sheep Canyon	MSH	4.5	moderate	views of Mount St. Helens
BEST HIKES FOR BIRDWATCHING					
21	Dark Meadow	DD	7.0	moderate to strenuous	meadow of wildlife and wildflowers
31	Cussed Hollow	LR	5.0	moderate	habitat for grouse, bobcats
34	Wright Meadow	LR	3.0	easy to moderate	nesting grounds for birds
35	Snagtooth Mountain	LR	3.5	easy to moderate	wildlife, excellent views
67	Gotchen Creek–Aiken Lava Bed East	MA	11.0	strenuous	fields of vanilla leaf and beargrass
BEST HIKES FOR PICKING BERRIES					
20	Sunrise Peak	DD	3.0	moderate	360-degree views, great at sunrise
45	Goat Lake–Jordan Basin	GR	12.0	strenuous	wildflower meadows, alpine lakes, peaks
46	Snowgrass Flat	GR	8.2	moderate to strenuous	wildflower meadows, views of Cascade volcanoes

No.	Hike Name	Area	Miles	Difficulty	Highlights
BEST HIKES FOR PICKING BERRIES					
60	Killen Meadows	MA	10.0	strenuous	mountain views, many types of meadows
69	Bird Mountain	IH	7.0	strenuous	exceptional mountain views, alpine lakes
73	Sleeping Beauty Peak	IH	3.0	moderate	great views, old-growth forest
HIKES THAT FEATURE LOCAL HISTORY					
72	Indian Racetrack	IH	5.0	moderate	meadow where Native Americans gathered
75	Lower Siouxon Creek	SS	6.5	easy to moderate	cabin used by firefighters in the 1930s
87	Harrys Ridge	MSH	8.0	moderate	home of man who refused to evacuate during eruption
99	Windy Ridge Trail	MSH	4.0	strenuous	old logging road used by evacuees during eruption
105	Ape Caves	MSH	2.6	easy	underground lava tubes discovered by a 1950s outdoor club
HIKES THROUGH WONDERFUL FORESTS					
4	Tatoosh Ridge	WP	8.0	moderate to strenuous	old-growth forest of Douglas-fir, hemlock, wildflowers
37	Quartz Creek	LR	8.0	moderate	old groves of Douglas-fir and western red cedar
48	Walupt Creek Loop	GR	12.0	moderate to strenuous	dense pine forests
58	Muddy Fork Lava Bed	MA	5.0	moderate to strenuous	large lava bed, open forests
103	Jackpine Shelter	MSH	1.0	easy	interpretive trail through ancient forest
HIKES WITH OUTSTANDING VIEWS					
1	High Rock	WP	3.5	moderate to strenuous	views from historic fire lookout
22	Juniper Ridge	DD	6.0	moderate to strenuous	views of South Cascade volcanoes
57	Potato Hill	MA	3.0	moderate	views of Mount Adams, Hamilton Butte
123	Hamilton Mountain	CG	9.0	moderate	views of waterfalls, Columbia River, Mount Hood
125	Beacon Rock	CG	2.0	moderate	views of Columbia River Gorge

Introduction

The more advanced we become with labor-saving technology, the less time we have to ourselves. All those timesaving tools merely open the door for time-eating traps at work and home. Americans are working more hours each year, with less vacation time taken, than they have at any time since World War II.

That helps explain why more and more hikers are forgoing multiday backpacking trips in favor of daylong outings. With fewer free hours—and more hobbies competing for that free time—hikers seem to favor trail excursions that can be done in a day.

To help modern hikers get their wilderness fix, we offer this new series: the Day Hiking series. We've set out to find the best routes in each region that can be enjoyed as a day trip. Of course, the length of day will vary, depending on where you start; drive times to, say, the Indian Heaven area will be considerably longer for hikers starting from Olympia than for those coming from Vancouver, Washington.

The book you hold focuses on the hiking routes found in the southern portion of Washington's Cascades, including those accessed off U.S. Highway 12 (White Pass Highway) and all points south. From the center of the William O. Douglas Wilderness to the Columbia River, the South Cascades cradle some of the most remarkable wildland trails in the country. This region is thick in human history and natural splendor.

The South Cascades are a land of violent birth. This is volcano country, through and through. The region boasts the looming volcanic peaks of Mount Adams and Mount St. Helens. The craggy teeth of the Goat Rocks Wilderness are remnants of a once massive volcano that towered thousands of feet higher than anything currently standing—even mighty Mount Rainier. Hikers will find broad expanses of black basalt lava beds sprawling around the flank of Mount Adams and filling the valleys near the Indian Heaven Wilderness. Of course, the still-smoking crater of Mount St. Helens is a constant reminder of the volcanic nature of this landscape.

The powerful forces of volcanism, though, aren't the only forces at work here. Wind and rain, snow and ice all shape this stunning landscape. Countless pothole lakes—lakes formed in broad catch basins in the volcanic rock and soil—fill the southern half of the William O. Douglas Wilderness and the entire expanse of the Indian Heaven Wilderness.

The South Cascades of Washington receive far fewer backcountry visitors than the regions farther north. I hope this book helps change that. The beautiful South Cascades warrant as much attention and appreciation as any other part of the state. More, in fact, as this rugged, remote country remains incredibly pristine.

USING THIS BOOK

These Day Hiking books strike a fine balance. They were developed to be easy to use while still providing enough detail to help you explore a region's backcountry. As a result, these guidebooks include all the information you need to find and enjoy the hikes, but leave enough room for you to make your own discoveries as you venture into areas new to you.

Opposite: Large bull elk in the winter

Ratings and Trail Facts

Every trail described in this book features a detailed "trail facts" section. Not all of the details here are facts, however.

Each hike starts with two ratings: each has a **rating** of one to five stars for its overall appeal, and each route has a **difficulty** rating on a scale of 1 to 5. Both are subjective, based on the author's impressions of each route, but the ratings do follow a formula of sorts. The overall rating is based on scenic beauty, natural wonder, and other unique qualities such as solitude potential and wildlife-viewing opportunities.

The difficulty rating is based on trail length, the steepness of the trail, and how difficult it is to hike. Generally, trails rated more difficult (4 or 5) are longer and steeper than average. But it's not a simple equation. A short, steep trail over talus slopes may be rated 5, while a long, smooth trail with little elevation gain may be rated 2.

To help explain those difficulty ratings, you'll also find the **round-trip mileage** (unless otherwise noted as one-way), total **elevation gain**, and **high point** for each route listed in the information blocks. The distances are not always exact mileages—trails weren't measured with calibrated instruments—but the numbers are those used by cartographers and land managers (who have measured many of the trails). The elevation gains report the cumulative difference between the high and low point on the route. It is worth noting that not all high points are at the end of the trail—a route may run over a high ridge before dropping to a lake basin, for instance.

Another subjective note you'll find in this information block is the hikable **season**. Many trails can be enjoyed from the time they lose their winter snowpack right up until they are buried in fresh snow the following fall. But snowpacks vary from year to year, so a trail that is open in May one year may be snow-covered until mid-July the next. The hiking season for each trail is an estimate based on past experience, but before you venture out, it's worth contacting the land manager to get a report on current conditions.

To help with trip planning, each hike provides details on what agency to **contact** for current trail conditions and permits, as well as which **maps** you'll want to have on your hike. Hikes in this guidebook use Green Trails maps, which are based on the standard 7.5-minute USGS topographical maps. Green Trails maps are aailable at most outdoor retailers in the state, as well as at many U.S. Forest Service visitor centers.

Given that we now live in a digital world, **GPS coordinates** for each trailhead are provided—use these both to get to the trail and to help you get back to your car if you get caught out in a storm or wander off-trail.

Finally, the **status** of several "endangered," "threatened," or "saved" trails is noted for trails that are in danger of disappearing due to lack of maintenance, or have been saved thanks to volunteer efforts. The imperiled trails may be officially recognized as trails in trouble, but not always. Sometimes, we listed trails as "threatened" or "endangered" even though land managers may consider them fine—this is especially true when destructive uses are allowed, such as motorcycle use of trails on steep terrain or in sensitive meadow or wetland areas.

You will also note small icons throughout the book. Trails that we found to be dog-friendly, kid-friendly, barrier-free (for people with disabilities), or of historical interest are marked by these icons. The icons are meant to be merely helpful suggestions, however, and should not be a limiting factor for your hiking. If you and the kids want to hike a trail that does not have a Kid icon, go for it! Same holds true for dogs, though you might want to check with the land manager before venturing out with your dog since canines are restricted in some areas, especially on trails outside the National Forest Service lands.

 Kid-friendly

 Dog-friendly

 Barrier-free

 Historical

 Endangered trail

 Saved trail

PLANNING AND ACCESS

The route descriptions provide a basic overview of what you might find on your hike, directions to get you to the trailhead, and then more detailed highlights of the actual trails you'll be exploring.

Of course, you'll need some of the information long before you ever leave home. As you plan your trips, several issues need to be considered. These include the following.

Permits and Regulations

You can't set off out your door these days without first making sure you're not breaking the rules. In an effort to keep our wilderness areas wild and our trails safe and well maintained, the land managers—especially the National Park Service and the U.S. Forest Service—have implemented a sometimes complex set of rules and regulations governing the use of public lands.

Virtually all trails in national forests in Washington (and Oregon) fall under the Region 6 Forest Pass Program. Simply stated, in order to park legally at any national forest trailhead in USFS Region 6 (Washington and Oregon), you must display a Northwest Forest Pass decal on your windshield. These sell for $5 per day or $30 for an annual pass good throughout Region 6. The Northwest Forest Pass is also required at most trailheads within the Mount St. Helens National Volcanic Monument.

In addition to the parking pass, when you hike in wilderness areas you must pick up and fill out a wilderness permit at the trailhead registration box (sometimes located at the wilderness boundary if the trail doesn't immediately enter a designated wilderness). These are free and unlimited (though that may change).

Weather

Mountain weather in general is famously unpredictable, but the Cascade Range stretches that unpredictability to sometimes absurd lengths. The high, jagged nature of the mountains, coupled with their proximity to the Pacific Ocean, makes them magnets for every bit of moisture in the atmosphere.

As the moist air comes rushing in off the Pacific, it hits the western front of the Cascades. The air is pushed up the slopes of the mountains, often forming clouds and eventually rain, feeding the wet rain forests that dominate the western slopes. By the time the airstream crests the Cascades and starts down the eastern slopes, the clouds have lost their moisture loads, leaving the east-side forests dry and filled with open stands of drought-resistant pine. This creates a "dryside ecosystem."

Where east meets west, the wet clouds hit the dry heat, often creating thunderstorms. Hikers on the trail must be aware of this potential, because the storms can brew up at any month of the year. Thunderstorms can also develop quickly with little warning, and a hiker stuck on a high pass becomes a good target for a lightning bolt.

To reduce the dangers of lightning, if thunderstorms are forecast or develop while you are in the mountains:

• Use a NOAA weather radio (i.e., a radio set

When lightning strikes a nearby ridge, seek shelter soon!

to tune in to one of the national weather forecast frequencies) to keep abreast of the latest weather information.

- Avoid travel on mountaintops and ridge crests.
- Avoid setting up camp in narrow valleys, gullies, or ridge tops. Instead, look for campsites in broad, open valleys and meadows, keeping away from large rock formations.
- Stay well away from bodies of water.
- If your hair stands on end, or you feel static shocks, move immediately—the static electricity you feel could very well be a precursor to a lightning strike.
- If there is a shelter or building nearby, get into it. Don't take shelter under trees, however, especially in open areas.
- If there is no shelter available, and lightning is flashing, remove your pack (the metal stays or frame are natural electrical conduits) and crouch down, balancing on the balls of your feet until the lighting clears the area.

Of course, thunderstorms aren't the only weather hazard hikers face. A sudden rainsquall can push temperatures down 15 or 20 degrees in a matter of minutes. Even if you're dressed for hot summer hiking, you should be prepared for such temperature drops and the accompanying soaking rain if you want to avoid hypothermia.

If the temperature drop is great enough, you can miss the rain and get hit instead by snow. I've seen snowstorms blow through the Cascades every month of the year, with as much as a foot falling on some routes in late August.

Besides fresh-fallen snow, summer hikers need to be aware of snowfields left over from the previous winter's snowpack. Depending on the severity of the past winter, and the weather conditions of the spring and early summer, some trails may melt out in June while others remain snow-covered well into August or beyond—some years, sections never melt out. In addition to treacherous footing and difficulties in routefinding, these lingering snowfields can be prone to avalanches or slides.

Road and Trail Conditions

Trails in general change little from year to year. Though they truly are manmade structures in rugged wilderness settings, trails really are durable. But change can and does occur, and sometimes it occurs very quickly. One brutal storm can change a river's course, washing out sections of trail (or access road) in moments. Wind can drop trees across trails by the hundreds, making the paths unhikable. And snow can obliterate trails well into the heart of summer.

Access roads face similar threats, and are in fact more susceptible to washouts and closures than the trails themselves. With this in mind, each hike in this book lists the land manager's contact information for each route included in this book, so you can call or email prior to your trip and ensure that your chosen road and trail are open and safe to travel.

Volunteer Trail Maintenance

On the topic of trail conditions, it is vital that we thank the countless volunteers who donate tens of thousands of hours to wilderness trail maintenance each year. The Washington Trails Association (WTA) alone coordinates upwards of 60,000 hours of volunteer trail maintenance each year.

As massive as the volunteer efforts have become, however, there is always a need for more. Our wilderness trail system faces ever-increasing threats, including (but by no means limited to) ever-shrinking trail funding, inappropriate trail uses, and conflicting land management policies and practices.

With this in mind, this guide includes several trails that are threatened and in danger of becoming unhikable. This "endangered trail" status is noted in the route descriptions, along with suggestions for how you can help these trails.

On the other side of the coin, we've also been blessed with some great trail successes in recent years, thanks in large part to that massive volunteer movement spearheaded

Nicole Mode enjoying a Washington Trails Association work party

by the WTA. We've noted these "saved trails," too, to help show you that individual efforts do make a difference. As you enjoy these saved trails, we hope you'll stop and consider the contributions made by your fellow hikers to help protect our trail resources.

Wilderness Ethics and Trail Giants

As wonderful as the volunteer trail maintenance programs are, they aren't the only way to help save trails. Indeed, these on-the-ground efforts provide quality trails today, but to ensure the long-term survival of our trails—and the wildlands they cross—we all need to practice sound wilderness ethics.

Strong, positive wilderness ethics embrace such principles as making sure you leave the wilderness as pure—or purer—than you found it. But it goes much deeper than that. Ensuring that our wildlands stay wild requires far more effort than simply picking up after ourselves when we go for a hike. The wilderness ethic must carry over into our daily lives. We need to make sure our elected officials and public land managers recognize and respond to our wilderness needs and desires. If we hike the trails on the weekend, but let the wilderness be neglected—or worse, abused—on the weekdays, we'll soon find our weekend haunts diminished or destroyed.

I want to add here a personal note. As I began my career as a guidebook author, I was blessed with the opportunity to learn from the men and women who helped launch the guidebook genre for The Mountaineers Books. Throughout the 1990s, I enjoyed many conversations with Ira Spring—we would talk for hours about our favorite trails and how we needed to diligently fight for those trails. I exchanged frequent correspondences with Harvey Manning, debating the best means of saving wildlands. I was advised and mentored by Louise Marshall. I worked alongside Greg Ball—founder of the WTA's volunteer trail maintenance program—for more than a decade.

In short, I served my apprenticeship with masters of the trail trade. From them, and from my own experiences exploring the wonderful wildlands of Washington, I discovered the pressing need for individual activism. When hikers get complacent, trails suffer. We must, in the words of the legendary Ira Spring, "get people onto trails. They need to bond with the wilderness." This "green bonding," as Ira called it, is essential in building public support for trails and trail funding.

As you get out and hike the trails you find described here, keep in mind the fact that many of these trails would have long ago ceased to exist without the phenomenal efforts of people like Ira Spring, Harvey Manning, Louise Marshall, and Greg Ball, not to mention all the other unnamed individual hikers who joined them in their push for wildland protection, trail funding, and strong environmental stewardship programs. When you get home, bear in mind the actions of those people, and then sit down and write a letter to your congressman, asking for better trail funding. Call your local Forest Service office and remind them that you've enjoyed the trails in their jurisdiction, and that you want to make sure all those routes remain wild and accessible for use by you and your children.

And if you're not already a member, consider joining an organization devoted to wilderness, backcountry trails, or other wild-country issues. Organizations like The Mountaineers, the Washington Trails Association, Volunteers for Outdoor Washington, Cascade Chapter of the Sierra Club, Conservation Northwest, the Cascade Land Conservancy, and countless others leverage individual contributions and efforts to help ensure the future of our trails and the wonderful wilderness legacy we've inherited.

ON THE TRAIL

Most hikers seek a sense of quiet solitude for themselves, or at least for their group, when they start up a trail. Yet our trails are being used by more hikers each year. To ensure that we preserve the serene experience we seek, we each must work to preserve the tranquility of the wildlands by being sensitive not only to the environment, but to other trail users as well.

General Trail Etiquette

The trails in this book are open to an array of trail users. Some trails are open to hikers only, but others allow hikers, horseback riders, mountain bikers, dog hikers, and—on occasion—motorcycles. When you encounter other trail users, whether they are hikers, climbers, trail runners, bicyclists, or horseback riders, the only hard-and-fast rule is that common sense and simple courtesy must be observed. It's hard to overstate just how vital these two things—common sense and courtesy—are to maintaining an enjoyable, safe, and friendly situation on our trails when different types of trail users meet.

With that Golden Rule of Trail Etiquette firmly in mind, there are other things you can do when you encounter other users to make your trip, and that of the others on the trail, most enjoyable:

- When hikers meet other hikers, the group heading uphill has the right-of-way. There are two reasons for this. First, on steep ascents, uphill hikers may be watching the trail before them and not notice the approach of descending hikers until they are face-to-face. More important, it is easier for descending hikers to break their stride and step off the trail than it is for those who have established a steady, hill-climbing plod. If, however, the uphill hikers are in need of a rest, they may step off the trail and yield the right-of-way to the downhill hikers, but this is the decision of the climbers alone.

- When meeting people employing other forms of trail recreation, hikers generally should yield since they are the most mobile and flexible users of the trail. For instance, when encountering a mountain biker or horseback rider, it is easier for hikers to step off the trail than for bikers to lift their bikes off into the brush or for horseback riders to get their animals off the trail. Horseback riders would actually put themselves and you at risk if they had to move their mounts off a steep trail.

- When hikers meet horseback riders, special consideration is called for to avoid startling the animals, which could cause a horse to throw its rider or sidestep in fright and stumble off the trail. When yielding, the hikers should step off the downhill side of the trail, unless the terrain makes this difficult or dangerous; in that case, move to the uphill side of the trail, crouching down a bit to stay below eye level of the horse so as not to spook it. Also, do not stand behind trees or brush if you can avoid it, as this could make you invisible to the animals until they get close, and then your sudden appearance could startle them. Rather, stay in clear view and talk in a normal voice to the riders. This calms the horses.

Sign at Bird Creek Meadows, Mount Adams

HIKING WITH DOGS

There's always something special about sharing the joys of the trail with good friends, but when one or more of those friends is your favorite canine companion, the experience is even more profound.

Hiking with dogs offers you a unique perspective on the natural world. A dog can alert you to dangers along rough trails, and show you things you might otherwise miss. For instance, a well-mannered, obedient dog can help you see more wildlife since dogs will often smell or hear animals long before you could see them.

The real benefit to hiking with dogs, though, is the sheer pleasure they bring. The absolute joy a dog experiences when hiking with its favorite humans is contagious. Just seeing a dog trotting happily up a trail, tongue lolling out and eyes shining with excitement, will elevate most people's moods, forcing them to share and revel in the dog's unabashed excitement and happiness as it frolics on the trail.

Of course, dogs can't be allowed to do as they please all the time. As a hiker, you are responsible for your own actions. As a dog owner, you have an added responsibility: your dog's actions.

* When hiking with your dog, you should have your dog on a leash—or under very strict voice command—at all times on the trail, around campsites, and wherever you are likely to encounter other people and animals. Strict voice command means your dog will immediately come back to heel when told, will stay at heel, and will refrain from barking.
* On meeting any other trail user, you and your dog must yield the right-of-way, stepping well clear of the trail to allow the other users to pass without worrying about "getting sniffed."
* If you meet horses on the trail, it is your first responsibility as dog owner to yield the trail, but you must also make sure your dog stays calm, does not bark, and does not make any move toward the horse. Horses can be easily spooked by strange dogs, and it is the dog owner's responsibility to keep their animal quiet and under firm control. Move well off the trail (go downhill off the trail when possible) and stay off the trail, with your dog held close to your side, until the horses pass well beyond you.

In practicing good canine trail etiquette, simply being friendly and courteous to other people on the trail goes a long way. If they have questions about your dog and/or her pack, try to be informative and helpful. Many of the folks unfamiliar with dogs will be reassured about the friendliness and trail-worthiness of your dog if they see the animal wearing a pack or reflective vest of some sort. Indeed, I have often encountered people on the trail who have been enchanted by the fact that Parka carries her own gear. If they have dogs, they'll often ask advice on getting their dogs trained to carry a pack, and if they are non-dog owners, they'll at least smile and pat her on the head.

Those of us who love to hike with our dogs must be the epitome of respectful, and responsible, trail users. When other hikers encounter dog hikers behaving responsibly, they will come away with a positive impression of dogs. In this way, we also help ourselves by preventing actions that could lead to additional trail closures or restrictions for dog hikers.

In short, as with all other forms of trail etiquette, common sense and courtesy are the order of the day.

- Stay on trails and practice minimum impact. Don't cut switchbacks (drop down across the neck of the switchback), as this promotes erosion and could destroy the trail. In fact, avoid taking any type of shortcut, and don't make new trails. If your destination is off-trail, leave the trail in as direct a manner as possible—that is, move away from the trail in a line perpendicular to the trail. Once well clear of the trail, adjust your route to your destination.
- Obey the rules specific to the trail you are visiting. Many trails are closed to certain types of use, including hiking with dogs or riding horses.
- Hikers who take their dogs on the trails should have the dog on a leash—or under very strict voice command—at all times. (For more on canine trail etiquette, see "Hiking with Dogs.")
- Avoid disturbing wildlife, especially in winter and in calving areas. Observe from a distance—even if you cannot get the picture you want from a distance, resist the urge to move closer to wildlife. This not only keeps you safer, but it prevents the animal from having to exert itself unnecessarily fleeing from you.
- Leave all natural things and features as you found them for others to enjoy.
- Never roll rocks off trails or cliffs—you never know who or what is below you.

These are just a few of the things hikers can do to maintain a safe and harmonious trail environment, and while not every situation is addressed by these rules, hikers can avoid problems by always practicing the Golden Rule of Trail Etiquette: Use common sense and courtesy toward others—those you see, and those who come after you.

Low-Impact Camping

In days gone by, wilderness travelers did as they pleased when hiking through the backcountry. Young, fragrant pine boughs were cut and stacked to create soft bedding, trenches were dug around tents to channel rainwater away from the shelter, and fires were lit to brighten the night and warm the camp.

As more and more people took to the hills, though, those actions began to leave large, noticeable scars on the land. Today, with millions of hikers flocking to the backcountry, such intrusive practices would leave the wilderness blighted for decades to come. To ensure we don't destroy the essence of the wild country we all enjoy visiting, hikers today are encouraged to employ the Leave No Trace (LNT) camping principles (see sidebar "Leave No Trace").

In short, these principles and practices are built around the idea that human visitors to the backcountry should "Leave only footprints, take only pictures." In fact, done right, even the footprints will be minimized.

Fires

One of the most important LNT practices involves fire.

Everyone loves a campfire. The acrid, sweet smoke wafts upward, stirring memories of childhood camping, roasting marshmallows, and sizzling hotdogs on sticks.

But campfires have no place in the backcountry. If everyone who enters the wilderness were to build a fire, the campsites would be filled with charcoal, and the forests would soon be picked clean of dead wood, leaving hordes of small critters with nowhere to scrounge for food (the insects that eat the dead wood provide meals for an army of birds and animals).

So, fires should be left to the car campgrounds with their structured fire pits and readily available supplies of firewood. Backcountry campers should stick to small pack stoves, even when regulations technically allow campfires. (In emergency situations, fires are not only allowed, but encouraged if it is a matter of survival.)

Waste

Perhaps the least talked about, but most important, Leave No Trace principle focuses on taking care of personal business.

The first rule of backcountry bathroom etiquette says that if an outhouse exists, use it. This may seem obvious, but all too often, folks find backcountry toilets are dark, dank affairs and they choose to use the woods rather than the rickety wooden structure provided by the land manager. It may be easier on your nose to head off into the woods, but this disperses human waste around the popular camping areas. Privies, on the other hand, keep the waste concentrated in a single site, minimizing contamination of area waters. The outhouses get even higher environmental marks if they feature removable holding tanks that can be airlifted out. These privies and their tanks may not be all that aesthetically pleasing, but they are a lot better than finding toilet paper strewn throughout the woods.

When privies aren't provided, the key factor to consider is location. You'll want to choose a site at least 200 to 300 feet from water, campsites, and trails. A location well out of sight of trails and viewpoints will give you privacy and reduce the odds of other hikers stumbling onto the site after you leave. Once you pick your place, start digging. The idea is to make like a cat and bury your waste. You need to dig down through the organic duff into the mineral soil below—a hole six to eight inches deep is usually adequate. When you've taken care of business, refill the hole and camouflage it with rocks and sticks—this helps prevent other humans, or animals, from digging in the same location before decomposition has done its job.

Water

To protect the wilderness water resources, hikers must camp at least 100 feet away from

lakeshores and stream banks. This not only lets other hikers—and animals—get to the water without having to bypass you, but it helps keep the water clean.

Even so, you'll want to treat your drinking water. Wherever humans have gone, germs have gone with them, and humans have gone just about everywhere. That means that even the most pristine mountain stream may harbor microscopic nasties like *Giardia* cysts, *Cryptosporidium*, or *E. coli*.

Treating water can be as simple as boiling it, chemically purifying it (adding tiny iodine tablets), or pumping it through one of the new-generation water filters or purifiers. (Note: Pump units labeled as filters generally remove everything but viruses, which are too small

Opposite: Sydney Mullock and Sailor sharing a hike together

to be filtered out. Pumps labeled as purifiers must have a chemical element—usually iodine—that kills the viruses after filtering all the other bugs out.) Never drink untreated water, or your intestines will never forgive you.

Cleanup

When washing your hands, first rinse off as much dust and dirt as you can in just plain water. If you still feel the need for a soapy wash, collect a pot of water from the lake or stream and move at least 100 feet away. Apply a tiny bit of biodegradable soap to your hands, dribble on a little water, and lather up. Use a bandanna or towel to wipe away most of the soap, and then rinse with the water in the pot. Follow the same procedure with washing up your cooking pots and dishes, making sure you eat all the food first. Never dump leftover food into the water or on the ground. If you can't eat it, pack it into a plastic bag and store with your other food (you'll want to learn the proper method for bear-bagging your food, described below under "Wildlife Encounters"). Anything that is packed in must be packed out—all leftovers, trash, and garbage, even biodegradable items like apple cores.

Wildlife Encounters

If you hike in Washington or Oregon, you'll be hiking in cougar and bear country—virtually every trail in the state pierces predator habitat. Black bears, which outnumber cougars ten to one in the Northwest, can be found in any forested area of the region, and cougars can be found anywhere deer can be found—that is, everywhere.

There are other predators prowling the backcountry, but these two are the biggest and most likely to cause concern when hikers encounter them. But an encounter with a cougar or bear doesn't have to be a negative experience. These critters rarely attack or even threaten humans, and in most of the few attacks that have

occurred, the human could have prevented the attack from happening with a little forethought and understanding of the animal.

Bears

There are an estimated 30,000 to 35,000 black bears in Washington, and the big bruins can be found in every corner of the state. The central and southern Cascades are especially attractive to the solitude-seeking bears. Watching the bears graze through a rich huckleberry patch, or seeing them flip dead logs in search of grubs, can be an exciting and rewarding experience—provided, of course, you aren't in the same berry patch. The bears tend to prefer solitude to human company, and will generally flee long before you have a chance to get too close. There are times, however, when the bears either don't hear hikers approaching, or they are more interested in defending their food source—or their young—than they are in avoiding a confrontation. These instances are rare. To further minimize the odds of an encounter with an aggressive bear, you can:

- Hike in a group, and hike only during daylight hours.
- Talk or sing as you hike. If bears hear you coming, they will usually avoid you. When they are surprised, they may feel threatened. So, make noises that will identify you as a human—talk, sing, rattle pebbles in a tin can—especially when hiking near a river or stream (which can mask more subtle sounds that might normally alert a bear to your presence).
- Be aware of the environment around you, and know how to identify "bear sign." Overturned rocks and torn-up deadwood logs often are the result of a bear searching for grubs. Berry bushes that are stripped of berries, with leaves, branches, and berries littering the ground under the bushes, show where a bear has fed. Bears use trees

Mama black bear and cub

as scratching posts and will often leave claw marks on trees; fur in the rough bark of the trees is a sign that says, "A bear was here!" Tracks and scat are the most common signs of a bear's recent presence.

- Stay away from abundant food sources and dead animals. Black bears are opportunistic omnivores and will scavenge food. A bear that finds a dead deer will hang around until the meat is gone, and it will defend that food against any perceived threat.
- Keep dogs on a leash and under control. Many bear encounters have resulted from unleashed dogs chasing a bear; the bear gets angry and turns on the dog; the dog gets scared and runs for help (i.e., back to its owner), and the bear follows right back into the dog owner's lap.

- Leave the perfume, hair spray, cologne, and scented soaps at home. Using scented sprays and body lotions makes you smell like a big, tasty treat. Any heavily scented clothing items (i.e., shirts with sweat and/or deodorant) should be suspended in bags (see below).
- Never eat or cook in your tent. The spilled food or even food odors can permeate the nylon material, essentially making your tent smell, at least to a bear, like last night's dinner.

- Never clean fish within 100 feet of camp.
- Always store all your food and other scented items in their own stuff sacks when preparing to hang them.
- Always suspend your food bags at least twelve feet in the air and eight to ten feet from the nearest tree trunk. In some popular backcountry campsites, the land managers provide wires, complete with pulleys, to help you do this, but you'll have to learn how to string your own rope to achieve these heights, too.

Cougars

Very few hikers ever see cougars in the wild. Not only are these big cats some of the most solitary, shy animals in the woods, but there are only 2,500 to 3,000 of them roaming the entire state of Washington. Still, cougars and hikers sometimes encounter each other. In these cases, the hikers should, in my opinion, count their blessings—they will likely never see a more majestic animal than a wild cougar.

To make sure the encounter is a positive one, hikers must understand the cats. Cougars are shy but very curious. They will follow hikers simply to see what kind of beasts we are, but they very rarely (as in, almost never) attack adult humans.

If you do encounter a cougar, remember that cougars rely on prey that can't, or won't fight back. So, as soon as you see the cat:

- Do not run! Running may trigger a cougar's attack instinct.

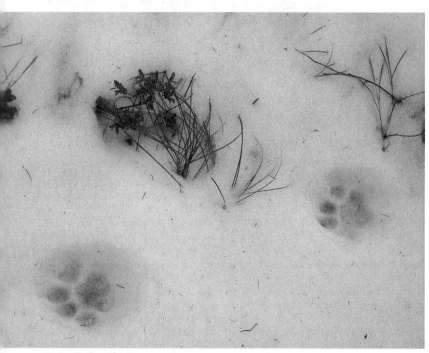

Cougar tracks in the snow

WHOSE LAND IS THIS?

All of the hikes in this book are on public land. That is, they belong to you and me and the rest of the citizenry. As fellow guidebook writer Craig Romano points out in *Day Hiking: Olympic Peninsula*, what's confusing is just who exactly is in charge of this public trust. Several different governing agencies manage the lands described in his guide and in this one as well.

The largest of the agencies, and the one managing most of the hikes in this book, is the U.S. Forest Service. A division of the Department of Agriculture, the Forest Service strives to "sustain the health, diversity, and productivity of the nation's forests and grasslands to meet the needs of present and future generations." The agency purports to do this under the doctrine of "multiple use"—the greatest good for the greatest number, frequently resulting in conflict. Supplying timber products, managing wildlife habitat, and developing motorized and nonmotorized recreation options have a tendency to conflict with each other. Some of these uses may not exactly sustain the health of the forest either.

The Gifford Pinchot National Forest, managed by the Forest Service, comprises over 1.3 million acres of land in the Cascades. Much of this forestland has been heavily logged. Eleven areas within the Gifford Pinchot National Forest, however, have been afforded stringent protections as federal wilderness areas, including Goat Rocks, Mount Adams, William O. Douglas, Indian Heaven, and Trapper Creek, as well as the Mount St. Helens National Monument—all of which are destinations for hikes in this guide.

Other public lands you'll encounter on the hikes in this book are Washington state parks, managed primarily for recreation and preservation; Washington State Department of Natural Resources lands, managed primarily for timber harvesting, with pockets of natural area preserves; and county parks, which are often like state parks but on a regional level.

It's important that you know who manages the land you'll be hiking on, for each agency has its own fees and rules. Confusing? Yes, but it's our land and we should understand how it's managed for us. And remember that we have a say in how our lands are managed, too, and can let the agencies know whether we like what they're doing or not.

- Stand up and face the animal. Virtually every recorded cougar attack of humans has been a predator–prey attack. If you appear as another aggressive predator, rather than as prey, the cougar will back down.
- Try to appear large; wave your arms or a jacket over your head. The idea is to make the cougar think you are the bigger, meaner beast.
- Pick up children.
- Maintain eye contact with the animal. The cougar will interpret this as a show of dominance on your part.
- Do not approach the animal; back away slowly if you can safely do so.

Gear

No hiker should venture far up a trail without being properly equipped.

Starting with the feet, a good pair of boots can make the difference between a wonderful hike and a horrible death march. Keep your feet happy, and you'll be happy.

But you can't talk boots without talking socks. Only one rule here: Wear whatever is most comfortable, unless it's cotton. Corollary to that rule: Never wear cotton.

Cotton is a wonderful fabric when your life isn't on the line—it is soft, light, and airy. But get it wet and it stays wet. That means blisters on your feet. Wet cotton also lacks any insulation value. In fact, when wet it sucks away your body heat, leaving you susceptible to hypothermia. So leave your cotton socks, cotton underwear, and even the cotton tee shirts at home. The only cotton I carry on the trail is my trusty pink bandanna (pink because nobody else I know carries pink, so I always know which is mine).

While the list of what you pack may vary from what another hiker on the same trail is carrying, there are a few things each and every one of us should have in our packs. For instance, every hiker who ventures more than a few hundred yards away from the road should be prepared to spend the night under the stars (or under the clouds, as may be more likely). Mountain storms can whip up in a hurry, catching sunny-day hikers by surprise. What was an easy-to-follow trail during a calm, clear day can disappear into a confusing world of fog and rain—or even snow—in a windy tempest. Therefore, every member of the party should have a pack loaded with the Ten Essentials, and a few other items that aren't necessarily essential but would be good to have on hand in an emergency.

The Ten Essentials

The following list includes items that everyone who ventures onto a trail or into the backcountry should have. You could add more, possibly, but these are the basics.

1. **Navigation (map and compass).** Carry a topographic map of the area you plan to be in and knowledge of how to read it. Likewise, a compass—again, make sure you know how to use it.

2. **Sun protection.** This should include sunscreen (SPF 15 or better), sunglasses, and physical sun barriers such as a wide-

---

DAY HIKER'S CHECKLIST
ALWAYS CARRY THE TEN ESSENTIALS
- See above

THE BASICS
- Daypack (just big enough to carry all your gear)

CLOTHING
- Polyester or nylon shorts/pants
- Short-sleeve shirt
- Long-sleeve shirt
- Warm pants (fleece or microfleece)
- Fleece jacket or wool sweater
- Wicking long underwear
- Non-cotton underwear
- Bandanna

OUTERWEAR
- Raingear
- Wide-brimmed hat (for sun/rain)
- Fleece/stocking hat (for warmth)
- Gloves (fleece/wool and shell)

FOOTWEAR
- Hiking boots
- Hiking socks (not cotton!). Carry one extra pair. When your feet are soaked with sweat, change into the clean pair, and rinse out the dirty pair and hang them on the back of your pack to dry. Repeat as often as necessary during the hike.
- Liner socks
- Extra laces
- Gaiters
- Moleskin (for prevention of blisters) and Second Skin (for treatment of blisters). Carry both in your first-aid kit.

OPTIONAL GEAR
- Camera
- Binoculars
- Reading material
- Fishing equipment
- Field guides (for nature study)
- Head net/mosquito net suit

Use good gear: hiking boots in water

brimmed hat, long-sleeved shirt, and long pants.

3. **Insulation (extra clothing).** This means more clothing than you would wear during the worst weather of the planned outing. If you get injured or lost, you won't be moving around generating heat, so you'll need to be able to bundle up.

4. **Illumination (flashlight/headlamp).** If caught after dark, you'll need a light to follow the trail. If forced to spend the night, you'll need it to set up emergency camp, gather wood, etc. Carry extra batteries and bulb.

5. **First-aid supplies.** Nothing elaborate needed—especially if you are unfamiliar with some of the uses. Make sure you have adhesive bandages, gauze bandages, some aspirin, etc. A Red Cross first-aid training course is recommended.

6. **Fire.** An emergency campfire provides warmth, but it also has a calming effect on most people. Without it the night is cold, dark, and intimidating. With it, the night is held at arm's length. A candle or tube of fire-starting ribbon is essential for starting a fire with wet wood. Matches are an important part of this essential—you can't start a fire without them. Pack them in a waterproof container and/or buy the waterproof/windproof variety. Book matches are useless in windy or wet weather, and disposable lighters are unreliable.

7. **Repair kit and tools.** A knife is helpful; a multitool is better. You never know when

you might need a small pair of pliers or scissors, both of which are commonly found on compact multitools. A basic repair kit includes such things as: a twenty-foot length of nylon cord, a small roll of duct tape, some one-inch webbing, and extra webbing buckles (to fix broken pack straps), and a small tube of instant adhesive like Superglue.

8. **Nutrition (extra food).** Pack enough that you'll have leftovers after an uneventful trip (those leftovers will keep you fed and fueled during an emergency).

9. **Hydration (extra water).** Figure what you'll drink between water sources, and then add an extra liter. If you plan on relying upon wilderness water sources, be sure to include some method of purification, whether it's a chemical additive such as iodine or a filtration device.

10. **Emergency shelter.** This can be as simple as a few extra-large garbage bags, or something more efficient such as a reflective space blanket or tube tent.

Enjoy the Trails

Above all else, I hope you will safely enjoy the trails in this book. These trails exist for our enjoyment, and for the enjoyment of future generations. We can use them and protect them at the same time if we are careful with our actions, and forthright with our demands on Congress to continue and further the protection of our county's wildlands.

Throughout the twentieth century, wilderness lovers helped secure protection for the lands we enjoy today. As we enter the twenty-first century, we must see to it that those protections continue, and that the last bits of wildlands are also preserved for the enjoyment of future generations.

Please, if you enjoy these trails, get involved. Something as simple as writing a letter to Congress can make a big difference.

A NOTE ABOUT SAFETY

Safety is an important concern in all outdoor activities. No guidebook can alert you to every hazard or anticipate the limitations of every reader. Therefore, the descriptions of roads, trails, routes, and natural features in this book are not representations that a particular place or excursion will be safe for your party. When you follow any of the routes described in this book, you assume responsibility for your own safety. Under normal conditions, such excursions require the usual attention to traffic, road and trail conditions, weather, terrain, the capabilities of your party, and other factors. Because many of the lands in this book are subject to development and/or change of ownership, conditions may have changed since this book was written that make your use of some of these routes unwise. Always check for current conditions, obey posted private property signs, and avoid confrontations with property owners or managers. Keeping informed on current conditions and exercising common sense are the keys to a safe, enjoyable outing.

— The Mountaineers Books

Opposite: Kloochman Rock

white pass corridor /
cowlitz river valley

U.S. Highway 12 stands as one of the primary east–west transportation corridors in Washington, crossing the Cascades at White Pass. This highway also serves as the northern gateway to the South Cascades. Hiking opportunities in this region range from forest river valleys to high alpine peaks. You will find trails in moss-laden old-growth forests and along high, sun-baked ridgelines.

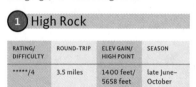

1) High Rock

RATING/ DIFFICULTY	ROUND-TRIP	ELEV GAIN/ HIGH POINT	SEASON
*****/4	3.5 miles	1400 feet/ 5658 feet	late June– October

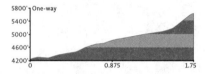

Map: Green Trails No. 301 Randle; **Contact/ Permits:** USFS Cowlitz Valley Ranger District, Packwood Office, (360) 494-0600 / Northwest Forest Pass; **GPS:** N46 39.986, W121 53.481

🏠 *Savvy hikers seeking stellar 360-degree views know to look for lookouts. The old fire lookout cabins (sometimes cabins-atop-towers) used by the Forest Service in the pre-satellite radar days were always situated atop high peaks with outstanding views in all directions. The sole purpose of these high lonesome structures was to provide fire lookouts a panoramic view of a broad swath of mountains so they could watch for smoke. As such, the old fire lookout stations are wonderful hiking destinations, and unlike many of the old sites, High Rock still has its tower (which is still used in season). As great as the views are, though, the mountain itself is even more astounding. High Rock is one of the more impressive stone formations on which you're ever likely to sit, not so much for its sheer height (5700 feet) but for its sheer north face (about 600 feet straight down).*

View of Mount Rainier from the High Rock lookout

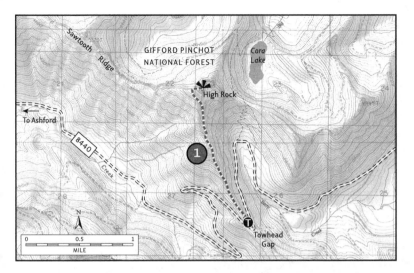

GETTING THERE

From Tacoma, drive State Highway 7 east to Elbe and continue on Highway 706 to Ashford. Continue east and turn right onto Kernahan Road. At about 1.5 miles, turn right onto Forest Road 85. Proceed 5.8 miles to FR 8440. Turn right and continue 4.5 miles to the trailhead on the left.

ON THE TRAIL

The trail begins near a clear-cut and rises 1400 feet through increasingly thin forest before opening to the grand spectacle at the top: a 1929-vintage fire lookout on the tip-top of what appears to be a massive, stone-walled ship's bow. Look straight ahead for one of the most magnificent views of Mount Rainier anywhere in Washington. Look straight down, about 1400 feet, for an overhead view of Cora Lake. You'll want to spend some time here watching Rainier make its own weather, which in turn performs magical shadow-and-light shows across the mountain's full south face; you see these displays in better detail here than from anywhere

inside Mount Rainier National Park.

High Rock is a favorite early-morning and late-afternoon hangout for nature photographers. The fire lookout, the only one left in the Cowlitz Valley Ranger District (and one of only three in the Gifford Pinchot National Forest), is staffed in the summer.

2 Purcell Lookout

RATING/ DIFFICULTY	ROUND-TRIP	ELEV GAIN/ HIGH POINT	SEASON
*****/5	7 miles (longer option 15 miles)	2600 feet/ 5442 feet	late June–October

5700' One-way
4700'
3700'
2700'
0   1.75   3.5

Map: Green Trails No. 310 Randle; **Contact/ Permits:** USFS Cowlitz Valley Ranger District, Packwood Office, (360) 494-0600 / Northwest Forest Pass; **GPS:** N46 34.886, W121 49.960

A clump of tiger lilies on the way up Purcell Mountain

To get to the site of the old Purcell Lookout, you have a choice: hike all the way from U.S. Highway 12, or let your car do part of the work. The Purcell Mountain Trail, which begins just west of the left-hand turn to Forest Road 63 (see Getting There directions), leads 7.6 pleasant miles up the mountain to grand views at the lookout. The better option, though, is to take the Purcell Lookout Trail for a shorter, but still rugged, day hike.

GETTING THERE

From Interstate 5 near Napavine, turn east onto U.S. Highway 12 and drive approximately 47 miles to Randle. Continue 6 miles east to the old highway (unmarked) on the left. Turn left (north) and drive about 1 mile to Forest Road 63. Turn left and drive north to FR 6310. Bear left on FR 6310, and you'll find the trailhead on the right in less than a mile.

ON THE TRAIL

Our route follows the shorter, but still rugged, Purcell Lookout Trail, which begins a couple

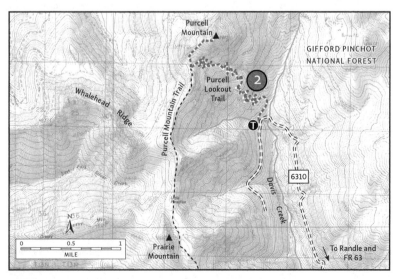

thousand feet higher on the mountain than the longer Purcell Mountain Trail.

From the trailhead, our path cuts straight to the chase, proving that shorter isn't always easier. This trail makes a direct assault on the high summit. After about an hour on the Purcell Lookout Trail, though, it might feel more like you're the one being assaulted.

The grade is steep, gaining 2100 feet (about half in an open, hot clear-cut) in about 3 miles. Here you join the main trail from the bottom and climb a more moderate 500 feet in the last 0.5-mile pitch to the lookout site. You get great views in all directions. Funny how they keep putting lookouts in places like this.

3 Pompey Peak

RATING/ DIFFICULTY	ROUND-TRIP	ELEV GAIN/ HIGH POINT	SEASON
***/4	3.5 miles	2000 feet/ 5180 feet	late June– October

Rocks on the summit of Pompey Peak

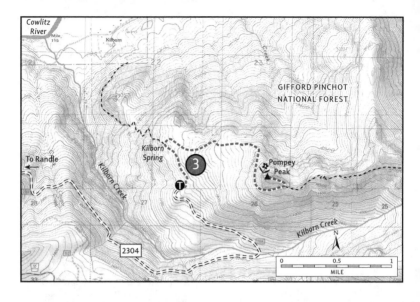

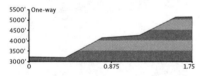

Maps: Green Trails No. 301 Randle, No. 302 Packwood, No. 334 Blue Lake; **Contact/ Permits:** USFS Cowlitz Valley Ranger District, Packwood Office, (360) 494-0600/Northwest Forest Pass; **GPS:** N46 29.986, W121 46.994

🏠 *Peak-baggers love the lookout-rich Cowlitz Valley. The number of high peaks that once housed fire watch stations in this deep, forested valley is astounding. This trail loops through some of those forests, past a brilliant, clear spring boasting nice campsites if you want to spend the night, and then on to the summit with its grand views of the upper Cowlitz Valley.*

GETTING THERE

From Randle, drive 1 mile south on Forest Road 25 and turn left (east) onto FR 23. Continue east for 3.5 miles on FR 23 and turn left (north) onto FR 2304. At 3.3 miles, stay right at the "Y" to continue uphill to the end of the road, where you find the trailhead on the left.

ON THE TRAIL

The trail leaves the end of the road and climbs gently through the forest for nearly a mile to reach the basin in which you'll find the clear, cool waters of Kilborn Spring. This is a fine place to rest and refresh yourself before the big push upward. A side trail comes in from the north here; this drops down into the Kilborn Creek Valley and out to Cline Road along the south side of the Cowlitz River.

From the spring, the trail climbs steeply at times up the northwest spine of Pompey Peak. As you near the 2-mile mark, the path swings south around the peak, finally cresting the summit from the southeast. From the top, enjoy expansive views north over the Cowlitz Valley, southeast to Mount Adams, and southwest to Mount St. Helens.

EXTENDING YOUR TRIP

From the peak, the trail continues east along the ridge for another couple miles between the Twin Sisters Peaks and past Castle Butte before dropping into a steep valley. The trail ends abruptly at the edge of the forest, both literally and figuratively—it dead-ends at the property line between the national forest and privately owned land. The landowner of the private parcel has clear-cut this spot.

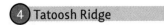

4 Tatoosh Ridge

RATING/ DIFFICULTY	ROUND-TRIP	ELEV GAIN/ HIGH POINT	SEASON
****/4	8 miles	2600 feet/ 5400 feet	July– October

Map: Green Trails No. 302 Packwood; **Contact/ Permits:** USFS Cowlitz Valley Ranger District, Packwood Office, (360) 494-0600 / Northwest Forest Pass; **GPS:** N46 42.783, W121 42.948; **Status:** Endangered

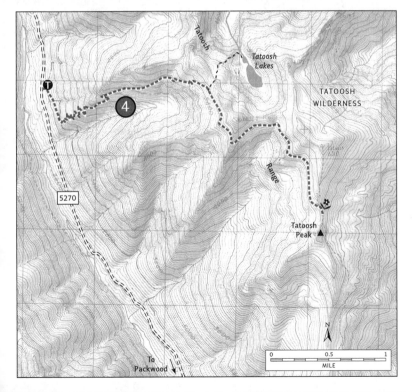

View of Mount Rainier from Tatoosh Ridge

Thick old-growth forest of Douglas-fir and hemlock line the lower trail, while ridgetop meadows and clear alpine vistas await you on the upper trail. The path climbs steeply and steadily, giving you a good workout. But the payoff for that work includes glorious views of Mount Rainier and the Goat Rocks Peaks, as well as the many rocky summits of the Tatoosh Range. You can look down on the shimmering waters of the Tatoosh Lakes, or if you are up for the extra effort, you can drop down a steep side trail to the lakeshore, finding great campsites and fabulous views from around the lake basin. The trail is a bit rough in places and can be hard to follow atop the ridge. It is in need of some TLC, so let the rangers know you'd like to see it treated well.

GETTING THERE

From Randle, drive east on U.S. Highway 12 through the town of Packwood. Near the east end of town, turn north onto Skate Creek Road (the Packwood Ranger Station sits on the south side of the highway, opposite Skate Creek Road). Drive 4 miles on Skate Creek Road and turn north (right) onto Forest Road 5270. Continue 7 miles up this road to the trailhead on the right. The trail is poorly marked, and the parking area consists of a wide spot in the road. The trail is located about 1.5 miles past a junction with FR 5270-990 on the left.

ON THE TRAIL

From the road, climb steeply, starting with a scramble up the road bank to dive into the forest. The path slants upward through the thick Douglas-fir forest, gaining elevation steadily as the trail settles into a long series of switchbacks. The old forest has a broken canopy, which lets plenty of sunshine filter through to the forest floor, meaning an abundance of forest wildflowers around the path. Look for vanilla leaf, Indian pipe, avalanche lilies, trilliums, Canadian dogwood, and more among the trees. As the trail climbs, the forest opens onto broad sidehill meadows filled with even more varied wildflowers.

At 2.5 miles, the trail crests the ridge and in a few hundred yards reaches a trail junction. To the left, a faint trail drops to the north, entering Mount Rainier National Park. Choose this side track if you want to descend to the Tatoosh Lakes. But the better views are found to the south. Follow the ridge-top track as it leads south to another trail junction.

Ramble along the ridge for another 1.5 miles to reach a rocky knob below the tall crown of Tatoosh Peak at the southern end of the ridge. From here, you have unsurpassed views of Mount Rainier, the Goat Rocks Peaks, Mount Adams, and on clear days, Mount St. Helens's abbreviated top.

5 Sand Lake

RATING/ DIFFICULTY	ROUND-TRIP	ELEV GAIN/ HIGH POINT	SEASON
***/2	6 miles	900 feet/ 5300 feet	June– November

Map: Green Trails No. 303 White Pass; **Contact/Permits:** USFS Naches Ranger District, (509) 653-2205 / Northwest Forest Pass; **GPS:** N46 38.684, W121 22.936

Bring the kids on this excursion— it's a great introduction to the Pacific Crest Trail (PCT) for youngsters. The elevation gain is minimal, the scenery is pretty, and the lake at the end of the hike offers a perfect swimming experience: While many wilderness lakes stay ice-cold throughout the summer, Sand Lake is just shallow enough for the sun to warm it to a comfortable temperature for cooling off during a hot summer hike. The smooth, sandy bottom is a comfort to boot-tired feet, too.

You'll pass Deer Lake on the way to Sand, and between them you'll find acres of wildflower meadows and cool stands of pine forests. Indeed, these are but two of a slew of lakes in the southern half of the William O. Douglas Wilderness worth visiting.

GETTING THERE

From Packwood, drive east on U.S. Highway 12 to White Pass. At the east end of the long parking strip on the north side of the highway, find the faint, unsigned, dirt road leading north to White Pass Campground on the northeast shore of Leech Lake. The Pacific Crest Trail–North trailhead is located just before the start of the campground loop.

ON THE TRAIL

The Pacific Crest Trail enters the forest and stays under cover of trees for most of its length. The steepest climbing of the hike occurs during the first mile, but don't fret—you'll gain just 400 feet in that mile.

From there, the trail levels considerably and the forest thins out, allowing lots of sunlight to filter down to the brush covering the forest floor. That's a blessing, as the sunshine sweetens the purple fruit that grows on that brush. Huckleberries! These forest berries aren't as thick or as big as those found in the open clearings and meadows throughout the wilderness, but they are delicious nonetheless. The berries are plentiful enough to snack on as you tread up the trail, even if they do throw off your stride (pick, step, pick, pick, step, pick, pick, pick, step).

The PCT veers west at 1.3 miles, just before reaching a junction with a small side trail on the right leading to Dog Lake (see Hike 6). Stay on the main track, though, and in another 0.7 mile reach a second spur trail, this time on the left. Take a few minutes to hike the 100 yards down this trail to Deer Lake. This forest-lined lake holds a good population of catchable (and keepable) trout, so bring along a fishing rod for you and the youngsters. The lake is frequently stocked with cutthroat trout, and there's also a sizable stock of brook trout residing here.

If you aren't fishing, jump back onto the PCT and continue north on the now-level path for another mile or so to Sand Lake. This last mile crosses several broad meadows (in early summer, the meadows are more like marshes), which offer the best chance of seeing big critters like deer and elk. Meadows push right up

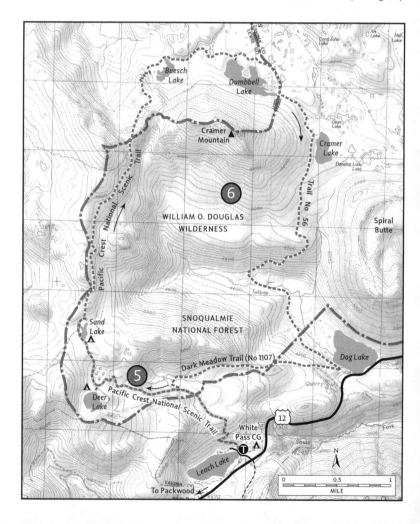

Hiker on the shore of Sand Lake

against Sand Lake, as do stands of timber.

The lake is actually a catch basin for run-off from melting snow. There is no permanent stream running into the lake, nor out of it. As snow melts, the water rolls into the lake basin where it gathers, swelling the lake in early summer. After most of the snow has melted off, the lake waters slowly recede as some evaporate and some percolate down through the porous volcanic soil.

Ideally, you'll visit here in late July to early August, when the waters are low enough to be off the lakeside trail but still high enough to be clear and cool. Folks who want to spend the night (it's a great destination for the kids' first backpacking trip) will find plenty of high, grassy campsites around the lake basin—just be sure to stay well back from the water so as not to intrude on the scenery and to protect the lake itself.

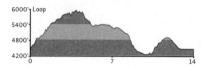

6 Cramer Mountain Loop

RATING/ DIFFICULTY	LOOP	ELEV GAIN/ HIGH POINT	SEASON
***/3	14 miles	1700 feet/ 5900 feet	June– October

Map: Green Trails No. 303 White Pass; **Contact/Permits:** USFS Naches Ranger District, (509) 653-2205 / Northwest Forest Pass; **GPS:** N46 38.684, W121 22.936

If you like water, this loop route should appeal to you. The William O. Douglas Wilderness boasts scores of lakes and hundreds of small ponds and tarns, and this loop takes advantage of many of those. You'll find all the great scenery that accompanies lakes, from rich foliage to great numbers of birds and small mammals. There are also a few big critters wandering the area, too, from massive mule deer to proud majestic wapati (aka Rocky Mountain elk).

GETTING THERE

From Packwood, drive east on U.S. Highway 12 to White Pass. At the east end of the long parking strip on the north side of the highway, find the faint, unsigned, dirt road leading north to White Pass Campground on the northeast shore of Leech Lake. The Pacific Crest Trail–North trailhead is located just before the start of the campground loop.

ON THE TRAIL

Start north on the PCT and in just over 2 miles, amble through the broad meadows east of Deer Lake. From Deer Lake, hike on north, finding Sand Lake in less than a mile.

Ground squirrel harvesting "hay" in meadows near Cramer Mountain

As you near Sand Lake (see Hike 5), broad meadows open all around you. Strolling into the Sand Lake basin, take note of the masses of wildflowers on the shoreline—lupines dominate, but there's a wealth of paintbrush, columbine, and assorted lilies, too. Also, check the bogs on the north end of the lake for a massive bog filled to overflowing with bog orchids.

Continuing north of Sand Lake, you'll find endless meadows and stands of silver fir forests before you reach Buesch Lake at 6 miles. As the PCT curves east around the north shore of Buesch, you'll reach a trail junction. Turn right off the PCT onto Trail No. 56 and hike down to the shore of Dumbbell Lake, in the shadow of Cramer Mountain. Cramer

Mountain sits across the lake from the trail, and many of the campsites along the north side of the lake provide bountiful views of this big cone-shaped peak.

Trail No. 56 curves south around the shores of Dumbbell and rolls straight south past Cramer Lake along the flank of Spiral Butte, to Dog Lake at 12.9 miles. A nearly flat Dark Meadow Trail (No. 1107) leads 1.6 miles west from Dog Lake back to the PCT just north of the trailhead at White Pass. Hike less than a mile south on the PCT to complete the 14-mile loop.

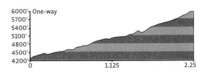

Map: Green Trails No. 303 White Pass; **Contact/Permits:** USFS Naches Ranger District, (509) 653-2205 / Northwest Forest Pass; **GPS:** N46 38.065, W121 18.199

This is a steep but short trail with incredible views and great wildlife viewing opportunities. The trail climbs relentlessly from the first step, first through cool forest and then finally, near the top, in open meadow. There are no views until the trail nears the summit, but deer and elk browse in the forest around the trail, and black bears frequent the area as well. An impressive array of

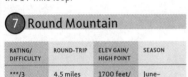

7 Round Mountain

RATING/ DIFFICULTY	ROUND-TRIP	ELEV GAIN/ HIGH POINT	SEASON
***/3	4.5 miles	1700 feet/ 5900 feet	June– October

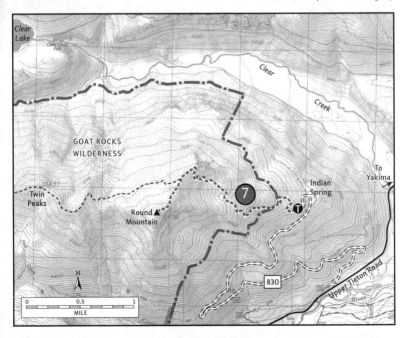

Views from Round Mountain east toward Rimrock Lake

birds is also found in this area; from cedar waxwings to golden eagles, the forests— and the skies above them—are filled with feathered beasts.

GETTING THERE

From Yakima, drive west on U.S. Highway 12 for about 40 miles and turn onto the Upper Tieton Road. Drive 2.8 miles and turn right onto Forest Road 830. Follow this to its end, about 5 miles, to find the trailhead.

ON THE TRAIL

From the trailhead, the route switchbacks up through forest to a trail junction in about 1.5 miles. The right fork leads to the Pacific Crest Trail by way of Twin Peaks, while the Round

Mountain route rolls straight ahead.

The last 0.5-mile climb to the top of Round Mountain is steep and strenuous, but it leads to a prominent knob with outstanding views of the eastern flank of the South Cascades. From the summit, look north to the cinder cone of Spiral Butte. Look down onto the blue waters of Rimrock and Clear Lakes (actually reservoirs), and look west to Goat Rocks Wilderness with its tall rocky spires and glaciated peaks.

8 Clear Fork–Lily Lake

RATING/ DIFFICULTY	ROUND-TRIP	ELEV GAIN/ HIGH POINT	SEASON
***/1	3 miles	200 feet/ 3600 feet	June–early November

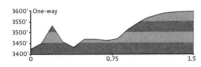

Map: Green Trails No. 303 White Pass; **Contact/Permits:** USFS Naches Ranger District, (509) 653-2205 / Northwest Forest Pass; **GPS:** N46 39.332, W121 29.171

  Paralleling the beautiful Clear Fork of the Cowlitz River, this

trail is flat and smooth, making it a wonderful hiking adventure for families with small children or for those who simply want to enjoy the wilderness without a lot of exertion. Over the entire trail length, the elevation gain is less than 300 feet. Walking ease doesn't correspond to a lack of interesting sights, though. The best and most dominant feature of this hike is the ever-beautiful Clear Fork of the Cowlitz River and the smaller Little Lava Creek on the other side of the valley. We enjoy simply listening to the river; watching the

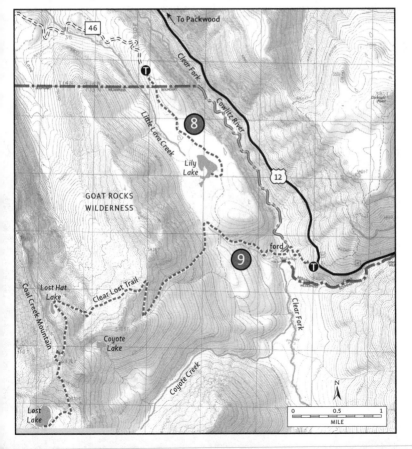

cold, clear water roll over the rocks; admiring the thirsty wildlife that gathers on its shores; or casting a fly into the river and feeling the raw energy of the strong, toothy trout that prowl the icy pools and eddies. In addition to the river, the trail leads to Lily Lake, a small meadow tarn that is the favorite haunt of muskrats and mule deer.

GETTING THERE

From Packwood, drive 4.6 miles east on U.S. Highway 12 and turn right (south) onto Forest Road 46. Continue 9.2 miles to the road's end and the trailhead.

ON THE TRAIL

The trail leaves the road-end trailhead and ambles gently east, darting into and out of the forests that line the valley floor. To the north, Highway 12 rides along the valley wall, so you might hear a bit of road noise, but generally the music of the tumbling river drowns out the less pleasant sounds.

Walk quietly along this path, and keep kids and dogs close at hand, and you might be surprised at the wildlife you'll find. Despite the proximity to the road, the valley bottom harbors a host of critters. Mule deer and even Rocky Mountain elk thrive here, as well as smaller beasts such as beavers, muskrats, and weasels. Because of the abundance of water, you'll also find a host of birds, both tiny tweeters such as juncos and big, soaring raptors such as redtail hawks and turkey vultures.

Lily Lake, at 1.5 miles, makes a fine picnic spot and turnaround point—though, if you want to go farther, the trail stretches on for many more miles, linking up with Clear Lost and other trails leading deep into the Goat Rocks Wilderness.

Lily Lake from the Clear Fork Trail

9 Clear Lost

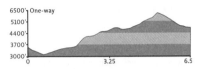

RATING/ DIFFICULTY	ROUND-TRIP	ELEV GAIN/ HIGH POINT	SEASON
****/5	13 miles	2600 feet/ 6376 feet	July–early October

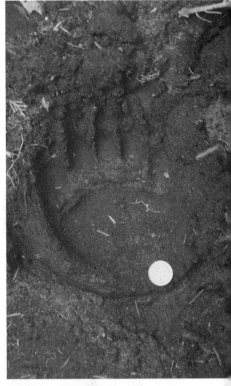

Fresh bear tracks dwarf a quarter.

Map: Green Trails No. 303 White Pass; **Contact/Permits:** USFS Naches Ranger District, (509) 653-2205 / Northwest Forest Pass; **GPS:** N46 37.543, W121 26.753

A steep descent and a cold-water ford in the first mile of the hike discourage a lot of hikers from pursuing the rewards offered by this trail. But if you wait until late July, when the snowmelt runoff has declined a bit and the water level in the creek has dropped, the ford isn't too difficult. By late August, wading the Clear Fork is relatively easy and even refreshing—especially on the return trip when the cool waters soothe trail-tired feet. Past the ford, the trail climbs relentlessly, leading hikers into high alpine country where both the trailside scenery and the expansive views increase in beauty with each step forward. The path leads past a pair of pretty mountain lakes and offers some fine camping for those who want more than a single day of exploring.

GETTING THERE

From Packwood, drive 17 miles east on U.S. Highway 12 to a poorly marked trailhead on the right. Pull off the highway into the wide turnout at 17 miles and find the trail starting on the right, behind the highway barrier.

ON THE TRAIL

The trail drops away from the highway, descending steeply through the forest to the banks of the Clear Fork of the Cowlitz River. No bridge exists here, so you'll need to do some wading—be extremely cautious, and keep in mind that early in the season, the water will generally get deeper and faster later in the day as the sun melts more snow.

Once across the river, the trail begins to gradually climb up the opposite wall of the Clear Fork Valley. As you gain elevation you gain views, and by the time you reach the subalpine meadows of Coyote Ridge you enjoy sweeping vistas that encompass Mount Rainier and all the long, green valleys between you and the mountain.

At 4.5 miles, the trail winds past Lost Hat Lake before climbing through broad hillside meadows to a trail junction near the summit of a 6376-foot knob atop Coal Creek Mountain. From here, the trail descends moderately to Lost Lake at 6.5 miles.

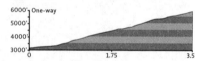

⑩ South Point Lookout

RATING/ DIFFICULTY	ROUND-TRIP	ELEV GAIN/ HIGH POINT	SEASON
***/4	7 miles	2900 feet/ 5980 feet	late June– October

[Elevation profile: One-way, from 3000' to 6000', horizontal axis 0 to 3.5, marked at 1.75]

Map: Green Trails No. 302 Packwood; **Contact/Permits:** USFS Cowlitz Valley Ranger District, Packwood Office, (360) 494-0600 / Northwest Forest Pass; **GPS:** N46 31.525, W121 40.043; **Status:** Endangered

👨‍👧 🏠 ❌ *You get both sides of the coin here: hiking through an old forest fire zone to a fire lookout site. You can see the place where men and women stood guard to try to protect the forests from fire, and you can see the effects of fire that wasn't contained. This route gets few visitors and as such offers a remarkable degree of solitude, but that lack of attention also means the trail is falling into disrepair. The route gets a bit brushy in places, and as it crests the open ridgeline below the summit, the path is very rough and hard to follow at times.*

GETTING THERE

From Packwood, drive 4 miles west on U.S. Highway 12 to a junction with Forest Road 20.

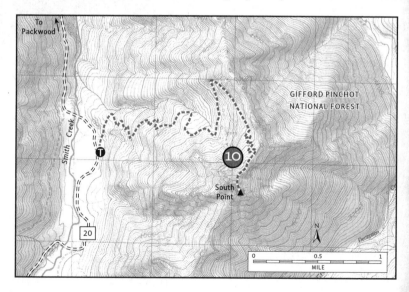

Opposite: Kim Brown near the summit of South Point, with Goat Rocks to the east

Turn left (south) onto this road and continue 4.9 miles to the trailhead on the left.

ON THE TRAIL

This is largely an open, sunlit trail thanks to an old forest fire that leveled much of the forest canopy and created a series of new wildflower meadows and deer-filled clearings. The forest is returning, but the timber is sparse still, leaving lots of sun-dappled terrain to explore.

The trail angles upward from the trailhead, riding switchbacks through the fire zone. After passing the old burn sites in the first 2 miles, the route loops north around the head of a small basin (a seasonal spring seeps out of the hillside above the trail, but generally not enough to be a stable water source).

Once on the ridgetop, the trail angles south once more, climbing moderately for 0.6 mile, then very steeply through a tight series of switchbacks to top out at the 5980-foot South Point summit, just 3.5 miles after leaving the trailhead.

Look for remains of the old lookout tower that stood here during the middle of this century. The adventurous hiker can scramble along an old trail (no longer maintained) that rides the crest of the South Point Ridge south for a few miles. There is no reliable source of drinking water along the entire trail, so be sure to carry all you need.

11 Dry Creek

RATING/ DIFFICULTY	ROUND-TRIP	ELEV GAIN/ HIGH POINT	SEASON
***/5	7 miles	2800 feet/ 3815 feet	late June– early November

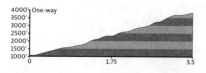

Map: Green Trails No. 303 White Pass; **Contact/Permits:** USFS Naches Ranger District, (509) 653-2205 / Northwest Forest Pass; **GPS:** N46 33.766, W121 42.555

Don't let the name fool you—this is no stroll along a forest brook. You'll dip your toes in Dry Creek within the first few minutes of this hike, then not see it again until you get back down from the long, steep climb ahead of you.

This steep forest trail offers few views and not much of interest other than thick second-growth fir forest, until near the route's end. But spectacular views await the patient and persistent. The 2800-foot elevation gain brings hikers to a vantage point that is unrivaled in the area. Once a Forest Service lookout tower stood here, but now all that is left are great views of the Cowlitz River Valley to the north and west; the high, craggy Smith Ridge to the east; and Goat Dike, a precipitous cliff, directly below on the north side of the ridge. On clear days the top of Mount Rainier can also be seen peeking up over the ridges to the north.

GETTING THERE

From Packwood, drive 4 miles west on U.S. Highway 12 to a junction with Forest Road 20. Turn left (south) onto this road and continue 0.5 mile to the trailhead on the right.

ON THE TRAIL

The trail begins by following the old roadbed a short distance before angling upward into the dense Douglas-fir forest. This young forest is dark and cool, which could be seen as a blessing, or a curse. It's a blessing because the trail climbs relentlessly from the start, weaving upward through endless switchbacks until sweat is running off you in rivers. If the forest were more open and sun-dappled, you'd surely bake on this steep ascent. The curse

View down to Dry Creek along the Dry Creek Trail

comes because even as the close canopy cools you, it also prevents any views outward.

For a full 3.4 miles, you'll hike under forest canopy. It's a pretty forest, full of birds and small critters. Finally, though, when you most ache for an open view, the trail crests the top of Smith Point and before you stretch the endless views you'd expect at a former look-out site, with Mount Rainier, Cowlitz Valley, the Goat Rocks, and all the peaks in the heart of the Gifford Pinchot National Forest spread out before you.

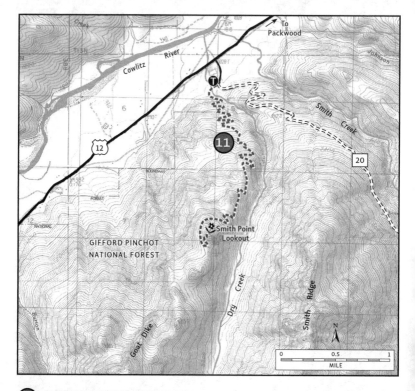

12 Ironstone–Burnt Mountain

RATING/ DIFFICULTY	ROUND-TRIP	ELEV GAIN/ HIGH POINT	SEASON
****/3	12 miles	850 feet/ 6596 feet	July– September

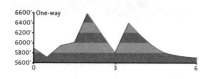

Maps: Green Trails No. 303 White Pass, No. 304 Rimrock; **Contact/Permits:** USFS Naches Ranger District, (509) 653-2205 / Northwest Forest Pass; **GPS:** N46 42.909, W121 9.961

Few times in life do hikers get the opportunity to enjoy a wonderful hiking adventure along a high, alpine ridge in a stunning wilderness area without first having to climb that ridge under their own steam. This is one of those rare opportunities. This route starts high from a road-end trailhead just outside the wilderness boundary, then rambles along the ridgeline of Burnt Mountain, onto the shoulder of Shellrock Peak, and then under the summit of Ironstone Mountain. Along the way, you'll explore wonderful ancient forests, cool forest glades, and flower-filled alpine meadows, and have ample opportunities to see wildlife and wide wilderness vistas—all without the *thigh-burning ascents and knee-grinding descents that usually are the prices paid for such stellar scenery.*

GETTING THERE

From White Pass, continue east on U.S. Highway 12 to Forest Road 1500, between Hause Creek and Riverbend Campgrounds at the east end of Rimrock Lake. Turn left (north) and follow FR 1500 for several miles before reaching FR 199. Turn left and find the Cash Prairie trailhead at the road's end after about 1.5 miles.

ON THE TRAIL

The Cash Prairie Trail rolls west through fragrant old forests and sun-dappled clearings for more than 1.7 miles to reach the lower flank of Burnt Mountain. From the east shoulder, the trail hooks around the meadows along the southside of the mountain, and a small scramble path leads hikers to the 6596-foot summit in less than 0.1 mile. This short off-trail excursion is generally worth the effort since the views from the summit are unmatched—you'll have a 360-degree view of all of the southern William O. Douglas Wilderness as well as south to the Goat Rocks and Mount Adams.

After leaving Burnt Mountain, the trail descends gradually into the forest, dropping to 5850 feet in a shallow saddle (2.7 miles out) between Burnt Mountain and Shellrock Peak. From here, the trail climbs once more, winding upward through the timber country to the

Rimrock Lake as seen from the Russell Ridge/Ironstone area

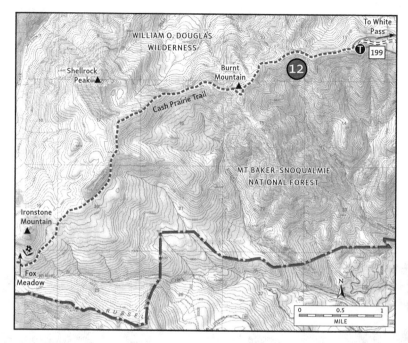

southern shoulder of Shellrock Peak (6350 feet) at mile 3.5. You'll find some broken views to the south, and nice looks north to the craggy summit of Shellrock, but push on for better scenery and more open vistas.

The trail descends gradually from this point on, rolling down the ridgeline through pretty forests to the south face of Ironstone Mountain. Here, at about 6 miles out, you'll break out into the broad expanse of Fox Meadow below the summit of Ironstone Mountain. Turn around in this wildflower field for the long, gradual climb back to the trailhead.

Map: Green Trails No. 303 White Pass; **Contact/Permits:** USFS Naches Ranger District, (509) 653-2205 / Northwest Forest Pass; **GPS:** N46 34.610, W121 21.493; **Status:** Endangered

❌ *This is wapiti country. For the uninitiated, wapiti is a Native American name for Rocky Mountain elk. These big, majestic beasts thrive along the eastern flank of the South Cascades, and come winter, hundreds of elk winter in the meadows of the Tieton River Valley. As the snow deepens, the elk move farther down the valley, feasting on the rich grasses that fill the*

13 Tieton Meadows

RATING/ DIFFICULTY	ROUND-TRIP	ELEV GAIN/ HIGH POINT	SEASON
***/4	3.5 miles	200 feet/ 3600 feet	May–November

meadows. Throughout the summer the elk disperse, though a few always seem to linger here, and come autumn the herds are back as the big bulls try to capture the attention of the cows during the rut. This is a magical time to visit the meadows as the lust-crazed bulls bugle challenges at each other. These melodious calls ring through the forests and meadows of the Tieton Valley through much of September. Of course, the meadows mean more than mere elk. Birds and beasts of all sizes, colors and species fill these rich fields. Exploring the meadows is an exercise in wildlife watching.

GETTING THERE

From Packwood, drive east over White Pass, then east on U.S. Highway 12 to Rimrock Lake, and turn south onto Clear Lake Road (Forest Road 1200). Continue about 3 miles, contouring around the west end of Clear Lake, before turning south onto FR 1207 (North Fork Tieton River Road). Drive south on FR 1207 to the trailhead at the road's end.

ON THE TRAIL

Shortly after you leave the trailhead, the path splits. Go left to follow Trail 1128. There is also a faint trail between the two established paths. This middle route is the fastest means straight up into the meadows, but it is old, rough, and poorly maintained, and will require bushwhacking.

The easier trail rolls up the south flank of the Tieton Valley, crossing the river in less than a quarter mile. You'll need to wade through the water (though the Forest Service sometimes has a footlog installed), but the river is seldom deep enough to cause problems. After crossing the river, the trail angles to the base of the southern valley wall to avoid the broad marshlands that fill the valley floor about a mile up from the road's end.

As you skirt the marshlands, stay quiet and listen—thousands of small birds thrive in the wetlands and adjoining forests. And where there are birds, there are hunters. Weasels, martens, bobcats, red foxes, and coyotes prowl these areas.

At about 1.5 miles, the primary trail turns sharply to the south and then east, climbing steeply away from the valley floor. Ignore that climb. Instead, veer to the right onto a primitive path away from the established trail and angle back down onto the floor, up-valley from the marshlands. In less than 0.25 mile, you'll be in extensive grass meadows. In spring and early summer, the meadows are awash in color as wildflower blooms fill the valley. Come autumn, the golden grasses rustle soothingly in the breeze.

Trail junction signpost in the Tieton Valley

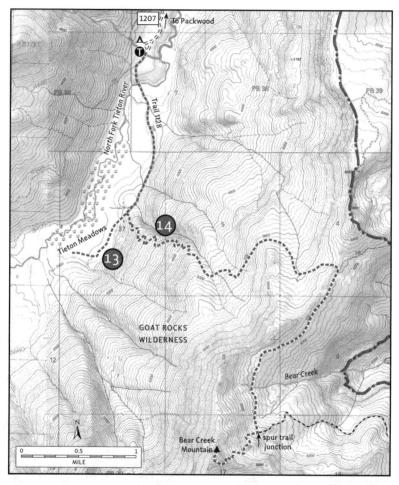

Hike as far as you like upvalley before turning back the way you came.

14 Bear Creek Mountain

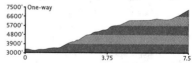

RATING/ DIFFICULTY	ROUND-TRIP	ELEV GAIN/ HIGH POINT	SEASON
****/5	15 miles	4000 feet/ 7337 feet	July– October

Map: Green Trails No. 303 White Pass; **Contact/Permits:** USFS Naches Ranger District, (509) 653-2205 / Northwest Forest Pass; **GPS:** N46 34.610, W121 21.493

After the first mile, you'll climb relentlessly, for much of the way in dense forests with few or no views. But the payoff for this thigh-burning, lung-tearing workout: incredible vistas from atop one of the highest peaks on the easternmost flank of the Goat Rocks.

GETTING THERE

From Packwood, drive east over White Pass, then east on U.S. Highway 12 to Rimrock Lake, and turn south onto Clear Lake Road (Forest Road 1200). Continue about 3 miles, contouring around the west end of Clear Lake, before turning south onto FR 1207 (North Fork Tieton River Road). Drive south on FR 1207 to the trailhead at the road's end.

ON THE TRAIL

The trail begins on the Tieton Meadow route described in Hike 13, rolling along Trail 1128 up the south flank of the Tieton Valley. After crossing the Tieton River at less than 0.25 mile (see Hike 13), Trail 1128 skirts the marshlands for another 0.75 mile, then angles away from the valley-bottom meadows and climbs steeply to the south, winding upward through the long series of switchbacks.

In the next 3.5 miles you'll stay under the

UNDERSTANDING ELK

Elk. Such a small, simple word for such a massive, majestic beast. I much prefer the Shawnee Indian name of *wapiti*, meaning "white rump." But a name is just a name and, wapiti or elk, these animals earn the respect and appreciation of anyone fortunate enough to see them in the wild.

But not all elk are created equal. Indeed, Washington boasts two distinct species of elk. Roosevelt elk, named for Theodore Roosevelt, are found on the Olympic Peninsula (hence their nickname, Olympic elk). In the Cascades—and points east—Rocky Mountain elk reign supreme.

Rocky Mountain elk are somewhat smaller than their Roosevelt cousins (a big Roosevelt bull may weigh more than a half ton), but they generally sport broader, heavier antler sets. A large part of this antler difference stems from the different habitats of each subspecies. Roosevelt elk tend to be in the foliage-rich rain forests of the Olympic Peninsula, so broad, heavy antlers become more problematic. Rocky Mountain elk thrive in the drier, more open forests of the Cascades, but they also move out over the plains of the eastern Cascade foothills and even out on to the desert steppes of the Columbia River Basin. Indeed, Rocky Mountain elk once existed in vast herds on the Great Plains, alongside the mighty American bison.

Elk of both types feed by browsing on a variety of vegetation, from grasses to berries to evergreen needles. The most impressive time to experience elk is autumn, when the herds are in rut—in other words, mating season. As with most ungulates, the elk males (bulls) fight among themselves to establish dominance and decide which bull gets to mate with the female elk (cows).

As part of the ritual, the bulls challenge each other by issuing ringing calls. Known as bugling, these calls can be an eerie trumpet tone that sends chills down the spine. Listening to the undulating high-pitched calls as twilight falls over a forest glade will get even the most unimaginative hiker thinking that they're lost in the forest primeval.

The best bet for experiencing wapiti in the South Cascades is along the trails in the White Pass and Mount St. Helens areas.

peer up to the summit crown to the west, and eastward out along the vast expanse of the eastern slope of the Cascades.

15 North Fork Tieton–Tieton Pass

RATING/ DIFFICULTY	ROUND-TRIP	ELEV GAIN/ HIGH POINT	SEASON
****/5	11.7 miles	2500 feet/ 5800 feet	July– November

Map: Green Trails No. 303 White Pass; **Contact/Permits:** USFS Naches Ranger District, (509) 653-2205 / Northwest Forest Pass; **GPS:** N46 34.610, W121 21.493; **Status:** Endangered

Deep pine forests dominate this route, offering an experience in dry-side ecosystems (see "Weather" in the introduction). The trail weaves around massive orange-tinged ponderosa pines and through fragrant spruce groves. Beavers and otters swim in the river below the trail, and owls, hawks, and eagles soar in the air overhead. Huge elk, mule deer, and black bear wander the hillsides around the trail, and snakes, coyotes, and cougars prowl the brush between the trees.

GETTING THERE

From Packwood, drive east over White Pass, then east on U.S. Highway 12 to Rimrock Lake, and turn south onto Clear Lake Road (Forest Road 1200). Continue about 3 miles, contouring around the west end of Clear Lake, before turning south onto FR 1207 (North Fork Tieton River Road). Drive south on FR 1207 to the trailhead at the road's end.

A Clark's nutcracker singing on a pine branch

forest canopy as the trail gains 2800 feet, reaching a trail junction at 4.7 miles out. Turn right and continue climbing, now moderately, along a ridgeline. This ridge crest leads into alpine meadow country as you climb west around the headwater basin of Bear Creek.

At 6.5 miles (6450 feet), you'll find a small spur trail leading southwest and the main trail veers east. Turn right onto this spur to scramble the last mile up the final 900 feet of elevation gain to the rocky summit of Bear Creek Mountain. Or simply enjoy the phenomenal views from this last trail junction. You can

ON THE TRAIL

From the riverside trailhead, stay right on Trail 1118 to climb along the north valley wall of the North Fork Tieton valley. The trail climbs gradually away from the water, gaining 600 feet in 1.2 miles to reach a trail junction. For the easiest climbing, stay left on the main trail (No. 1118) as it continues to parallel the river, while gradually ascending the valley wall. The trail crosses several small creeks but stays mostly in pine forest for the next 3 miles with few views beyond the pine trunks. Early-season hikers may enjoy blooming beargrass and some patches of crimson columbine, but in midsummer it's a dry forest devoid of color beyond the ever-present greens and browns.

That changes as the trail turns steeper until, at 4.9 miles, it reaches the Pacific Crest Trail (PCT) at Tieton Pass, elevation 4800 feet. Turn north and follow the PCT through forest glades and gardens of wildflowers, while still gaining elevation. In another 3 miles hiking farther north and east, you'll be 1000 feet higher (5800 feet elevation) and will have crossed some pretty meadows with wonderful views of Tieton Peak to the south.

At that point, near Hidden Spring—some 8 miles from the trailhead—leave the PCT and start a steep descent along Trail 1117 back to the Tieton River Valley. This trail drops 2000 feet in 2.5 miles. Great views are found on the first 0.5 mile, but after that

Hiking through old-growth along the North Fork Tieton Trail

the trail plunges into tree-lined switch-backs with few views.

Trail 1117 ends at the junction with the North Tieton River Trail (No. 1118). Turn left and retrace your steps over the 1.2 miles to the trailhead.

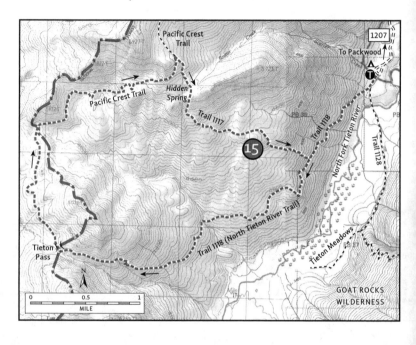

Opposite: Jumbo Mountain

dark divide / cispus area

There's really nothing dark about this wonderful wild region. The sunlit meadows that top the long, broad ridges are bright and colorful with fields of wildflowers. The name Dark Divide can be traced back to nineteenth-century gold prospector John Dark, who explored this broad region that divides Mount Adams and Mount St. Helens.

16 Cispus Braille Trail

RATING/ DIFFICULTY	ROUND-TRIP	ELEV GAIN/ HIGH POINT	SEASON
**/1	1 mile	0 feet/ 7337 feet	May– October

Map: Green Trails No. 333 McCoy Peak; **Contact/Permits:** USFS Naches Ranger District, (509) 653-2205 / Northwest Forest Pass; **GPS:** N46 26.323, W121 51.156

♿ *Barrier-free trails are generally designed for folks with mobility concerns—people in wheelchairs or with walking limitations. This unique forest path serves those forest visitors admirably, but it does far more than that. It also opens a wonderful Northwest forest up to the visually impaired. Even hikers who are completely blind can enjoy this remarkable trail.*

GETTING THERE
From Randle, drive 1 mile south on Forest Road 25 and then turn left (east) onto FR 23 (Cispus Road). Continue on FR 23 to its junction with FR 28. Bear right on FR 28, cross the Cispus River, turn right onto FR 76, and continue to the Cispus Environmental Center. Parking is on the left near the Elderberry Lodge.

ON THE TRAIL
It's hard to believe this area was leveled twice by forest fires, but it's true. But those fires are in the past, and the forest has recovered beautifully. This barrier-free interpretive trail explores the new forest and explains the changes wrought by the fires, as well as the processes of recovery.

Trail guide pamphlets are available at the Cispus Environmental Center, and the interpretive signs along the route are printed in bold, easy-to-read lettering and in braille. A guide rope is strung along the right side of the

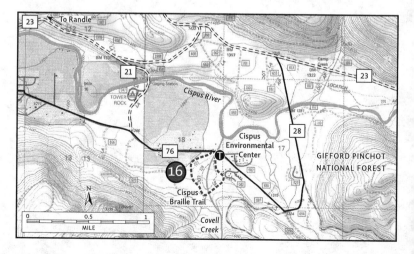

Guide ropes pass a nurse log along the Cispus Braille Trail.

trail; it helps the visually impaired move from station to station. The compacted-dirt trail is smooth and free of those toe-grabbing roots so often found on forest trails.

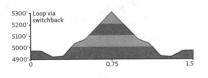

17 Burley Mountain

RATING/ DIFFICULTY	ROUND-TRIP	ELEV GAIN/ HIGH POINT	SEASON
**/2	1.5 miles	400 feet/ 5304 feet	July– October

5300' Loop via
5200' switchback
5100'
5000'
4900'
0   0.75   1.5

Map: Green Trails No. 333 McCoy Peak; **Contact/Permits:** USFS Cowlitz Valley Ranger District, Randle Office, (360) 497-1100/Northwest Forest Pass; **GPS:** N46 23.991, W121 52.212

This is an easy walk up to a picturesque fire lookout. Along the way, you'll find huckleberries in abundance along the track, and views that get increasingly better as you climb the slight grade. You have the option of hiking the old dirt road, or following a short trail that loops around the other side of the peak on its way to the summit. Either way, the views are grand and the walking is easy and highly enjoyable.

GETTING THERE

From Randle, drive 1 mile south on Forest Road 25 and then turn left (east) onto FR 23 (Cispus Road). Continue on FR 23 to its junction with FR 28/21. Bear right on FR 28/21, cross the Cispus River, turn right onto FR 76, and continue past the Cispus Environmental Center to FR 77 on the left (see Hike 16). Follow FR 77 for about 7.5 miles, then turn left onto the dirt track of FR 7605. The trailhead is found in another 1.5 miles at the start of Spur Road 7605-086.

ON THE TRAIL

Start up the dirt track of the spur road, enjoying a pleasant forest hike. After about 0.25 mile, your options double: You can stay on the road as it swings right into one long switchback to climb to the lookout atop the summit. (This way is easier walking for small legs and chatty hikers since two hikers can walk abreast.) Or you can go left onto a small single-track trail that swings out along the northern side of the mountain before attaining the summit.

Both options entail a half-mile of walking, and both offer the same bounty of huckleberry bushes and glorious views. Your best bet? Choose one track for the way up, and the other for the way down.

Distant view of the Burley Mountain lookout

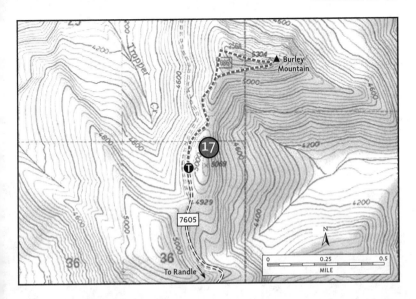

To Randle

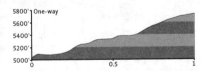

18 Hamilton Buttes

RATING/ DIFFICULTY	ROUND-TRIP	ELEV GAIN/ HIGH POINT	SEASON
***/2	2 miles	700 feet/ 5772 feet	May– October

Map: Green Trails No. 334 Blue Lake;
Contact/Permits: USFS Cowlitz Valley
Ranger District, Randle Office, (360) 497-
1100/Northwest Forest Pass; **GPS:** N46
23.467, W121 37.074

*Mount Adams, Mount Rainier, the Goat
Rocks, and the Tatoosh Range are all
visible from this 5800-foot peak. The views
are stunning and well worth the short hike
up. The trail is a bit rough, but the distance*
*is short enough that you can enjoy a good
stretch of the legs, bask in the grand views,
and still only invest a few short hours out of
your hectic schedule.*

GETTING THERE
From Randle, drive 1 mile south on Forest
Road 25 and turn left (east) onto FR 23 (Cispus Road). Continue to a junction with FR 22.
Turn left onto FR 22, drive 4.1 miles, and turn
right onto FR 2208. Continue 2.6 miles and
turn right onto FR 78. Follow FR 78 2.5 miles
to FR 7807. Bear left and continue on FR 7807
for 3 miles to Spur Road 7807-29. Drive to the
trailhead at the end of the road.

ON THE TRAIL
This trail doesn't pierce pristine wilderness,
as you'll soon realize walking through the
scars of human activity on the lower section.
The beauty of the route, though, awaits you
at trail's end, which is important to remember
while hurrying over the first half mile of the

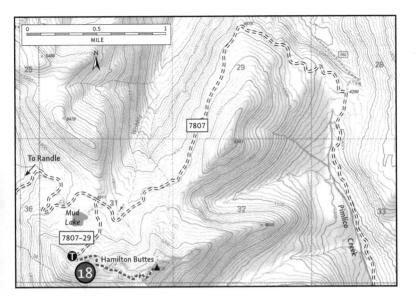

trail. In this early section the route follows an old access road, and the views are restricted by dense second-growth forest and alder thickets.

After leaving that old road and starting up the single-track path along Hamilton Buttes, your enjoyment level increases exponentially until you reach the summit at 5772 feet, a former lookout site. This is a great trail for late-afternoon hiking—it's short enough that you can enjoy the sunset from the summit, hurry down, and be back at your vehicle before the evening twilight completely fades into darkness.

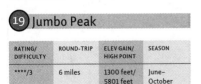

19 Jumbo Peak

RATING/ DIFFICULTY	ROUND-TRIP	ELEV GAIN/ HIGH POINT	SEASON
****/3	6 miles	1300 feet/ 5801 feet	June–October

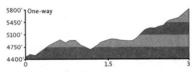

Maps: Green Trails No. 333 McCoy Peak, No. 334 Blue Lake; **Contact/Permits:** USFS Cowlitz Valley Ranger District, Randle Office, (360) 497-1100/Northwest Forest Pass; **GPS:** N46 20.123, W121 44.603; **Status:** Rescued

⭐ *Jumbo is one of the big boys of the vast Dark Divide Roadless Area. Not that Jumbo is a massive mountain, but rather, it's one of the big highlights of the incredibly scenic and wild roadless area that stretches across a network of ridges and peaks in the heart of the Gifford Pinchot National Forest. This route, like many of those of the Dark Divide, still faces the threat of excessive motorized use, but the ongoing efforts of trail*

Opposite: A hiker watches the sunset on Mount Adams from Hamilton Buttes.

advocates have defeated several attempts by motorcycle groups to rebuild these trails to make motorized travel easier. The rugged route is worth protecting, since the pristine meadows atop the ridges are very fragile and slow to heal—not to mention wonderfully scenic.

GETTING THERE

From Randle, drive 1 mile south on Forest Road 25 and turn left (east) onto FR 23. Continue south about 25 miles on FR 23, turning right (south) onto FR 2324. Drive to the road-end trailhead.

ON THE TRAIL

From the trailhead, head west as the path winds around the side of the ridge and slowly winds around the southern flank of Sunrise Peak. At just a mile out, you'll find a trail fork. Go left to descend gently about 400 feet in a quarter mile to a 4700-foot meadow-filled saddle on the ridge between Sunrise and Jumbo.

At the saddle, you'll find another fork. Stay left to climb again, still heading south-southwest to ascend the ridge leading toward the hulk of Jumbo. The trail rolls upward through open stands of forest and broad

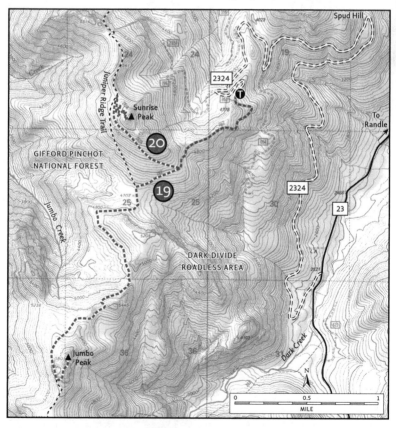

Jumbo Mountain from the approach to Sunrise Peak

expanses of wildflower meadow, becoming steep at times. When the trees part, you'll enjoy long views out over the blue-green world of the Dark Divide Roadless Area, including back north to Sunrise Peak, south to Jumbo, and east to Mount Adams.

The trail runs along the western flank of Jumbo's summit crown. At about 3 miles out, you can leave the trail and scramble upwards on a boot-beaten path, to the top of the mountain for outstanding views in all directions. Dark Mountain looms to the south, and Adams is ever present on the eastern horizon.

20 Sunrise Peak

RATING/ DIFFICULTY	ROUND-TRIP	ELEV GAIN/ HIGH POINT	SEASON
****/3	3 miles	1400 feet/ 5892 feet	June– October

Maps: Green Trails No. 333 McCoy Peak, No. 334 Blue Lake; **Contact/Permits:** USFS Cowlitz Valley Ranger District, Randle Office, (360) 497-1100/Northwest Forest Pass; **GPS:** N46 20.123, W121 44.603; **Status:** Rescued

The name tells you when to visit: Come early so you can be up on the summit as the sun rises in the east, bringing the massive snowcone of Mount Adams to life. Seeing the sun throw brilliant golden light onto the snowy white peak first thing in the morning is a wonderful way to start a day. But, fortunately

View north to Juniper Ridge from Sunrise Peak

for sleepyheads, it's not the only time to experience the magic of this route. Sunrise can be enjoyed at high noon and even at sunset—indeed, some of my favorite moments on Sunrise are at sunset, as the last rays of the day cast long, dark shadows across the deep valleys and sprawling ridges of the Dark Divide Roadless Area.

GETTING THERE
From Randle, drive 1 mile south on Forest Road 25 and turn left (east) onto FR 23. Continue south about 25 miles on FR 23, turning right (south) onto FR 2324. Drive to the road-end trailhead.

ON THE TRAIL
Following the Jumbo Peak Trail (Hike 19), head west as the path winds around the side of the ridge and slowly winds around the southern flank of Sunrise Peak. When you reach the trail junction at 1 mile out, turn right.

You'll find yourself now skirting the meadow-rich flank of Sunrise Peak, climbing steadily upward at the trail rolls up the southwestern face of the mountain. In just 0.5 mile, the trail reaches the long north–south route of the Juniper Ridge Trail (see Hike 22). But rather than join this picturesque path, look for a boot-built path to the right (east) and follow it up the steep western face of Sunrise.

The trail winds up a tight series of switchbacks, gaining the final 400 vertical feet in less than a quarter mile to put you atop the peak. Enjoy the 360-degree views for as long as your schedule allows, as you'll seldom find better.

21 Dark Meadow

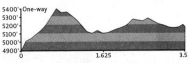

RATING/ DIFFICULTY	ROUND-TRIP	ELEV GAIN/ HIGH POINT	SEASON
*****/4	7 miles (longer option 12 miles)	500 feet/ 5400 feet	July– October

Map: Green Trails No. 333 McCoy Peak;
Contact/Permits: USFS Cowlitz Valley Ranger
District, Randle Office, (360) 497-1100/

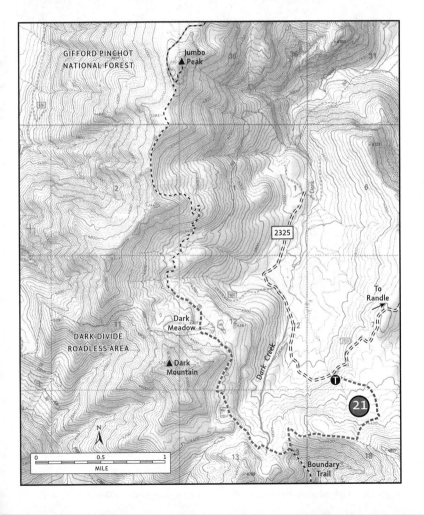

Lupines blooming in Dark Meadow

Northwest Forest Pass; **GPS:** N46 16.537, W121 44.611; **Status:** Rescued

The poorly named Dark Meadow is one of the bright spots of the entire Dark Divide Roadless Area. The trail passes through deep old forest, ascending modestly to high meadow-rimmed ridgelines.

As the trail ascends, the views begin to develop, and the thick fir forest thins and fades away entirely when the trail enters Dark Meadow near the ridge top. The stunning meadow is filled with wildflowers, panoramic vistas, and a wide variety of wildlife. The views encompass Mount Adams, Mount St. Helens, and Jumbo Peak just to the north.

GETTING THERE

From Randle, drive 1 mile south on Forest Road 25 and then turn left (east) onto FR 23. Continue south on FR 23 for nearly 25 miles, turning right (south) onto FR 2325. Drive 5.3 miles on this road, and locate a small, unmarked trail on the left (west) side of the road, elevation 3900 feet.

ON THE TRAIL

From the road, head up the faint boot trail as it climbs gradually through the trees and forest glades. If you lose the path, just keep climbing, knowing that you'll eventually reach the ridge-top trail no matter where you crest the ridge.

The path leads upward, slanting southeast. The trees give way to forest glades, laced with fruit-rich huckleberry brambles, and then broader fields of berries. Soon, even the huckleberry bushes fall back and the trail enters long, sweeping meadows atop the ridge.

At the junction with the Boundary Trail, turn right and hike north along the long ridgeline on the flank of Dark Mountain. The trail drops off the ridge and enters the broad, shallow cirque of Dark Meadow about 2.8 miles from the car, and for the next half mile the trail crosses this fragrant flower field.

EXTENDING YOUR TRIP

Continue north on the ridge-top trail, reaching Jumbo Peak (see Hike 19) about 2.5 miles past the meadow.

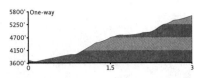

Map: Green Trails No. 333 McCoy Peak; **Contact/Permits:** USFS Cowlitz Valley Ranger District, Randle Office, (360) 497-1100/ Northwest Forest Pass; **GPS:** N46 23.792, W121 45.917

★ *Ridge-top meadows stretching for miles await you here, though you'll work to reap those rewards. The trail climbs steeply from the low valley bottom to the high ridgeline, but once aloft on those airy plains, you'll stroll through endless fields of flowers, basking in the glorious views of the South Cascades peaks, from the mammoth volcanoes—Mount Rainier, Mount Adams, Mount St. Helens, and even Oregon's Mount Hood—to the modest little knobs and knolls that make up the heart of the range—Juniper Peak, Jumbo Peak, Sunrise, Dark Mountain, etc.*

GETTING THERE

From Randle, drive 1 mile south on Forest Road 25 and then turn left (east) onto FR 23. Continue south 9 miles and turn right onto FR 28. Continue 1 mile and turn left onto FR 29. Four miles down FR 29, turn left onto FR 2904, and in another 4 miles look for the trailhead on the right (south) side of the road at about 3600 feet elevation.

ON THE TRAIL

The Juniper Ridge Trail (No. 261) climbs south from the trailhead, passing through an old clear-cut before ascending through long, looping switchbacks up the snout of the ridge. For more than 2 miles, the trail climbs, offering

22 Juniper Ridge

RATING/ DIFFICULTY	ROUND-TRIP	ELEV GAIN/ HIGH POINT	SEASON
★★★★★/4	6 miles (longer option 14 miles)	1900 feet/ 5611 feet	July– October

Dennis Long on Juniper Ridge, with views of the Cispus River Valley

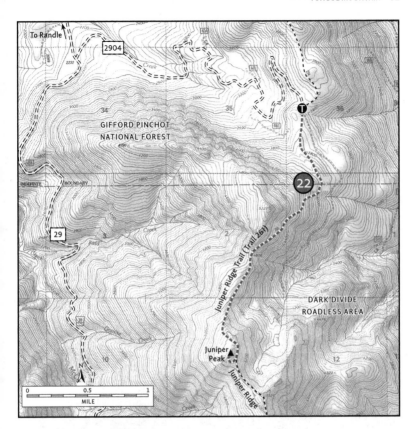

frequent photogenic views out over the forest and mountains to the north. The path rolls in a long, straight ascent from here, following the ridgeline through long fields of wildflowers to reach the sun-roasted top of Juniper Peak at 3 miles.

Stop and rest here. Take lots of pictures and pass some time dozing in the sun or just gazing out over the grand panoramas laid out before you. Mount Rainier dominates the northern skyline. The ragged line of the Goat Rocks Peaks, punctuated at their southern end by the tall cone of Mount Adams, captures the eastern horizon. Nearby, Sunrise Peak and Shark Rock can be seen looking south across the long, green valleys of the Dark Divide.

EXTENDING YOUR TRIP

Continue south along the ridgeline—all the way to Sunrise Peak (7 miles from the trailhead) if you have the time and energy—before returning to the trailhead.

23 Tongue Mountain

RATING/ DIFFICULTY	ROUND-TRIP	ELEV GAIN/ HIGH POINT	SEASON
***/3	3 miles	1200 feet/ 4838 feet	July– October

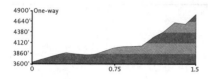

Map: Green Trails No. 333 McCoy Peak;
Contact/Permits: USFS Cowlitz Valley Ranger District, Randle, Office, (360) 497-1100/ Northwest Forest Pass; **GPS:** N46 23.792, W121 45.917

You'll be wagging your tongue over both the workout and the views after you enjoy this route. The workout comes by way of the last 0.75 mile to the summit, but you'll definitely earn the payoff you'll find at the top: stunning views of the Cispus River Valley and the peaks of the Dark Divide Roadless Area.

GETTING THERE

From Randle, drive 1 mile south on Forest Road 25 and then turn left (east) onto FR 23. Continue south on FR 23 for 9 miles, then turn right onto FR 28. Continue 1 mile and turn left onto FR 29. Four miles down FR 29, turn left onto FR 2904, and in another 4 miles look for the trailhead on the left (north) side of the road—opposite the Juniper Ridge Trail (Hike 22)—at about 3600 feet elevation.

ON THE TRAIL

The trail heads north from the road, climbing just 400 feet in a mile. The path angles gently upward through sunlight-filled forests to a trail junction at 1 mile. While the main trail drops off to the left, descending to the Cispus River, our trail goes right.

Look for the faint path leading upward on the right, around the 4000-foot elevation

Dennis Long about to summit Tongue Mountain

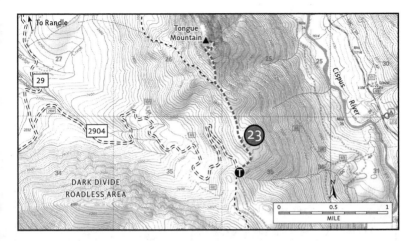

level. This is the summit trail, leading up the last 0.5 mile to the top of Tongue Mountain (4838 feet). This last 838 feet of climbing is steep and, as you break out of the forest onto sun-drenched meadow slopes, hot! But from the summit you'll love the views out over the Cispus River Valley to the north and the many long arms of the Dark Divide, a network of high, wild ridges in the heart of the forest between Mount Adams and Mount St. Helens.

24 Langille Peak

RATING/ DIFFICULTY	ROUND-TRIP	ELEV GAIN/ HIGH POINT	SEASON
****/4	5 miles	2100 feet/ 5372 feet	July– October

Map: Green Trails No. 333 McCoy Peak; **Contact/Permits:** USFS Cowlitz Valley Ranger District, Randle Office, (360) 497-1100/ Northwest Forest Pass; **GPS:** N46 22.901, W121 49.824

A forest of thick Douglas-fir (punctuated by fat, juicy huckleberries) runs for nearly 2 miles here before it begins to thin and open up into broad, windswept meadows on the ridge top. This trail—one of the long octopus arms that comprise the wild, remote Dark Divide region of the forest—stays high and open during most of the route's remainder. Early-summer hikers find the snow melted and wildflowers in full bloom. In addition to the bonanza of color underfoot, the Langille Ridge Trail is renowned for its beautiful vistas of distant peaks and valleys. Mount St. Helens, Mount Adams, and Mount Rainier can all be seen on clear days, and the deep, dark valleys on either side of the ridge give this area a true feeling of wilderness, even without an official wilderness designation.

GETTING THERE

From Randle, drive 1 mile south on Forest Road 25 and then turn left (east) onto FR 23. Continue to a junction with FR 28. Turn right (south) on FR 28, drive 6.8 miles, and turn left onto FR 2809. Continue to the trailhead near the road's end.

ON THE TRAIL

Climbing away from the trailhead, the Langille Ridge Trail soon loops into a series of long, sweeping switchbacks. The trail climbs steadily and steeply, staying mostly in forest as it heads south up the snout of Langille Ridge. The forest canopy is open enough, however, that huckleberries can be found all along the route, though

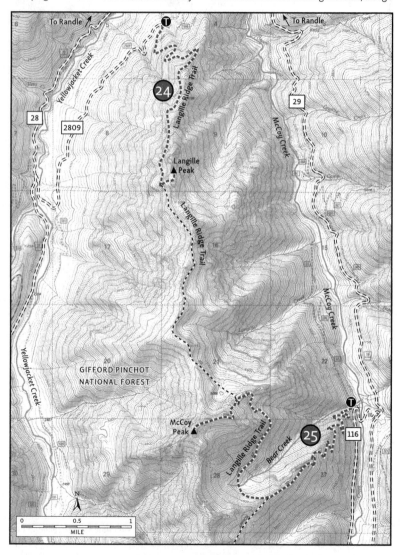

Views of fog-draped forest slopes from Langille Peak

the picking is scarce enough that it's not worth trying to collect the fruit in quantity. Just grab a few to snack on as you climb.

After the first 0.75 mile of switchbacks, the path straightens out a bit and angles south along the flank of Langille Peak proper. At just over 2 miles you are into the meadows that grace the upper slopes of the peak, and at around 2.2 miles you should look for a boot track on the left, leading upward through the meadows toward the summit of the peak. If you don't want to be a summit-seeker, simply stop and rest in the wildflower fields here. Otherwise, push upward to the 5372-foot summit (or at least the ridgeline just before the true summit) for stellar views east to Juniper Ridge and its many peaks: Juniper Peak, Tongue Mountain, Sunrise Peak, and Jumbo.

25 McCoy Peak

RATING/ DIFFICULTY	ROUND-TRIP	ELEV GAIN/ HIGH POINT	SEASON
****/4	8.4 miles	3200 feet/ 5856 feet	July– October

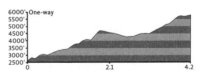

Map: Green Trails No. 333 McCoy Peak; **Contact/Permits:** USFS Cowlitz Valley Ranger District, Randle Office, (360) 497-1100/Northwest Forest Pass; **GPS:** N46 19.991, W121 47.618

Leaves of the false hellebore, commonly found along Langille Peak

This may be the steepest climb in the entire Dark Divide Roadless Area. It is certainly the steepest climb that is sustained for more than a few miles—you'll be huffing every step of the way up this 4-plus-mile monster, but once you top out, your worries are behind you and you can enjoy the breathtaking (!) views from this towering peak in this scenery-rich part of the Gifford Pinchot National Forest.

GETTING THERE

From Randle, drive 1 mile south on Forest Road 25 and then turn left (east) onto FR 23. Continue to a junction with FR 28. Turn right (south) on FR 28 and in less than a mile go left onto FR 29. Follow FR 29 several miles to a junction with Spur Road 29-116 on the right (just after crossing Jumbo Creek). Turn right onto Spur 116, cross McCoy Creek, and find the trailhead on the west side of the road.

ON THE TRAIL

Tighten your laces, because you're starting into the switchbacks immediately. From the trailhead at 2600 feet, you'll be climbing steeply through forest and meadow for the first 1.7 miles, where you reach a trail junction, elevation 4600 feet. That's right: 2000 feet of gain in 1.7 miles! Thankfully, that's not only the worst of the climbing, it's the start of the best scenery.

Turn right at the trail junction and head north on the Langille Ridge Trail as it sweeps around the head of the Bear Creek valley. After a mile of traversing the headwall, the trail climbs through hillside meadows for another half mile to reach your next junction. Here, at 5200 feet, a small spur trail cuts hard left (west), while the long Langille Ridge Trail leads off to the north.

Take the spur and mount those last 600 vertical feet in the final mile to attain your goal: the summit of McCoy Peak and the astounding views presented there. Look north to Langille Peak, and east to Sunrise Peak and the rest of the Juniper Ridge summits. Farther east is Mount Adams, and to the southwest is Mount St. Helens.

26 Bishop Ridge

RATING/ DIFFICULTY	ROUND-TRIP	ELEV GAIN/ HIGH POINT	SEASON
***/5	9 miles	3600 feet/ 5200 feet	July–October

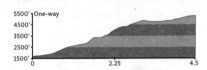

Maps: Green Trails No. McCoy Peak, No. 334 Blue Lake; **Contact/Permits:** USFS Cowlitz Valley Ranger District, Randle Office, (360) 497-1100/Northwest Forest Pass; **GPS:** N46 25.938, W121 45.756

Hikers might feel like there's no end in sight on the long, steep climb that characterizes the Bishop Ridge Trail. But really, the trail does level off. You just need to put in the miles! The trail levels out somewhat on the ridge and then leapfrogs from one ridge-top meadow to another, passing through intermittent sections of dense fir forest. So really, whatever the effort required, it's worth it, if you enjoy exploring lush forest ecosystems.

GETTING THERE
From Randle, drive 1 mile south on Forest Road 25 and then turn left (east) onto FR 23. Continue about 10 miles to the trailhead, which is a couple miles beyond North Fork Campground.

ON THE TRAIL
The trail climbs away from the Cispus River Valley, winding up the steep wall of Bishop Ridge. You'll soon lose yourself in the rich forest as the trail climbs, moderately most of the way, until it levels out between Slickrock Creek and Smoothrock Creek (apparently named by the most unimaginative geographers in the world).

After a mile or so, the trail breaks out of

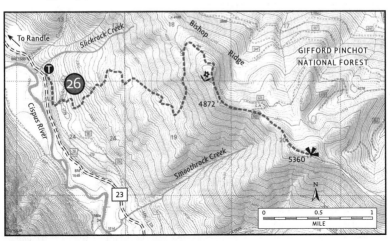

Vanilla leaf–lined Bishop Ridge Trail

the forest periodically, thrusting you into sun-filled sloping meadows before running back under the eaves of the woods. About 3 miles into the hike, you'll reach the ridge crest at 4872 feet.

From this point on, the climbing slows considerably, while the scenery gets more and more impressive. Lots of birds and wildlife fill the forest and meadows atop this ridge, loving the endless interface between clearing and woodland cover. Stop and listen frequently if you really want to enjoy the wildlife—birdsong can usually be heard, and deer are frequently seen browsing the sun-ripened vegetation.

At around 4.5 miles, you'll find yourself atop a small knoll at 5200 feet, with the best views of the trek. Look north to Castle Butte, and west down into the blue valley of the Cispus.

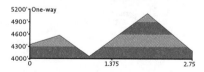

27 Hat Rock–Yellow Jacket Pass

RATING/ DIFFICULTY	ROUND-TRIP	ELEV GAIN/ HIGH POINT	SEASON
***/3	5.5 miles	1200 feet/ 5200 feet	June– October

Map: Green Trails No. 333 McCoy Peak; **Contact/Permits:** USFS Cowlitz Valley Ranger District, Randle Office, (360) 497-1100/Northwest Forest Pass; **GPS:** N46 25.938, W121 45.756

The Yellow Jacket–Hat Rock Trail allows you to enjoy the beauty of the southern end of

Langille Ridge and the views from Hat Rock. You'll find a small tarn awaiting you at Yellow Jacket Pass, a broad, flat forest glade between Straight Creek and French Creek.

GETTING THERE

From Randle, drive 1 mile south on Forest Road 25 and then turn left (east) onto FR 23. Continue to its junction with FR 28. Turn right (south), drive 7.8 miles, and turn left onto FR 2810. Continue to the trailhead just before the road's end.

ON THE TRAIL

The trail climbs steeply the first mile to attain the top of Langille Ridge. Here, turn

Hat Rock as seen from near Yellow Jacket Pass

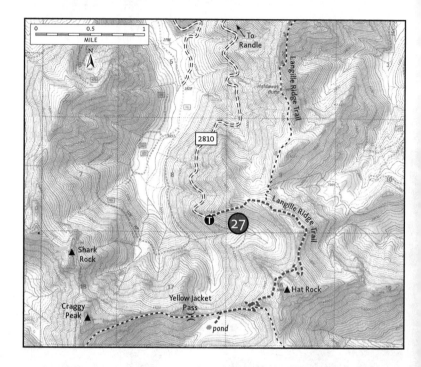

right onto the Langille Ridge Trail and sweep southeast in a long arc around the bowl of a creek basin to reach the flank of Hat Rock about 2 miles out.

Savor the views of Mount St. Helens and Mount Adams as you hike, since the summit of Hat Rock is fairly inaccessible—it requires a steep, rocky scramble that demands skill and experience.

Rather than attempt the top of Hat Rock, press on south to Yellow Jacket Pass at around 2.75 miles from the trail. A small pond sits amid the forest meadows here, making a fine turnaround. Between the trees you'll enjoy views of Craggy Peak and Shark Rock.

28 Spring Creek–Green Mountain

RATING/ DIFFICULTY	ROUND-TRIP	ELEV GAIN/ HIGH POINT	SEASON
***/3	8.2 miles	1200 feet/ 5107 feet	June– October

Map: Green Trails No. 334 Blue Lake; **Contact/ Permits:** USFS Cowlitz Valley Ranger District,

Opposite: Meadows along Spring Creek, with views of Mount Adams

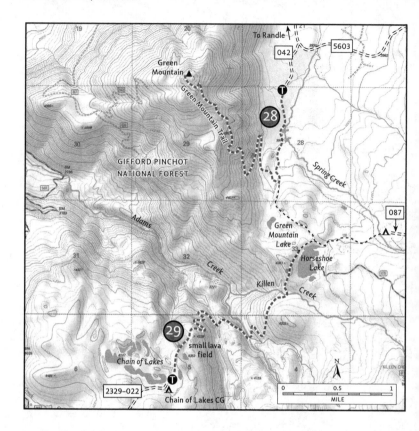

Randle Office, (360) 497-1100/Northwest Forest Pass; **GPS:** N46 19.830, W121 34.440

![icon] *This trail leads through small meadows, old fir forest, and huckleberry patches along the Spring Creek valley, before taking you on a moderate climb to the summit of the large, forested peak of Green Mountain.*

GETTING THERE

From Randle, drive approximately 1 mile south on Forest Road 25 and turn left (east) onto FR 23. Continue to the junction with FR 21. Turn left onto FR 21, drive to the Adams Fork Campground, and then turn left (south) onto FR 56. Cross the Cispus River and veer left, continuing 3.2 miles to FR 5603. Turn right and drive 2.8 miles to Spur Road 5603-042. Turn right onto the spur road and follow it about a half mile to the road's end and the trailhead.

ON THE TRAIL

Head up the trail as it wonders through the meadows, marshlands, and forests of the Spring Creek valley. The initial going is scenic forest ecosystems, filled with birds and beasts—including clouds of mosquitoes if you come too early in the year (i.e., July). After about 1.8 miles of nearly flat strolling along the valley bottom, turn right onto the Green Mountain Trail and begin your workout.

This trail winds moderately upward, following the southeast spine of the mountain. But don't fret too much about the climb—the pitch is pretty gentle. In the 2.3 miles to the summit (from the trail junction in the valley bottom), you'll gain a modest 1100 vertical feet. There are wonderful views awaiting you at the top, with mighty Mount Adams dominating the scene.

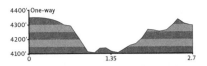

Map: Green Trails No. 334 Blue Lake; **Contact/ Permits:** USFS Cowlitz Valley Ranger District, Randle Office, (360) 497-1100/Northwest Forest Pass; **GPS:** N46 17.578, W121 35.759

29 High Lakes Ramble

RATING/ DIFFICULTY	ROUND-TRIP	ELEV GAIN/ HIGH POINT	SEASON
***/2	5.4 miles	200 feet/ 4329 feet	June– November

Set in the middle of a broad meadow and thin forest, the Chain of Lakes lie strung out like a strand of jewels in Gifford Pinchot National Forest. Sparkling blue-green waters reflect the glacier-covered north face of Mount Adams. Huckleberries, wild strawberries, and an assortment of mushrooms thrive in the area around the lakes, and wildlife—from white-tailed deer and black bear to deer

Chain of Lakes in the High Lakes region

mice and blackbirds—linger close by to feed on the bountiful harvest.

This route is on the border of the Mount Adams Wilderness, sharing many features with nearby routes to Takhlakh Lake (Hike 55) and Council Bluff (Hike 56).

GETTING THERE

From Randle, drive 1 mile south on Forest Road 25 and turn left (east) onto FR 23. Continue to a junction with FR 2329. Turn left and drive south to Spur Road 2329-022. Turn left and drive to the end of the road at Chain of Lakes Campground. The trailhead is on the east end of the campground.

ON THE TRAIL

The trail climbs gently east away from the campground. Before heading out the main trail, though, you might want to stroll the trails that weave between the six or seven lakes and ponds that make up the Chain of Lakes network. You might find yourself in the company of deer, elk, or even a black bear taking advan-

tage of the huckleberry fields that fringe the lakes. If nothing else, you'll surely see—and hear—an assortment of birds, from small twitterers to big kingfishers and raptors.

Once you commit to the main trail, you'll head east, dropping slowly—nearly imperceptibly—through broad meadows and open stands of forest to cross the wide Adams Creek valley. A thin strand of lava bed stretches across the eastern side of the valley showing you the black basalt that dominates the geology here.

The trail leaves the Adams Creek valley, skirts a small knoll, and leads to Horseshoe Lake at 2.7 miles out. You could arrange a car shuttle to here if you want a short one-way walk since there is road access to the other side of Horseshoe, but your best option is to just rest at the lake, then return the way you came.

Special Note: While mushrooms are common in the lakes basin and along Adams Creek, unless you are skilled in identifying mushrooms, don't eat any of them. While some are delicious, others are deadly.

Opposite: Mossy rocks along the Lower Lewis River

lewis river region

The Lewis River serves as a main artery for the rich forestlands south of the Dark Divide and flanking the Mount St. Helens country. This area offers some of the South Cascades' most scenic riparian trails, and some of the richest forest ecosystems in all of Washington. You'll find cathedral forests of old-growth Douglas-fir and cedar flanked by frothy whitewater chasms. Climb rolling hills and steep ridges to find glorious views. Wildlife, ranging from small bobcats to big bull elk, shares this wonderful landscape with you.

30 Spencer Butte

RATING/ DIFFICULTY	ROUND-TRIP	ELEV GAIN/ HIGH POINT	SEASON
***/2	3 miles (3 miles one-way with shuttle)	800 feet/ 4247 feet	June–November

Map: Green Trails No. 365 Lone Butte; **Contact/Permits:** USFS Mount St. Helens National Volcanic Monument, (360) 247-3900 / Northwest Forest Pass; **GPS:** N46 10.560, W121 55.596

A broad, flower-filled meadow lies just to the west of this trailhead. Spend a few minutes exploring fragrant Spencer Meadow before turning south and hiking down the trail. If you arrive early in the morning, you will probably find deer, elk, or both grazing in the lush forest clearing. If you don't see any of these big animals in the meadow, keep your eyes open as you hike up the butte trail.

GETTING THERE
From Cougar, drive about 30 miles east on Forest Road 90 to the Lewis River Camp-

ground and the junction with FR 93. Turn left (north) and continue 19 miles to the trailhead on the left. If you so desire, you can leave a shuttle car at the upper-elevation trailhead, found 3 miles south of the preferred northern trailhead where this hike begins.

ON THE TRAIL
The trail begins in Spencer Meadow and ends on Spencer Butte, gaining 800 feet in 1.5 miles. That's pretty easy going for a scenery walk through prime wildlife habitat.

From the lower trailhead on the north end of the butte, drop into Spencer Meadows and follow the trail south as it crosses the wildflower fields and starts upward after less than 0.25 mile. The trail climbs gently along the northern spine of the butte, moving upward through open forestlands. The views in the lower sections of trail are limited to the local scenery, but that's plenty scenic. The forest is rich in flora and fauna. Huckleberries provide sweet treats late in the summer, while bulbous beargrass blooms brighten the way early in the season.

The views start to show after hiking more than a mile, and the last 0.25 mile of climb provides wonderful views, which culminate in summit vistas at 1.5 miles. The 800 feet of elevation gain proves just enough to provide some startlingly clear views of distant peaks: from Mount Rainier to Mount Hood, and from Mount Adams to Mount St. Helens. If you missed spotting deer, elk, or black bear earlier, scan the forest and valleys closer to you—this might be your opportunity. The butte top is carpeted with wildflowers in early summer.

Turn around at the top, or continue another 1.5 miles south to the southern trailhead if you arranged a shuttle.

Special Note: Although this trail is outside the official boundary of Mount St. Helens National Volcanic Monument, the monument office administers the whole area.

Cirrus clouds over Mount St. Helens

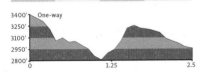

31 Cussed Hollow

RATING/ DIFFICULTY	ROUND-TRIP	ELEV GAIN/ HIGH POINT	SEASON
***/3	5 miles	600 feet/ 3400 feet	May– November

Map: Green Trails No. 365 Lone Butte; **Contact/Permits:** USFS Mount St. Helens National Volcanic Monument, (360) 247-3900 / Northwest Forest Pass; **GPS:** N46 10.387, W121 55.541

The gentle Cussed Hollow Trail weaves across the headwater basins of several tributaries of Cussed Hollow Creek, pro- *viding an unmatched forest exploration. Because of its relatively low elevation, the route is snowfree early in the summer, making it a fine early-season option for hikers tired of winter snow.*

GETTING THERE

From Cougar, drive about 30 miles east on Forest Road 90 to the Lewis River Campground and the junction with FR 93. Turn left (north) and continue 18.8 miles to the trailhead on the right.

ON THE TRAIL

From the trailhead, head north, crossing the first of several creeks within the first 0.25 mile. You'll soon swing east and start a slow, descending traverse around first one, then another of

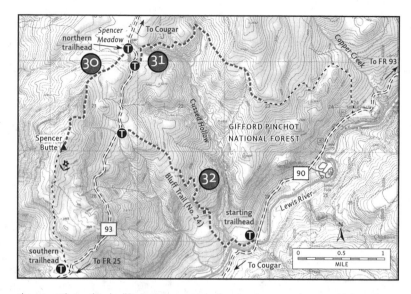

the many tributary headwall basins in the upper Cussed Hollow Valley. The trail stays within the forest canopy for its entire length, with occasional sun-bolts coming through the trees. But this is a woodland walk, so plan on enjoying the

Noble fir cones, a favorite fall treat of the Douglas squirrel

forest environment when you visit here. Grouse are common (listen for the "whoomp! Whoomp! WHOOMP!" calls) and bobcats are frequently present, hunting those big birds.

As the trail passes the 1-mile mark, it starts to head uphill once more, still winding in and out of various creek basins. At around 2.5 miles, the trail sweeps out around the ridge on the east flank of Cussed Hollow. As you leave the Hollow, pick a place and turn back at any time. If you continue on, the trail descends into the Copper Creek valley and ends at FR 90.

Special Note: Although this trail is outside the official boundary of Mount St. Helens National Volcanic Monument, the monument office administers the whole area.

32 Spencer Creek (Bluff) Trail

RATING/ DIFFICULTY	ROUND-TRIP	ELEV GAIN/ HIGH POINT	SEASON
**/4	6 miles (3 miles one-way with shuttle)	1800 feet/ 3400 feet	June– November

Mount Adams view from the Bluff Trail

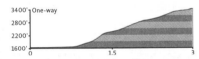

Map: Green Trails No. 365 Lone Butte;
Contact/Permits: USFS Mount St. Helens
National Volcanic Monument, (360) 247-3900
/ Northwest Forest Pass; **GPS:** N46 3.648,
W121 58.327; **Status:** Endangered

❌ *This forgotten trail suffers from neglect in the form of disuse. Too many hikers ignored the short trail up the canyon wall above the Lewis River, and the land managers have taken notice, it seems. The path provides a pleasant walk in the woods, but it is getting rough and brushy. It would be great to see these small remnant trails restored for day hikers to enjoy. In the meantime, it's rough but still enjoyable as a place to explore the recuperative power of nature. The forest is young and regrowing, and the wildlife is flocking back.*

GETTING THERE

From Cougar, drive east on Forest Road 90 past the Lewis River Campground to the trailhead. The trailhead is located just after the bridge on the north side of the Lewis River on the left.

ON THE TRAIL

The Bluff Trail (No. 24) is relatively short but steep. This route parallels the Lewis River downstream for a quarter mile, crosses the mouth of Cussed Hollow Creek, turns steeply uphill, and then ends at FR 93 at 3 miles.

During the climb up the ridge face, pause often to enjoy the startlingly beautiful southern and eastern views of Mount Adams, the Lewis River drainage, and Hungry Peak. If shuttle cars are available, you only need to hike one way, since Forest Road 93 is very accessible. Otherwise, turn around at the top of the route where you hit the upper trailhead and retrace your steps back to the valley floor, which will allow you to really enjoy the views.

Special Note: Although this trail is outside

the official boundary of Mount St. Helens National Volcanic Monument, the monument office administers the whole area.

33 Craggy Peak

RATING/ DIFFICULTY	ROUND-TRIP	ELEV GAIN/ HIGH POINT	SEASON
****/3	11 miles	1800 feet/ 5275 feet	June– October

```
5400' One-way
4900'
4400'
3900'
3400'
    0              2.75              5.5
```

Maps: Green Trails No. 365 Lone Butte, No. 333 McCoy Peak; **Contact/Permits:** USFS Mount St. Helens National Volcanic Monument, (360) 247-3900 / Northwest Forest Pass; **GPS:** N46 12.801, W121 54.980

Bear with us. This may not be the type of trail most hikers think of when they plan a "wilderness" *outing. Yes, this isn't wilderness. This is a forest that has been heavily impacted by humans, but which still has a wild beauty that is worth the effort to enjoy this long, forest ramble.*

The thick forest canopy here effectively shuts out most of the potential views from the early part of the trail, but that's okay. This is a beautiful forest to hike in. The old-growth fir, hemlock, and cedar forest is home to countless species of wildlife. If you want more to look at than forest, you will enjoy the small flower-filled meadows dotting the route. These lush green fields also offer the best long-distance views; the top of Mount Rainier occasionally "peaks" up in the north.

GETTING THERE

From Cougar drive about 16 miles east on Forest Road 90 to the east end of Swift Reservoir, and turn left (north) onto FR 25. Continue north to its junction with FR 93, 0.5 mile past

Mama and baby mountain goats on Craggy Peak

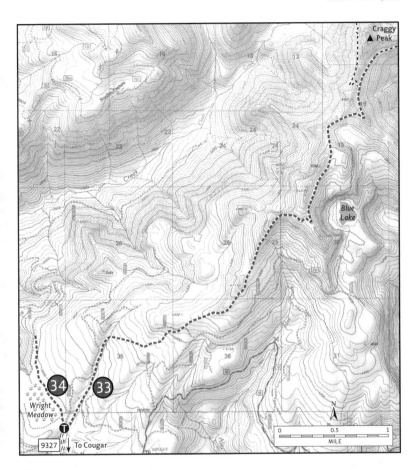

the Muddy River Bridge. Turn right (east) onto FR 93 and continue 12 more miles to FR 9327. Turn left (north) onto this road and drive 0.5 mile to the trailhead on the right.

ON THE TRAIL

Leave the trailhead on the shoulder of Wright Meadow and start upward into the forest. The trail soon gains the crest of the long ridge, heading north, and stays there.

You'll find the path intersecting old logging roads as the forest shifts periodically from old second-growth, to young third-growth, to ancient cathedrals. You'll notice a few clear-cut scars at times. Still, nature has a miraculous way of curing itself, and under the scars you'll find wonderful wild country to explore. Deer wander this woods, and a host of small animals scurry underfoot or flutter overhead.

By the time you hit the 2-mile mark, you're atop the fairly pristine ridge, now dancing in and out of wildflower meadows. At around 3 miles, you skirt the ridge high above Blue Lake, enjoying views down onto the sparkling waters. Then it's on to the head of the Straight Creek Basin, nestled on the south slope of Craggy Peak.

At about 5 miles, the trail splits. Go right for grand views up the wildflower-lined slope of Craggy to its craggy summit—and down into the deep bowl of Straight Creek Basin. Or go left and slide along the west flank of Craggy for beautiful views north of the fin of Shark Rock. Either way, 0.5 mile of walking covers the best views along each path.

Special Note: Although this trail is outside the official boundary of Mount St. Helens National Volcanic Monument, the monument office administers the whole area.

34 Wright Meadow

RATING/ DIFFICULTY	ROUND-TRIP	ELEV GAIN/ HIGH POINT	SEASON
****/2	3 miles	100 feet/ 3400 feet	June– October

Map: Green Trails No. 365 Lone Butte; **Contact/Permits:** USFS Mount St. Helens National Volcanic Monument, (360) 247-3900 / Northwest Forest Pass; **GPS:** N46 12.801, W121 54.980

This hike is less an established trail to follow as a region to explore. There is a trail, but to really experience the richness of the meadows, you need to explore the areas around the trail. Move quietly and lis-

ten: Birds use this area as nesting grounds, and as places to hunt, whether it's for grass seeds, small insects, or big rodents. And yes, critters roam here too, from ground squirrels to weasels, coyotes, and cougars—as well as the ever-present black-tailed deer.

GETTING THERE

From Cougar, drive about 16 miles east on Forest Road 90 to the east end of Swift Reservoir and turn left (north) onto FR 25. Continue north to its junction with FR 93, 0.5 mile past the Muddy River Bridge. Turn right (east) onto FR 93 and continue 12 more miles to FR 9327. Turn left (north) onto this road and drive 0.5 mile to the trailhead on the left.

ON THE TRAIL

The Wright Meadow Trail heads northwest away from the trailhead, slicing along the eastern side of a marshland at the bottom of the meadow. If you follow the trail, you'll find yourself back on FR 9327 in about a mile—the road loops wide around the meadow, while our trail slices across it.

Turn around the road and head back the way you came, but rather than stick to the path, angle off to the left (north) and explore the gently sloping meadow above the trail. Move quietly and check behind stands of trees to see what wildlife lurks there. If you lack routefinding skills, simply stick to the trail and follow it back to the trailhead. But if you know how to use a map and compass, and you can keep yourself heading in the right direction, move a ways off the trail to see what lies beyond.

Special Note: Although this trail is outside the official boundary of Mount St. Helens National Volcanic Monument, the monument office administers the whole area.

Old-growth forest along the Wright Meadow Trail

35 Snagtooth Mountain

RATING/ DIFFICULTY	ROUND-TRIP	ELEV GAIN/ HIGH POINT	SEASON
*****/2	3.5 miles	700 feet/ 4900 feet	June– October

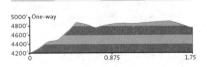

Maps: Green Trails No. 365 Lone Butte, No. 333 McCoy Peak; **Contact/Permits:** USFS Mount St. Helens National Volcanic Monument, (360) 247-3900 / Northwest Forest Pass; **GPS:** N46 14.883, W121 48.927

No crooked smiles here: You'll be sporting a full-on Cheshire Cat toothy grin as you find yourself hiking along under the craggy summit of Snagtooth Mountain. After all, this route provides a very pleasant walk with some better-than-average views. The trail is a good choice when time is limited or weather is less than perfect. Many of the best vistas along the route are found close in to the trailhead, and they are not dependent on crystal-clear skies.

GETTING THERE

From Cougar, drive east on Forest Road 90 to the Lewis River Campground and the junction with FR 93. Turn left (north) onto FR 93 and

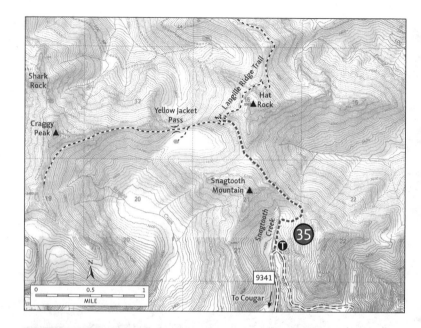

Upper summit cliffs of Snagtooth Mountain

drive to its junction with FR 9341. Turn right (east) and drive to the trailhead on the left.

ON THE TRAIL

The trail heads up the Snagtooth Creek valley, paralleling the creek briefly before climbing onto the wall above the waterway. In the first 0.5 mile, you'll get well clear of the creek and then climb right out of the creek basin itself as the trail moves up on the upper reaches of Snagtooth Mountain. The trail sticks to the eastern face of the mountain, providing astounding views north and east, as well as west up onto the face of Snagtooth. **Note:** It is possible to scramble to the summit of Snagtooth, but extreme care should be taken when navigating loose rocks and scree.

The trail runs under the summit face at around 1 mile, then continues north, climbing past the peak to join the southern end of Langille Ridge near Yellow Jacket Pass (see Hike 27) at 1.75 miles. Turn around at the trail junction, or head up to the pass before returning home.

A male western tanager in open forest of firs

36 Quartz Ridge–Summit Prairie

RATING/ DIFFICULTY	ROUND-TRIP	ELEV GAIN/ HIGH POINT	SEASON
***/3	6 miles	1800 feet/ 5245 feet	June–October

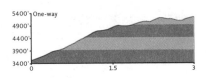

Maps: Green Trails No. 365 Lone Butte, No. 333 McCoy Peak; **Contact/Permits:** USFS Mount St. Helens National Volcanic Monument, (360) 247-3900 / Northwest Forest Pass; **GPS:** N46 11.868, W121 46.877

It's always a good sign when your trail starts in a well-named place. We start this hike at Summit Prairie, a beautiful location with a well-earned name. The trail rides the crest of the stunning Quartz Creek Ridge, running through wonderful forest and broad wildflower meadows. You can meander at will for 1 mile, or 5, along the ridgetop meadows as you enjoy the views down into the deep valleys of Quartz and French Creeks.

GETTING THERE

From Cougar, drive about 30 miles east on Forest Road 90 to find FR 9075 on the left. Turn onto FR 9075 and follow it to the trailhead at road's end.

ON THE TRAIL

The Summit Prairie trailhead provides access to a gentle hike along the crest of Quartz Creek Ridge—gentle, that is, after you make the steep and dusty climb on the first mile of the route. You'll switchback through a long series of tight turns for that first mile, and then suddenly crest out on

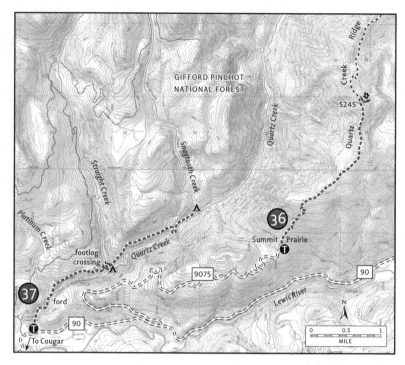

the ridge top. Fortunately, during the initial climb, the surrounding forest is thick and shady, which keeps hikers from baking in the hot summer sun. There are even a few huckleberries along the route to provide nourishment.

At the ridge top the walking is easy, and the views are spectacular. The network of broad, meadow-topped ridges of the Dark Divide sprawls across the scenery to the west, the white summits of Mount Adams and Mount Rainier punctuate the vistas to the east and north, and the beautiful valley of the Lewis River stretches away to the south.

You'll be able to wander for miles, but at about 3 miles out, you'll cross the high point of the ridge at 5245 feet. Keep going or turn back—there's no wrong answer here.

EXTENDING YOUR TRIP

If you do want more mileage, press on another 1.5 miles to find spectacular views and stunning meadows in the basin above Deer Creek.

37 Quartz Creek

RATING/ DIFFICULTY	ROUND-TRIP	ELEV GAIN/ HIGH POINT	SEASON
***/3	8 miles	500 feet/ 2500 feet	June– November

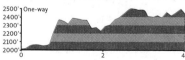

Map: Green Trails No. 365 Lone Butte; **Contact/Permits:** USFS Mount St. Helens

National Volcanic Monument, (360) 247-3900 / Northwest Forest Pass; **GPS:** N46 10.959, W121 50.935

The Quartz Creek route is a river trail, but not a river valley trail. Sure, it follows the creek upstream, but it doesn't exactly parallel it. This path weaves in and out of side canyons and up and down small rises and ridges, always working upstream, but seldom coming very close to the waters of Quartz Creek. When it does dip down and access the creek, however, the views are stunning.

The creek is a rugged, swift mountain river teeming with trout. Several good campsites are easily accessible, many of them near the shores of the creek, and the scenery near and away from the river is spectacular. The side canyons and ravines are often cut down the middle by rushing tributary creeks that thunder through narrow slots and bound over steep drops. The forest that shades the entire route is dominated by deep, old groves of Douglas-fir and western red cedar, and the high, shimmering cliff walls of Quartz Canyon are beautiful.

GETTING THERE

From Cougar, drive east on Forest Road 90 to the Quartz Creek Bridge. The trailhead is on the left.

ON THE TRAIL

The trail rolls up and down as it meanders up the Quartz Creek valley for several miles. The first mile actually makes use of an ancient miner's road, though nature has reclaimed most of the old roadbed, leaving just a single track to follow. You might still find a few rusty hulks along the path, though—the last dingy remains of miners' broken dreams.

The trail crosses Platinum Creek at about 0.75 mile. No bridge exists, so you'll need

Quartz Creek

to ford the creek. This is generally easily accomplished **unless** the creek is swollen with snowmelt early in the year. As with all river crossings, use extreme caution.

At 2 miles, the trail brings you to the second river crossing, though this time there is (usually) a stable footlog to bridge Straight Creek. The forest adjoining Straight Creek is mostly old second-growth, but it's grown up nicely. Just across the creek, you'll find the first of the fine campsites that dot this route.

Push on another 2 miles, passing yet another old (1970s-era) clear-cut full of young trees and then more ancient forest. You'll find the third creek crossing, at Snagtooth Creek, 4 miles out. There are campsites here for those who want them, and for day hikers, Snagtooth

makes a wonderful place to stop and rest before turning back.

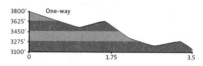

38 French Creek

RATING/ DIFFICULTY	ROUND-TRIP	ELEV GAIN/ HIGH POINT	SEASON
****/4	7 miles	700 feet/ 3800 feet	June– November

Map: Green Trails No. 333 McCoy; **Contact/ Permits:** USFS Mount St. Helens National Volcanic Monument, (360) 247-9900 / North-

An American dipper rests on a rock in French Creek.

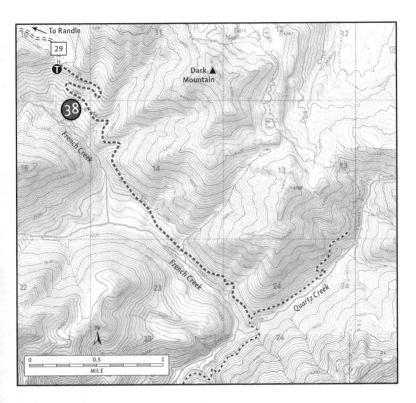

west Forest Pass; **GPS:** N46 16.669, W121 47.655; **Status:** Threatened

Few people visit this trail, so you *should have the deep-forest path to yourself. The route descends gradually from the road-end trailhead, dropping into the French Creek valley and eventually ending at a junction with Quartz Creek Trail alongside that stunningly pretty river.*

GETTING THERE

From Randle, drive 1 mile south on Forest Road 25 and then turn left (east) onto FR 23. Continue to its junction with FR 28. Turn right (south) on FR 28, and in 1.2 miles turn

left (southeast) onto FR 29. Drive south to the road's end and the trailhead.

ON THE TRAIL

From the trailhead, start down through the hillside meadows and soon enter thick forests as the path descends into the French Creek valley. The trail drops gradually, crossing a few tributary creeks in the first mile. At just over 1.5 miles, you'll move close enough to the tumbling waters of the creek to hear the aquatic music.

The trail, now in dense old forest, slides down along the creek at times in the third mile, reaching the Quartz Creek Trail at 3.3 miles. A short way farther along this new trail, and you'll find grand views of Quartz Creek itself. Find a place to sit and relax while enjoying the riparian delights before heading back *up* the trail.

39 Badger Peak

RATING/ DIFFICULTY	ROUND-TRIP	ELEV GAIN/ HIGH POINT	SEASON
**/1	1.75 miles	700 feet/ 5664 feet	March– November

Map: Green Trails No. 333 McCoy; **Contact/ Permits:** USFS Mount St. Helens National Volcanic Monument, (360) 247-3900 / Northwest Forest Pass; **GPS:** N46 17.704, W121 53.336

A rough road and short trail may deter you from making this hike, but remember the great views and solitude that await at the top. Badger Ridge Trail, steep in places and a bit primitive, traverses the ridge on the north flank of Badger Mountain. There are pleasant views from the trail, but the best panoramas of the surrounding forests and mountains are found at the top of Badger Mountain.

GETTING THERE

From Randle, drive 1 mile south on Forest Road 25 and then turn left (east) onto FR 23. Continue to the road's junction with FR 28. Take a right (south) turn onto FR 28 and drive 13 miles to FR 2816. Turn left (east) and follow FR 2816 for 4.4 miles to the trailhead. **Note:** Last 4.4 miles are rough and narrow; use of a high-clearance vehicle is recommended.

ON THE TRAIL

From the trailhead, head south along the Badger Ridge Trail. In 0.75 mile, the path splits; take the rough left-hand trail. This little rough-hewn trail climbs almost straight to the

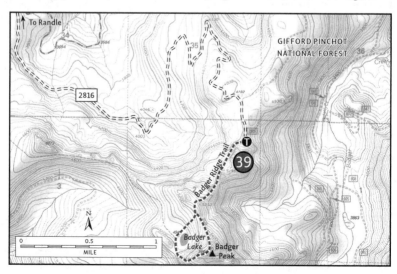

View of Mount St. Helens from the summit of Badger Peak

summit, a short (approximately 0.5 mile) but strenuous scramble. The summit is a great place to recuperate, however. Once home to a fire lookout station, the 5564-foot peak offers views ranging from Mount Rainier to Mount St. Helens. The most impressive sight is Pinto Rock, the craggy remains of a long-gone volcano.

When it's time to leave the summit, drop off the south side of the peak by way of a faint game trail/boot-built trail. This path drops quickly to a well-established trail. Turn right and stride out to Badger Lake. Turn right around the north shore of the lake, and follow the trail back to the main Badger Ridge Trail and that trail fork that led you to the summit. Continue on, and soon you'll be back at the trailhead.

40 Curly Creek

RATING/ DIFFICULTY	ROUND-TRIP	ELEV GAIN/ HIGH POINT	SEASON
****/1	1 mile	100 feet/ 1250 feet	March–November

Map: Green Trails No. 365 Lone Butte; **Contact/Permits:** USFS Mount St. Helens National Volcanic Monument, (360) 247-3900 / Northwest Forest Pass; **GPS:** N46 3.648, W121 58.327

  A pair of waterfalls is visible from this broad, compact-gravel trail.

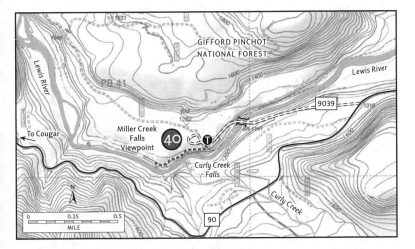

Climbing through a thick stand of Douglas-fir and noble fir, the route breaks into the open at a viewpoint overlooking Curly Creek Falls, a pretty cascade on the Lewis River. Enjoy the crashing water before moving up the trail to a second viewing platform. At this point the scenery consists of Miller Creek Falls, a smaller cascade that is as picturesque as Curly Creek Falls. The trail doesn't provide river access, but it is a good place to watch the falls and the autumn anglers trying to catch spawning steelhead trout.

GETTING THERE

From Cougar, drive about 20 miles east on Forest Road 90 to its junction with FR 9039. Turn left (north) onto this road and continue 0.75 mile. Cross the Lewis River and then turn into the parking area on the left, just beyond the bridge.

ON THE TRAIL

The trail is a wide, well-traveled path from the trailhead downstream. In just over a

Opposite: Curly Creek Falls

quarter mile, you'll find a grand view across the Lewis River to the wonderful cascades of Curly Creek. Move on a little farther, and better viewing can be found.

41 Big Creek Falls

RATING/ DIFFICULTY	ROUND-TRIP	ELEV GAIN/ HIGH POINT	SEASON
****/1	1.5 miles	300 feet/ 1900 feet	March– November

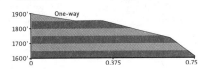

Map: Green Trails No. 365 Lone Butte; **Contact/Permits:** USFS Mount St. Helens National Volcanic Monument, (360) 247-3900 / Northwest Forest Pass; **GPS:** N46 5.634, W121 54.436

Along this trail, interpretive signs offer information on the flora, fauna, and geography of the area, but you won't need signs to figure out that this land

Big Creek Falls

is beautiful and wild. The wide, compacted trail meanders through ancient Douglas-fir forest before reaching the viewing platform overlooking the falls.

GETTING THERE

From Cougar, drive about 25 miles east on Forest Road 90 up the Lewis River Valley to the well-marked trailhead on the left.

ON THE TRAIL

Start down the wide, well-groomed trail, and as you near the viewing area you'll hear crashing water echoing through the tall trees. Once you see it, the falling white water is awe-inspiring. The waterfall leaps into view as you round the last bend of the trail and immediately grabs your attention. The sight of the falls, the sound of the crashing water, and the mute vibrations caused by the pounding water dominate your senses. It is a wonderful experience.

42 Speed onto Lewis River

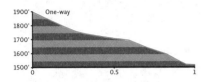

RATING/ DIFFICULTY	ROUND-TRIP	ELEV GAIN/ HIGH POINT	SEASON
***/2	2 miles	400 feet/ 1900 feet	March– November

Map: Green Trails No. 365 Lone Butte; **Contact/Permits:** USFS Mount St. Helens National Volcanic Monument, (360) 247-3900 / Northwest Forest Pass; **GPS:** N46 6.129, W121 54.389

If you want to reach the beautiful Lewis River quickly, this is your trail. In the spring and fall, ocean-running steelhead return en masse. Even if you don't plan on fishing, we recommend bringing a pair of polarized sunglasses to help you peer into the swirling cold water and spot the big fish. Look for ripples as the fish lunge up from under big rocks to snatch insects off the surface of the river.

GETTING THERE
From Cougar, drive about 25 miles east on Forest Road 90 up the Lewis River Valley to the well-marked trailhead on the left (about a mile past the Big Creek Falls trailhead, Hike 41).

ON THE TRAIL
The trail drops steeply from the road into the Lewis River Basin, slicing through thick old-growth pine and fir forest. Anglers love this trail because it takes them right to water that's chock-full of big rainbow, brown, and brook trout. Hikers who don't fish will still love the path since it provides a beautiful walk down to a front-row seat on the beautiful riparian world.

Late in the year, it might be possible to ford the river and continue your trek on the Lower Lewis River Trail found on the north side of the river. But don't force the ford—it's better to simply sit back, relax, and enjoy the river music for a while before climbing back the way you came.

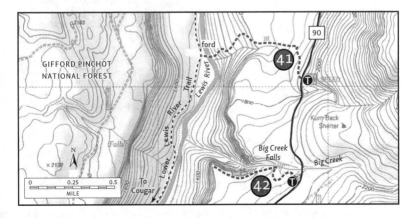

Huge old-growth firs near the Lewis River

The climb back up to the car is a workout, so go slow and enjoy the deep-forest environment.

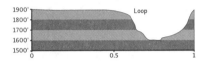

43 Cedar Flats Nature Trail

RATING/ DIFFICULTY	ROUND-TRIP	ELEV GAIN/ HIGH POINT	SEASON
**/1	1 mile	400 feet/ 1900 feet	March– November

```
1900'                          Loop
1800'
1700'
1600'
1500'
     0                0.5                  1
```

Map: Green Trails No. 365 Lone Butte; **Contact/Permits:** USFS Mount St. Helens National Volcanic Monument, (360) 247-3900 / Northwest Forest Pass; **GPS:** N46 6.695, W122 1.099

Looping through a cathedral forest of massive western red cedars and Douglas-fir, this trail offers a lesson in forest ecology. There are countless examples of life springing from death. Huge logs lie across the valley floor—the remains of ancient trees that finally died of age. Vibrant, young trees now grow from these great logs, nourished by the decaying wood of the old giants. Lush mosses, lichens, and ferns carpet the forest and give the trail an emerald glow. From the second half of the trail, you can enjoy views of the Muddy River.

GETTING THERE

From Cougar, drive east on Highway 503 (Forest Road 90) to FR 25, at Pine Creek Information Station. Turn left and drive 6 miles to the trailhead on the right.

Old-growth Douglas-fir and cedar in the Cedar Flats Nature Area

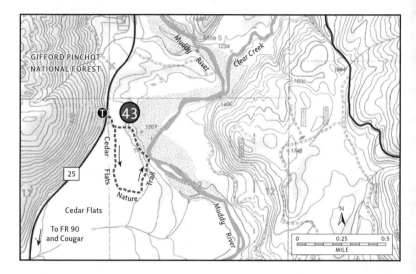

ON THE TRAIL

Enjoy the hike counterclockwise to really get the most out of the experience. This direction will provide you the most enjoyable viewing, as you can look out onto the Muddy River while you complete the short loop. This picturesque river meanders across the broad glacier-carved valley, routinely changing course with each big winter storm. The river channel is lined with gravel and sandbars, which serve as favorite drinking lounges for the herds of elk that winter near here. Keep on an eye out for the big beasts from mid-October (after the breeding season) to late spring.

Opposite: Mount Gilbert and the Goat Rocks from the Pacific Crest Trail

goat rocks region

The core of this region is the Goat Rocks Wilderness, but the beauty of the Goat Rocks goes beyond the politically set boundaries of that protected area. The high spine of the Goat Rocks stands as a distinctive landmark seen from much of the South Cascades, but once upon a time, that long string of craggy rocks was much grander. Indeed, today's "Goat Rocks" were once merely the flank of a 12,000-foot volcano that has eroded away after an eruption some 2 million years ago. The designated wilderness area encompasses the remaining peaks, the tallest of which are Gilbert Peak (8184 feet) and Old Snowy Mountain (7880 feet). The trails included below as part of the Goat Rocks Region stretch out into the surrounding valleys and ridges that are part of the great Goat Rocks world.

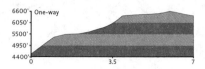

Map: Green Trails No. 303 White Pass; **Contact/Permits:** USFS Cowlitz Valley Ranger District, Packwood Office, (360) 494-0600 / Northwest Forest Pass; **GPS:** N46 38.584, W121 22.753

It's unfortunate that prior abuses of the Shoe Lake Basin have forced the area to be closed to camping, but the lake and the trails to it are pretty enough that a long day hike to the area is well worth the effort. Campers overran Shoe Lake in the 1980s, and the fragile meadows around the pond were crisscrossed with social trails and dotted with bare-earth tent sites. In the years since camping has been prohibited, the vegetation has slowly recovered, though faint trails still show through the wildflowers.

This trail which runs along Hogback Mountain is a classic example of what most

44 Shoe Lake

RATING/ DIFFICULTY	ROUND-TRIP	ELEV GAIN/ HIGH POINT	SEASON
****/3	14 miles	2200 feet/ 6600 feet	July–October

Shoe Lake Basin

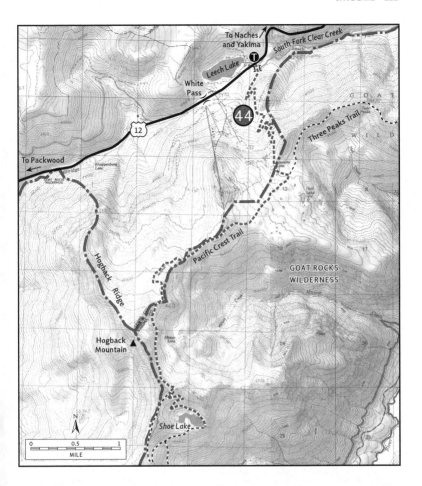

folks think of when they hear Pacific "Crest" Trail—*a faint footpath through alpine meadows hugging the side of a knife-edged ridge.*

GETTING THERE

From Packwood, drive east on U.S. Highway 12 to White Pass. The Pacific Crest Trail–South trailhead is located just east of the ski area on the south side of the highway.

ON THE TRAIL

The Pacific Crest Trail angles southeast for the first 2.5 miles, skirting the edge of the White Pass Ski Area. This initial section climbs modestly through open pine forests, gaining 1000 feet in those 2.5 miles, to a junction with the Three Peaks Trail. There, our route bears west and the forests open even more, as the trail weaves between sun-dappled woods and sun-filled meadows.

At 3.5 miles, a short spur trail leads north to the top of the ski lifts. The PCT, though, continues southwest along the east flank of Hogback Mountain.

This remnant of the once-great Goat Rocks Volcano is a jagged peak with long, knife-sharp ridges leading north and south from the summit. The trail hugs the southern ridge, contouring along the 6400-foot level. A few wildflowers struggle for survival on this steep slope, but mostly the trail slides across scree slopes and pika-playgrounds on the curving ridge wall.

At just over 6 miles from the trail, the PCT crosses a narrow shoulder of the mountain at 6600 feet. Pause here to soak up the incredible views before you—the horseshoe-shaped Shoe Lake lies 400 feet below, while far beyond the lake to the southeast is the cliff-lined Pinegrass Ridge.

From the ridge top, it's another 0.5 mile down to the lakeshore, and then there's a 0.5-mile trail around the lake to explore. Wildflower meadows surround the lake, with a small grove of shade-providing evergreens on the peninsula in the center of the lake's horseshoe. Those who insist on camping nearby should return to the PCT and continue south about a mile to Hidden Spring Camp.

45 Goat Lake–Jordan Basin

RATING/ DIFFICULTY	ROUND-TRIP	ELEV GAIN/ HIGH POINT	SEASON
*****/5	12 miles	2000 feet/ 6600 feet	July– October

Maps: Green Trails No. 302 Packwood, No. 303 White Pass, No. 304 Blue Lake, No. 335

Walupt Lake; **Contact/Permits:** USFS Cowlitz Valley Ranger District, Packwood Office, (360) 494-0600 / Northwest Forest Pass; **GPS:** N46 28.012, W121 31.645

The trail up through Jordan Basin to Goat Lake makes a wonderful outing for all hikers, but the open meadows and modest climbs are perfect for wildflower lovers and photographers. Why? Well, this route offers nearly everything you could want on an alpine ramble: vast wildflower fields, stunning panoramas that include towering glaciated peaks, high alpine meadows, cold alpine lakes, tons of birds and wildlife, and a good chance at solitude despite the incredible beauty of the route.

GETTING THERE
From Packwood, drive west on U.S. Highway 12 for 2 miles and turn left (south) onto Forest Road 21 (Johnson Creek Road). Continue about 15.5 miles on the sometimes-rough gravel road before turning left (east) onto FR 2150, signed Chambers Lake Campground. In 3.5 miles, turn right onto a short dirt road that leads into the trailhead parking area, just above the Chambers Lake Campground.

ON THE TRAIL
Start up the Goat Ridge Trail (No. 95) as it climbs the snout of Goat Ridge. The first 1.5 miles ascend through old pine and fir forests. The airy woodlands present an open canopy with lots of sunshine reaching the forest floor. Taking advantage of that plentiful light is a mass of huckleberry bushes. The berries aren't as big and juicy as some found in more open meadows, but the fruit offers a tasty treat to hikers plodding up the steep trail.

A small side trail branches off to the left at 1.5 miles—this is merely a scenic alternative that loops out around the steep west slope

Bob Chesterman departing the Goat Lake basin

of Goat Ridge while the main trail hugs the meadow-dotted east side of the ridge. Just over 0.5 mile down the main trail, the secondary trail rejoins it (at 1.1 miles long, the alternative trail is more than a mile longer than the main route).

Just after the first trail junction, the forest begins to open up, first with small forest glades scattered along the ridge, and finally the trees give way to broad, rolling meadows as the trail crosses under a large talus slope at 3 miles. Above this point, the trail climbs steeply into the flower-filled meadows. The views gradually improve as you ascend until, at 4.5 miles, the trail crosses over Goat Ridge in a deep saddle under Hawkeye Point. This ridge provides outstanding views west into the wildflower wonderland of Jordan Creek Basin to the west and Goat Creek basin to the east.

From the ridge crossing, the trail traverses around the upper basin of Goat Creek to reach Goat Lake at 6 miles. There are a few campsites along the shores of the intensely cold lake. The lake is nestled in a north-facing rocky cirque and frequently has an ice shelf covering a portion of the water year-round.

46 Snowgrass Flat

RATING/ DIFFICULTY	ROUND-TRIP	ELEV GAIN/ HIGH POINT	SEASON
****/4	8.2 miles	1600 feet/ 5800 feet	July– October

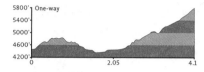

Maps: Green Trails No. 302 Packwood, No. 303 White Pass, No. 304 Blue Lake, No. 335 Walupt Lake; **Contact/Permits:** USFS Cowlitz Valley Ranger District, Packwood Office, (360) 494-0600 / Northwest Forest Pass; **GPS:** N46 27.851, W121 31.140

The trail climbs through some of the most spectacular wildflower meadows in the state, and presents some of the most wonderful views a hiker could imagine. Volcanoes loom on all sides: Mount Rainier, Mount Adams, Mount St. Helens, and on clear days, even Mount Hood can be seen far to the south. But it's not just the big snow-capped cones that are seen. Lesser volcanoes—perfectly formed cinder cones—can be seen scattered throughout the southern Cascades, in addition to the ancient volcanic peaks of the Goat Rocks. Actually, the peaks along the Goat Rocks Crest are the last remaining bits of an ancient volcano that formed and collapsed long before the current peaks poked up.

GETTING THERE

From Packwood, drive west on U.S. Highway 12 for 2 miles and turn left (south) onto Forest

Wildflower-filled meadows beyond Snowgrass Flat

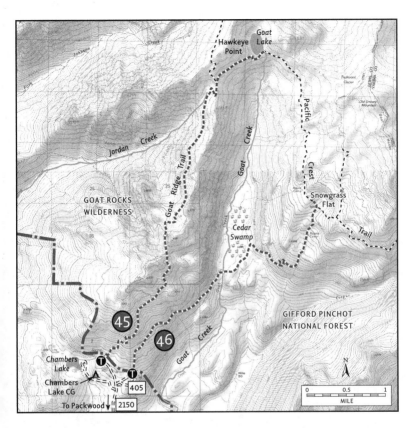

Road 21 (Johnson Creek Road). Continue about 15.5 miles on the sometimes-rough gravel road before turning left (east) onto FR 2150, signed Chambers Lake Campground. In 3 miles, turn right onto Spur Road 2150-040 and, shortly, right again on Spur 2150-405. Drive to the trailhead (signed Berry Patch) at the road's end, about 20 miles from Highway 12.

ON THE TRAIL

A short spur trail leads west from the trailhead, and in less than 0.25 mile it joins the Snowgrass Flat Trail (No. 96). Starting out in heavy forest cover, the trail crosses Goat Creek near the 2-mile mark and swings into a cedar swamp.

This swamp is one of the reasons I recommend early autumn as the prime hiking season. By waiting until September to enjoy this hike, you'll find the high pass snow-free and the swamp will be mostly bug-free. Hike in August, and there will likely be snowfields at the pass, and swarms of blood-hungry mosquitoes in the swamp. Of course, the marsh is a mere quarter mile long, so if you do come here in the summer months, a bit of bug dope and a fast pace will protect you from the worst of the bugs.

Once past the wetlands, the trail climbs 1100 feet in the next 2 miles to reach the lower meadows of Snowgrass Flat at 4.1 miles.

EXTENDING YOUR TRIP

You can link this route with Goat Lake (Hike 45) by way of the Pacific Crest Trail to create a 14-mile loop, or you can turn south at Snowgrass Flat and head out onto the PCT for endless adventures.

Map: Green Trails No. 335 Walupt Lake; **Contact/Permits:** USFS Cowlitz Valley Ranger District, Packwood Office, (360) 494-0600 / Northwest Forest Pass; **GPS:** N46 25.387, W121 28.277

47 Nannie Ridge–Sheep Lake

RATING/ DIFFICULTY	ROUND-TRIP	ELEV GAIN/ HIGH POINT	SEASON
****/4	9 miles	1800 feet/ 5800 feet	July–October

This trail offers a bounty of purple gold: an endless tangle of huckleberry bushes. During every visit in late summer, I slow my hiking so I can pick as many ripe berries as possible while still making some trail mileage. Of course, berries aren't always ripe,

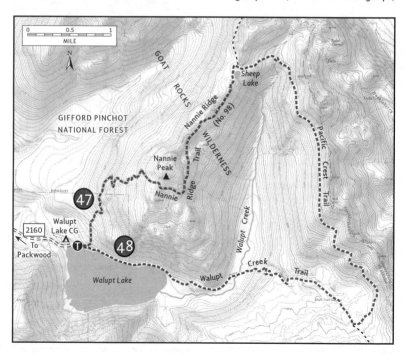

Sheep Lake and meadows on Nannie Ridge

so it's a good thing this trail offers far more than ripe fruit. It provides stunning views of the peaks of the South Cascades, including the near-perfect cone of Mount Adams, and ample opportunity to witness wildlife.

GETTING THERE

From Packwood, drive west on U.S. Highway 12 for 2 miles and turn left (south) onto Forest Road 21 (Johnson Creek Road). Continue about 19 miles on the sometimes-rough gravel road before turning left (east) onto FR 2160, signed Walupt Lake Campground. The trailhead is about 5 miles farther on at the end of this road near the pretty campground on the shores of Walupt Lake.

ON THE TRAIL

The trail begins near the eastern end of the campground. The Nannie Ridge Trail (No. 98) climbs north through dense pine forests for more than a mile, crossing a couple of shallow creeks (often dry late in the year) and gradually gaining elevation. One problem you might encounter is that the area's abundant volcanoes have dumped a lot of light ash into the dirt, leaving it gritty and powdery. In fact, by midsummer, the dirt trail is churned into several inches of billowy dust.

As the trail nears the 1.5-mile point, the forests begin to open with spacious clearings scattered throughout. Here's where the fun begins. Hit the trail in late August, and you'll find these clearings a deep shade of purple, provided you get there before the other hikers and the bears.

At 3 miles, the trail tops the ridge crest just below the summit of Nannie Peak. A short, 0.5-mile way trail leads to the summit of the peak, and it is well worth the effort to scramble up this boot-beaten path to enjoy the outstanding views, and wonderful mountaintop meadows. The views are dominated by the big three southern volcanoes—Mount Rainier to the north, Mount Adams to the south, and Mount St. Helens to the southwest—but the jagged crests of the Goat Rocks peaks to the northeast are also not to be missed.

The trail continues east from Nannie Peak, along but just below the crest of Nannie Ridge, dropping several hundred feet below the ridge for a while in order to avoid some towering cliffs. At 4.4 miles, you'll find Sheep Lake at the junction with the Pacific Crest Trail. The best campsite is on the knoll to the south of the lake where you'll enjoy evening views of alpenglow on Mount Adams. The lake is large enough to be clear and cool, but shallow enough that the summer sun takes the bone-chilling cold out of the snowmelt water. That makes it a fine place to turn around and return home.

48 Walupt Creek Loop

RATING/ DIFFICULTY	LOOP	ELEV GAIN/ HIGH POINT	SEASON
*****/4	12 miles	1800 feet/ 5800 feet	July– October

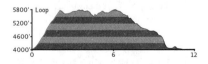

Map: Green Trails No. 335 Walupt Lake; **Contact/Permits:** USFS Cowlitz Valley Ranger District, Packwood Office, (360) 494-

0600 / Northwest Forest Pass; **GPS:** N46 25.387, W121 28.277

More a triangle than a loop, this route offers breathtaking views from the summit of Nannie Peak—just as you might expect from the site of a former fire lookout tower. There's more than views to this hike, though. You'll find wonderful wildflower meadows along the crest of Nannie Ridge (see Hike 47), a clear, cold swimming experience in Sheep Lake, a walk along the spine of the Cascades on the Pacific Crest Trail, and a cool forest hike in the Walupt Creek valley.

The trail is short and gentle enough to enjoy as a long day hike, but the fine (though few) campsites at Sheep Lake, with their astounding views of Mount Adams (especially at sunset, when the alpenglow has the snowy peak of Adams aflame with orange light), can be too tempting to pass up, as many backpackers can attest.

GETTING THERE

From Packwood, drive west on U.S. Highway 12 for 2 miles and turn left (south) onto Forest Road 21 (Johnson Creek Road). Continue about 19 miles on the sometimes-rough gravel road before turning left (east) onto FR 2160, signed Walupt Lake Campground. The trailhead is about 5 miles farther on at the end of this road, near the pretty campground on the shores of Walupt Lake.

ON THE TRAIL

The loop can be hiked in either direction, but I prefer to do it clockwise—you'll find yourself facing more views this way as you hike. The trail begins near the eastern end of the campground. The Nannie Ridge Trail (No. 98) climbs north through dense pine forests for more than a mile, crossing a couple of shallow creeks (often dry late in the year) and gradually gaining elevation.

As the trail nears the 1.5-mile point, the forests begin to open with spacious clearings scattered throughout. The trail continually steepens over the next mile, and deep ruts cut many of the switchbacks—be sure to stay on the true trail, and don't use the shortcuts or the braided sections of trail (braided trails are sections where hikers and horses have created multiple, parallel trails that weave back and forth together, forming a broad network of trails instead of one simple path).

At 3 miles, the trail tops the ridge crest just below the summit of Nannie Peak. The views include Mount Rainier to the north, Mount Adams to the south, Mount St. Helens to the southwest, and the jagged crests of the Goat Rocks peaks to the northeast.

The trail continues east from Nannie Peak, along but just below the crest of Nannie Ridge, dropping several hundred feet below the ridge for a while in order to avoid some towering cliffs. At 4.4 miles, you'll find Sheep Lake at the junction with the Pacific Crest Trail. The best campsite is on the knoll to the south of the lake where you'll enjoy evening views of alpenglow on Mount Adams.

To complete the loop, turn south on the Pacific Crest Trail and hike along meadows and ponds. Backpackers should note that if Sheep Lake fills up with campers, there are some fine sites along the headwaters of Walupt Creek just 0.5 mile down the PCT from the lake.

As the PCT weaves past a cluster of small ponds 4 miles south of Sheep Lake, turn right

Lichen-draped trees along Walupt Creek

onto the Walupt Creek Trail. The trail follows the southern fork of the creek about 3.5 miles back to the trailhead at Walupt Lake.

49 Coleman Weedpatch

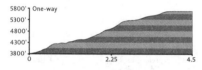

RATING/ DIFFICULTY	ROUND-TRIP	ELEV GAIN/ HIGH POINT	SEASON
***/4	9 miles	1900 feet/ 5700 feet	July– October

Map: Green Trails No. 335 Walupt Lake; **Contact/Permits:** USFS Cowlitz Valley Ranger District, Packwood Office, (360) 494-0600 / Northwest Forest Pass; **GPS:** N46 25.376, W121 30.059

What the trail namers call weeds, most of us call wildflowers. The meadows visited by this trail are home to some of the finest wildflower displays in the country, and the views beyond aren't too bad either. Look up from the brilliant blooms, and you'll see Mount Adams on one side, Mount Rainier on another. The jagged crest of the Goat Rocks peaks stretches to the north, and

Raindrops cling to an avalanche lily.

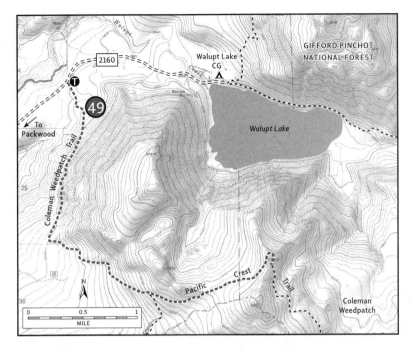

the deep blue waters of Walupt Lake lie below your feet, straight down the steep ridge wall.

GETTING THERE

From Packwood, drive west on U.S. Highway 12 for 2 miles and turn left (south) onto Forest Road 21 (Johnson Creek Road). Continue about 19 miles on the sometimes-rough gravel road before turning left (east) onto FR 2160, signed Walupt Lake Campground. The Coleman Weedpatch trailhead is about 3 miles down this road on the right.

ON THE TRAIL

Dense forest shelters the first section of the Coleman Weedpatch Trail as it climbs gradually to the southwest, along the flank of a steep ridge. At 1.5 miles, the trail steepens consider-

ably, but the climb is still modest—you'll gain a touch over 1000 feet elevation in the next 1.5 miles. During this stretch, the trees thin and the forest is broken by the occasional forest glade. The Pacific Crest Trail is reached at 3 miles, and here is where the fun really begins. Turn left (east) on the PCT and hike into the splendid country before you.

Meadows, speckled with small groves of stunted subalpine evergreens, line the high route. Between the trees, acres of "weeds" sprout colorful blossoms throughout the summer—paintbrush, lupine, phlox, mountain daisies, heather, and columbine are a few of the plentiful flowers that grace these fields.

From the point where you join the PCT, you'll hike about 1.5 miles through these open meadows with good views of Mount Adams and the smaller volcanoes along its base.

The best views are found at 4.5 miles from the trailhead where the PCT crosses the top of a prominent knoll on the ridge crest. The top of this bluff offers an excellent place for lunch as you soak in the panoramic views—all around the slopes of the hill at your feet are wildflower meadows, and beyond are the snow-capped peaks of Mount Adams and the Goat Rocks.

The PCT descends into forest after leaving the top of the bluff on the ridge crest, so turn back the way you came.

Map: Green Trails No. 302 Packwood; **Contact/Permits:** USFS Cowlitz Valley Ranger District, Packwood Office, (360) 497-1100 / Northwest Forest Pass; **GPS:** N46 37.601, W121 35.354

50 Mosquito Lake–Three Peaks

RATING/ DIFFICULTY	ROUND-TRIP	ELEV GAIN/ HIGH POINT	SEASON
***/3	10 miles	1700 feet/ 4900 feet	July–October

Don't let the name scare you: This is a fine trail with only a few bugs, at least compared to some of the other routes in the South Cascades. Most of the trail stays well clear of water bodies, so the skeeter population is relatively low. The first section of trail is far from spectacular, but there are unbeatable views once you climb into the

A pair of elk pause in a small meadow.

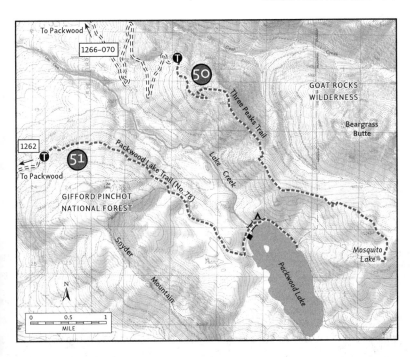

beautiful high country on the second half of the route.

GETTING THERE

From Packwood, drive 2 miles east on U.S. Highway 12 and turn right (south) onto Forest Road 1266. Continue to the end of the road where there is a large barrier. The trail begins on Spur Road 1266-070.

ON THE TRAIL

Start the hike by walking up the old dirt road. You'll soon come to a relatively new section of trail climbing steeply away from the old road. Follow this reconstructed trail for nearly 0.5 mile through dense forest before erupting out of the trees onto the upper section of the road. Another short walk

(well, about 0.5 mile of walking, actually) along the roadway leads to the start of the true Three Peaks Trail.

Here, the payoffs begin. Once you hit the end of the road and venture out on the ridgetop trail, the scenery becomes increasingly more awesome. Indeed, the trail really improves shortly after it enters the Goat Rocks Wilderness about 3 miles from the car. The forest gets brighter—old-growth with a varied canopy to let in more light—and the views start to open up more.

You'll find a great vista down into the Packwood Lake basin and south to Johnson Peak. Be sure to carry plenty of water, since there is no water at the trailhead and the only water along the route is at the turnaround point near Mosquito Lake.

51 Packwood Lake

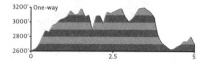

RATING/ DIFFICULTY	ROUND-TRIP	ELEV GAIN/ HIGH POINT	SEASON
***/2	10 miles	600 feet/ 3200 feet	late May– November

Map: Green Trails No. 302 Packwood;
Contact/Permits: USFS Cowlitz Valley Ranger
District, Packwood Office, (360) 494-0600 /
Northwest Forest Pass; **GPS:** N46 36.502,
W121 37.627

Sometimes, even the most gung-ho hiker needs a break—just a gentle walk through the woods, followed by a leisurely swim and a relaxing afternoon alongside a cool lake. Packwood Lake is the perfect place to practice this laid-back trail lifestyle, especially late in the spring and early in the autumn when the hordes of summer hikers have gone home, freeing up the lake's popular campsites and excellent fishing opportunities.

GETTING THERE

From Packwood, follow U.S. Highway 12 to
the east end of town and turn southeast onto

The closed ranger station at Packwood Lake

Forest Road 1262 (next to the former USFS Packwood Ranger Station). Continue southeast on FR 1262 for 6 miles to the trailhead parking lot.

ON THE TRAIL

The Packwood Lake Trail (No. 78) weaves through old second-growth forests for 4 miles along a deep river valley, with views limited to the trees around you. As the trail nears this broad, low-elevation lake, you'll find peek-a-boo views up the valley to the jagged crest of Goat Rocks.

At 4.6 miles, the trail reaches an old ranger station at the west end of the lake (2900 feet). A wide wooden bridge crosses the outlet stream. You'll pass the campground just after crossing the bridge. The trail continues around the end of the lake and leads east along the north side of the mile-long lake. Many campsites can be found along the lake, with great views up onto the Goat Rocks peaks.

52 Glacier Lake

RATING/ DIFFICULTY	ROUND-TRIP	ELEV GAIN/ HIGH POINT	SEASON
***/2	4 miles	800 feet/ 2905 feet	late June– October

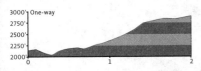

Map: Green Trails No. 302 Packwood; **Contact/Permits:** USFS Cowlitz Valley Ranger District, Packwood Office, (360) 494-0600 / Northwest Forest Pass; **GPS:** N46 32.739, W121 37.329

Climbing just 800 feet in 2 miles, this is one of the best trails in the South Cascades for families and kids. Not only is the going easy, but it's also a pretty hike that ends at a beautiful alpine wilderness lake. The trail follows Glacier Creek through old Douglas-fir and hemlock forest to a rock-filled basin around the cold, clear waters of Glacier Lake. Late-summer hikers find bushels of huckleberries growing along the route, and anglers can try for the big rainbow trout that lurk in the depths of the lake.

GETTING THERE

From Packwood, drive 2.1 miles west on U.S. Highway 12 to a junction with Forest Road 21. Turn left (south) onto this road and continue 5 miles. Turn left onto FR 2110 and drive 0.5 mile to the trailhead on the right.

ON THE TRAIL

You'll enjoy a variety of ecosystems along this short trail. To get started, you stride up an ancient logging road as it climbs through a stand of second-growth timber. Before long, the young forest gives way to ancient stands of Douglas-fir and hemlock, and then those massive trees fade away as you climb into the steep-walled Glacier Creek valley.

As you near the lake basin about 2 miles in, you'll encounter a massive jumble of boulders. Geologists say this wall of rock fell as a huge landslide sometime before Columbus sailed, creating a dam across Glacier Creek and creating Glacier Lake.

A rough path circles the lake, accessing the top casting locations for anglers and also offering the best views of the lake and lake basin.

 53 Johnson Peak–Lily Basin

RATING/ DIFFICULTY	ROUND-TRIP	ELEV GAIN/ HIGH POINT	SEASON
***/4	12 miles (longer option 14.5 miles)	1900 feet/ 6100 feet	late June–October

Map: Green Trails No. 302 Packwood;
Contact/Permits: USFS Cowlitz Valley Ranger District, Packwood Office, (360) 494-0600 / Northwest Forest Pass; **GPS:** N46 33.845, W121 35.993

The worst part of this moderate climb is knocked off in the first few miles. After that, the trail rambles along a beautiful, rugged ridge to the west flank of 7487-foot Johnson Peak before turning sharply south to intercept the Angry Mountain Trail.

GETTING THERE

From Packwood, drive 2 miles west on U.S. Highway 12 to a junction with Forest Road 48. Turn left (south) onto this road and continue 10 miles to the trailhead on the right.

ON THE TRAIL

The trail climbs slowly and steadily from the trailhead, traversing the slope above Glacier Lake for nearly a mile before topping out on

An avalanche of avalanche lilies in Lily Basin

Opposite: Glacier Creek

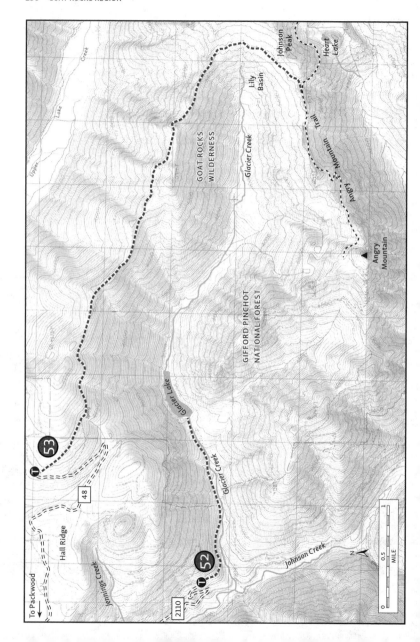

the long ridge leading east. You'll follow the forested ridge for 4 miles to the lower flank of Johnson Ridge. As you stride out under the west face of Johnson, the forest opens onto broad but steep wildflower meadows.

At this point, you are circling the upper reaches of Lily Basin—the headwaters of Glacier Creek (see Hike 52). Find a nice place to stop and rest in these sweet wildflower meadows, or press on to the 6-mile mark where the trail intercepts the Angry Mountain Trail. Turn around there for a 12-mile trek.

EXTENDING YOUR TRIP

From the trail junction, turn right to continue west along the ridgeline as it drops gently to a saddle, before climbing to the summit of Angry Mountain, about 2.5 miles from the junction.

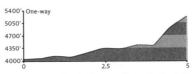

Maps: Green Trails No. 304 Rimrock, No. 303 White Pass, No. 335 Walupt Lake; **Contact/Permits:** USFS Naches Ranger District, (509) 653-2205 / Northwest Forest Pass; **GPS:** N46 33.845, W121 35.993

Most hikers enter the Goat Rocks Wilderness from the western side, but those who come in from the east find the wilderness just as beautiful and wild, and much less crowded. The Surprise Lake Trail is one of the few that enter from the east, and it is also one of the most gentle and scenic.

GETTING THERE

From Yakima, drive west on U.S. Highway 12 for 33.2 miles and turn left onto Tieton River Road. Drive 3.5 miles, passing Rimrock Lake, and turn left onto Forest Road 1000. Continue 14 miles to the trailhead parking area at Conrad Meadows.

54 Surprise Lake

RATING/ DIFFICULTY	ROUND-TRIP	ELEV GAIN/ HIGH POINT	SEASON
***/4	10 miles	1200 feet/ 5255 feet	late June– October

Elephant's head, camas, and bog orchids in Conrad Meadows

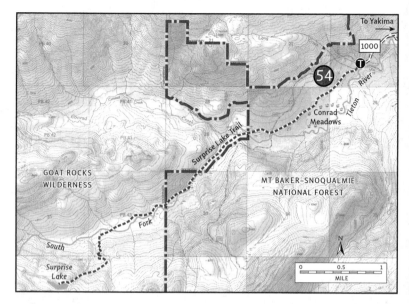

ON THE TRAIL

The trail climbs gradually from Conrad Meadows—a broad, grassy meadow in the valley bottom—to the high alpine lake at trail's end. Along the way it passes through a seemingly endless series of forest meadows. These elk pastures are broken up by beautiful stands of ponderosa pine and spruce forests, and are home to not only elk but also white-tailed and mule deer and a host of small critters.

Indeed, so great is the number of meadows that many hikers find it more enjoyable to leave the trail altogether and journey up to the lake by going cross-country through the forest glades. This is a great place to practice your off-trail rambling, but before leaving the trail, be sure you have map and compass and the skill to use them effectively.

The first 3.5 miles of trail thread through these patchwork wildflower meadows, but the upper end of the route is enclosed in denser forests until, near the lake, the route breaks out into alpine clearings. Above the pretty little lake loom some of the great craggy peaks that give the Goat Rocks Wilderness its name. With a pair of binoculars and a little patience, it's possible to spot the creatures themselves. Mountain goats scramble among the rocky slopes high above the lake, jumping lightly about the cliffs that lie between the forest and the glaciers. Look for them on the bare rocks above green fields of moss and grass.

There are good campsites at the lake and along the numerous meadows farther down the trail. If you choose to camp in a meadow, though, wander as far off trail as is reasonable and look for a campsite that is sheltered from the trail by a stand of trees. This will shield your camp from other hikers so they can continue to enjoy their sense of solitude in this wild, beautiful area.

Opposite: Mount Adams rises over a field of lupines along the Pacific Crest Trail.

mount adams area

Mount Adams stands as the sentinel of the eastern flank of the South Cascades. After Mount St. Helens blew her top in 1980, Mount Adams was left as the most perfect "snow cone" in the Washington Cascades. The big, symmetrical volcano rises 12,277 feet tall, on the boundary between National Forest Service lands (Gifford Pinchot National Forest) and the Yakama Indian Reservation. The mountain can be seen from virtually every ridge and peak south of Mount Rainier and north of the Columbia River, making it a wonderful landmark by which to navigate. But the impact of Adams goes beyond that. Over the course of thousands of years, Mount Adams (and its small cinder cone siblings scattered around its base) unleashed several lava flows. Those rivers of molten rock hardened into broad, black fields of basalt lava. Today, many of those lava beds serve as stark reminders of what happened in the past, and what could happen again.

55 Takhlakh Lake Loop

RATING/ DIFFICULTY	LOOP	ELEV GAIN/ HIGH POINT	SEASON
***/2	3 miles	90 feet/ 4460 feet	late June– October

Map: Green Trails No. 334 Blue Lake; **Contact/ Permits:** USFS Mount Adams Ranger District, (509) 395-3400 / Northwest Forest Pass; **GPS:** N46 16.593, W121 35.950

Here's one for the kids. The trail is short, but it offers a great lesson in the volcanic history of the region. It explores the shore of Takhlakh Lake and climbs into a small band of basalt lava that flowed from Mount Adams thousands of years ago.

GETTING THERE

From Randle, drive 1 mile south on Forest Road 25 and then turn left (east) onto FR 23. Continue 32 miles to a junction with FR 2329. Turn left and drive east about a mile to the Takhlakh Lake Campground.

ON THE TRAIL

From the campground on the southwestern side of the lake, head east along the lakeshore trail, enjoying the cool forest and blue waters as you walk. At the southeast corner of the lake, the trail splits. The forest pierced by the trail boasts a bounty of huckleberry bushes (the fruit typically ripens here in mid-August), and you'll pass several small glades carpeted with shimmering green leaves of vanilla leaf plants.

At the junction, turn right and climb a short 0.5 mile south through the forest before curving eastward and edging up into a band of black basalt lava. This rock is jagged and tends to get quite hot during the sunny days of summer, so make sure the kids are warned to be careful—you might even consider having them wear gloves if they want to handle the volcanic rock and scramble on the mounds of lava.

The trail loops through the end of the lava field and curves back down to the trail junction at the lakeshore, about 2 miles from the start. You can now either hike the 0.5 mile back to the trailhead on the trail you came in on, or you can turn right and follow the other side of the lake and hike a mile, looping all the way around the lake to return to your car after a 3-mile walk.

Opposite: Mount Adams reflected in Takhlakh Lake

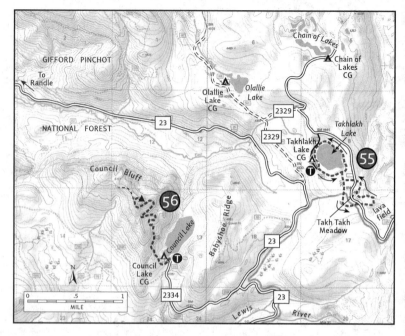

56 Council Bluff

RATING/ DIFFICULTY	ROUND-TRIP	ELEV GAIN/ HIGH POINT	SEASON
**/2	3 miles	1000 feet/ 5180 feet	late June– October

Map: Green Trails No. 334 Blue Lake; **Contact/
Permits:** USFS Mount Adams Ranger District,
(509) 395-3400 / Northwest Forest Pass;
GPS: N46 15.774, W121 37.949

 *Sure it's a road walk, but the road has
been largely reclaimed by the forest,*

*and the destination is a view-rich summit
that once held a fire lookout station. The
route is easy enough that kids of all ages will
be able to enjoy the walk, and when the hike
is over everyone can take a cool dip in Council Lake down at the trailhead.*

GETTING THERE

From Randle, drive 1 mile south on Forest
Road 25 and then turn left (east) onto FR 23.
Continue some 30 miles to a junction with FR
2334. Turn right and drive west about a mile to
the Council Lake Campground. Park near the
point where the road is gated.

ON THE TRAIL

Walk around the road gate (make sure you
don't block the gate with your car), and start
hiking up the small dirt road. The route winds

upward for 1.25 miles, to where the road ends; from there a small dirt track continues on for the last 0.25-mile climb to the summit.

Council Bluff has a long, attractive summit. Explore the length of the summit ridge (about 0.1 mile) and enjoy the fantastic views east to

The north cliffs of Council Bluff

Council Lake and Mount Adams beyond before returning the way you came.

57 Potato Hill

RATING/ DIFFICULTY	ROUND-TRIP	ELEV GAIN/ HIGH POINT	SEASON
****/3	3 miles	550 feet/ 5387 feet	late June– October

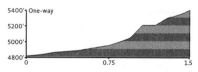

Map: Green Trails No. 334 Blue Lake; **Contact/Permits:** USFS Mount Adams Ranger District, (509) 395-3400 / Northwest Forest Pass; **GPS:** N46 19.525, W121 30.361

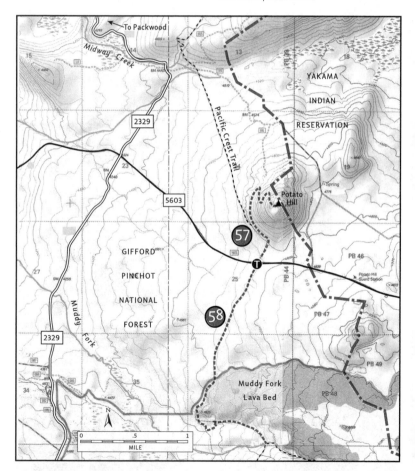

Mount Adams and the Muddy Fork Lava Flow as seen from Potato Hill

This is a good place for kids to come and explore. The Pacific Crest Trail ducks the western face of Potato Hill, but the gentle cone can be climbed without much effort or difficulty. The scramble to the top is worth the effort, as it brings wonderful views of Mount Adams and the volcanic landscape of the country north of the mountain. One of the most impressive sights is the sprawling Muddy Fork Lava Bed that seems *to flow from the perfect cone of Red Butte (7200 feet) on Adams's northeast slope.*

Potato Hill is centered on a north–south fault line that also runs under Mount Adams, and around 110,000 years ago, the mountain was formed when an eruption of basalt lava spewed out of the fissure along this fault line. The cinder cone that was left behind became Potato Hill.

GETTING THERE

From Packwood, drive south on Forest Road 21 for 17 miles to a junction with FR 2160. Turn left (east) onto FR 2160 and continue 1.8 miles, crossing the Cispus River, and turn right (southwest) onto FR 56. In 1.8 miles, leave FR 56 by bearing left (south) onto FR 2329. In 5.5 miles, turn left at a junction with FR 5603 and drive 2 miles to the trailhead.

ON THE TRAIL

The Pacific Crest Trail heads north from the trailhead with the perfect cone of Potato Hill in sight all the way. The trail is relatively level and well maintained, and the vegetation is mostly low trees and brush. The trail traverses around the base of Potato Hill and explores some pretty wildflower meadows before reaching an old dirt road within 0.5 mile of the trailhead.

Rather than hike to the road, pick a place to scamper off-trail and start up the gentle slope of the mini volcano. Be sure to stay on the western face of the peak, as the entire eastern side is within the Yakama Indian Reservation and is off limits to non–tribal members. The boundary isn't marked, but by staying on the west and southwest sides, you'll remain on public land.

The sparse vegetation on the slopes makes climbing a warm experience when the sun is out, but it also means the top of the peak is always in sight—a quick glance up lets you know how much farther you've got to climb to

get to the summit. If the 500-foot gain tires you, pull up for a breather and enjoy the wonderful views to the south and west. In addition to the beauty of Mount Adams, you'll see other prominent peaks, including Green Mountain and Hamilton Butte to the west.

58 Muddy Fork Lava Bed

RATING/ DIFFICULTY	ROUND-TRIP	ELEV GAIN/ HIGH POINT	SEASON
***/4	5 miles	500 feet/ 4900 feet	late June– October

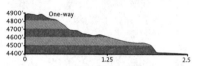

Map: Green Trails No. 367S Mount Adams; **Contact/Permits:** USFS Mount Adams Ranger District, (509) 395-3400 / Northwest Forest Pass; **GPS:** N46 19.531, W121 30.349

Mount Adams, at 12,276 feet, dominates the South Cascades and provides the most dramatic scenery of the region, thanks to the mountain's mighty prominence. The mountain is a standout destination also for the massive basalt lava beds that cover large portions of the surrounding landscape. This relatively young volcano initially formed nearly a million years ago, about 3 miles southeast of its current location. That first cone was ground down by glaciers during the long succession of ice ages that swept the region, while the "hot spot" that gave birth to the mountain shifted northwest as plate tectonics and continental drift rearranged the landscape.

GETTING THERE

From Packwood, drive south on Forest Road 21 for 17 miles to a junction with FR 2160. Turn left (east) onto FR 2160 and continue 1.8

View of massive lava flow

miles, crossing the Cispus River, and turn right (southwest) onto FR 56. In 1.8 miles, leave FR 56 by bearing left (south) onto FR 2329. In 5.5 miles, turn left at a junction with FR 5603 and drive 2 miles to the trailhead.

ON THE TRAIL

Start hiking south on the Pacific Crest Trail and begin a gradual descent through open forests and sun-filled clearings toward Muddy Fork Creek. After 2 miles, in which you'll descend 400 feet, the trail suddenly encounters a large, black wall. This is the lava bed. The rapidly cooling lava, as it flowed from the mountain, stopped in place, forming a high wall of jagged basalt.

For the next half mile or so, the trail skirts around this broad, black jumble. If you have gloves and a very fine sense of balance, you

might scramble the 20 or so feet up the edge of the basalt so you can look across the expanse of the massive lava bed, the Muddy Fork Lava Bed.

Explore along the edge at your leisure before heading north again the way you came.

59 Burnt Rock

RATING/ DIFFICULTY	ROUND-TRIP	ELEV GAIN/ HIGH POINT	SEASON
****/4	13 miles	1400 feet/ 6100 feet	late June– October

View of the Adams Glacier from the Pacific Crest Trail

Map: Green Trails No. 367S Mount Adams;
Contact/Permits: USFS Mount Adams Ranger
District, (509) 395-3400 / Northwest Forest
Pass; **GPS:** N46 16.156, W121 34.715

*Burnt Rock is an appropriate name for the
black mound of basalt piled up near Sheep
Lake. The rock is one of the many upthrusts
of volcanic rock in this area of massive lava
beds, and Sheep Lake is a cool pool of sparkling
water nestled in the folds of lava near the base
of Burnt Rock. The trail passes a few small
barren lava beds, some deep old-growth pine
and cedar forests, and fields of huckleberries
big enough to satisfy the hunger of a battalion
of bears and an army of hikers.*

The berries of Mount Adams are legend-
*ary for their size, their number, and their
sweet sun-enriched flavor. Berry bushes line
this route from start to finish, sometimes in
small clumps in the open forest, sometimes
in vast berry patches in the clearings. It's a
wonderful thing to be able to hike all day,
nibbling on juicy fruit as you walk, with
wonderful views of the snow-capped mountain before you.*

GETTING THERE

From Randle, drive south on Forest Road 25.
One mile from Randle, bear left onto FR 23 and
drive 32 miles to a junction with FR 2329 (signed
Takhlakh Lake Campground) and turn left onto
FR 2329. Continue 3.5 miles to the West Fork
trailhead on the right, elevation 4700 feet.

HIKING WITH KIDS

School just let out for summer and the kids are already bored and restless. What do you do? Take a hike!

This Day Hiking series features many scenic-but-gentle trails laced throughout our state lands and national forests and parks, offering wilderness adventures perfect for families with young kids. With the abundance of these easy-to-moderate hiking trails, there is no reason for anyone to miss out on the enjoyment of hiking. This pastime has grown to be truly a sport for people of all ages, all abilities.

Check out hikes such as Sand Lake (Hike 5) or Council Bluff (Hike 56) for great kid-friendly adventures.

The woods are full of things kids of all ages find fascinating. Besides bugs, birds, and animals there are all sorts of relics of human history to discover and explore, from rusting railroad spikes and mining equipment, to old fire lookouts and foresters' cabins. There are fascinating geologic formations and countless forms of water bodies—streams, creeks, seeps, marshes, tarns, ponds, lakes, and waterfalls.

Before heading out to discover your own great trail experiences, though, there are some things to consider. First and perhaps most important are the ages of the kids and their physical condition (not to mention your own). If you are new to hiking, or have been away from it for a while (like, since the kids were born), or if your kids are under fourteen years old, stick to trails of less than 1 mile in length. Both you and the kids will find this to be long enough, and many of the trails in that range offer plenty to see and experience.

Once the trip is planned, parents can do a few things to make sure their kids have fun—for instance, never hike with just one child. Kids need companions to compete with, play with, and converse with. One child and a pair of adults makes a hike seem too much like work for the poor kid. But let your child bring along a friend or two, and all will have the time of their lives.

When starting out on the trail, adults need to set goals and destinations that are attainable for everyone. Kids and adults alike are more likely to enjoy the hike if they know there is a specific destination rather than just an idea of "going until we feel like turning back."

Then, when hiking, make sure to take frequent breaks and offer the kids "energy food" consisting of a favorite cookie or tasty treat. These snacks serve two purposes: The kids will be motivated to make it to the next break site, knowing they will get a good-tasting treat; and the sugar will help keep the kids fueled up and energized on the trail. For maximum benefit, make the energy foods a special treat that the kids maybe don't get as often as they'd like. You can also keep the kids sugared-up with huckleberries when they are in season. Pack plenty of water, too, to wash down the snacks and to replace what is lost as sweat.

Finally, let the kids explore and investigate the trail environment as much as they like. Patience is more than a virtue here—it's a necessity. Take the time to inspect the tadpoles in trailside bogs, to study the bugs on the bushes, and to try spotting the birds singing in the trees. Just let the kids be kids. If you can then share in their excitement and enthusiasm, everyone will have a great time on the trail.

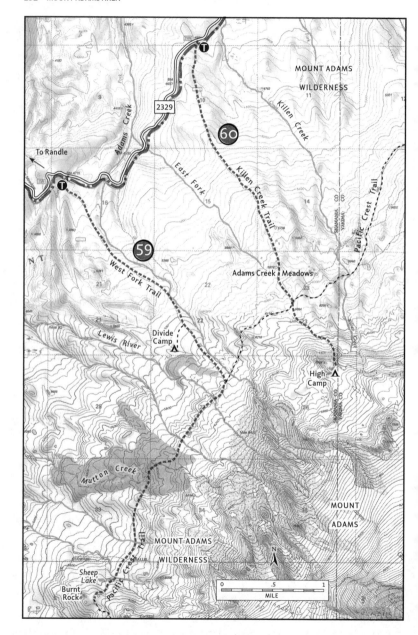

ON THE TRAIL

The trail begins at the Mount Adams Wilderness boundary and climbs modestly through old-growth pine and spruce forests for nearly 2 miles. In the first mile, a small lava bed can be seen through the trees to the right of the trail—it looks like a black gravel pile from a distance, but if you scramble over for a closer look, you'll find it is more like a black boulder pile. Huge blocks of jagged basalt rock are piled haphazardly around the field, left by a flow of molten lava coming from a vent in the side of the mountain. The route occasionally drops close to the crashing waters of the West Fork of Adams Creek, but generally stays on the slope above.

At 1.8 miles, you'll pass a small side trail—this leads south about 0.5 mile to a pretty campsite at the edge of a meadow known as Divide Camp. A mile past this spur trail, the West Fork Trail ends in broad meadow at a junction with the Pacific Crest Trail. High above the PCT to the east is the white monolith of Adams Glacier, headwaters of Adams Creek.

Turning south on the PCT, you'll hike along the upper edge of the heather-filled meadow, staying near the line where lush meadow gives way to a world of rock and ice.

The trail stays near the 6100-foot level for nearly 1.5 miles before crossing a 0.5-mile wide lava bed. You'll want to make sure you stay on the trail as it cuts through this jumble of lava, as the black rocks of the bed are brittle, and often razor sharp.

The Pacific Crest Trail descends gradually just past the lava bed, dropping to another trail junction at 5700 feet (6.1 miles from the trailhead). Stay left to remain on the PCT, and in another 0.25 mile you'll reach the small pool of Sheep Lake. Good campsites can be found here. An alternative is to bear right at the last trail junction and hike about a mile through open meadows, crossing Riley Creek, to the west side of Burnt Rock.

Deer, elk, and mountain goats frequent the meadows between Burnt Rock and Sheep Lake; with plenty of huckleberries in the well-watered meadows, bear are also frequent visitors to the area. Please use proper bear-bagging techniques when camping here.

60 Killen Meadows

RATING/ DIFFICULTY	ROUND-TRIP	ELEV GAIN/ HIGH POINT	SEASON
****/5	10 miles	2300 feet/ 6900 feet	late June– October

Map: Green Trails No. 367S Mount Adams; **Contact/Permits:** USFS Mount Adams Ranger District, (509) 395-3400 / Northwest Forest Pass; **GPS:** N46 17.308, W121 33.151

Meadows: Lush, green meadows filled with fragrant wildflowers and juicy berries. High, alpine meadows with low, hardy heathers and grasses. Rocky subalpine meadows littered with rocks and patches of slow-melting snow. This route explores a rich cornucopia of meadow types. But these natural pasture lands for wildlife aren't the only draws to this route. From start to finish, the trail here offers outstanding views of Mount Adams and its many personalities. The rocky cliff faces, the crevasse-torn glaciers, the flowing white snowfields, and the noble crown of the summit are all visible most of the way up the trail.

GETTING THERE

From Randle, drive 1 mile south on Forest Road 25. At the first main road junction, bear left onto FR 23 and drive 32 miles to a junction

View from near High Camp, looking toward Mount Rainier

with FR 2329 (signed Takhlakh Lake Campground) and turn left onto FR 2329. Continue 6 miles to the Killen Creek trailhead on the right, elevation 4580 feet.

ON THE TRAIL

Step onto the trail and immediately enter a wonderland of color. Wildflowers grace the meadows and open forest along the trail for most of its length, and throughout much of the hiking season. Early on, the bulbous blooms of beargrass wave you on, while later in the summer the trail is lit with brilliant displays of gaudy colors, thanks to the prolific wildflowers including paintbrush, marsh marigolds, shooting stars, columbine, and lupine, to name just a few. The trail climbs gradually through forest clearings and open, sun-dappled stands of old-growth for the initial 2 miles before running into a denser, cooler forest of old-growth.

At just over 2.5 miles, the trail crosses a stream in the meadow, East Fork Adams Creek, and reaches the first of the countless possibilities for camping. This is the start of the meadow country, and the broad fields around East Fork Adams Creek are quite properly known as the Adams Creek Meadows.

At just over 3 miles, the Killen Creek Trail dead-ends at the Pacific Crest Trail, at 6100 feet elevation, amidst heather meadows with wide-open views of Mount Adams. A faint way trail leads seemingly straight toward the summit from this junction. This is the route to High Camp, a rocky plateau at the edge of the life zone—the line where vegetation gives way to a world of rock and ice. High Camp, at 6900 feet, is often crowded on hot August weekends, so it's usually best to camp lower and visit High Camp merely as a side trip.

61 Horseshoe Meadow

RATING/ DIFFICULTY	ROUND-TRIP	ELEV GAIN/ HIGH POINT	SEASON
****/4	11 miles	1900 feet/ 6100 feet	late June– October

Map: Green Trails No. 367S Mount Adams; **Contact/Permits:** USFS Mount Adams Ranger District, (509) 395-3400 / Northwest Forest Pass; **GPS:** N46 10.209, W121 37.750

The trail climbs through dry, cathedral-like old-growth pine forests, and traverses meadows of wildflowers. The trail knifes through jagged piles of basalt in massive, old lava beds, and slides under massive glaciers hugging the upper slopes of the mountain.

GETTING THERE

From Trout Lake, drive north on Forest Road 23 for about 13.5 miles and turn right onto a small dirt road marked PCT–North Trailhead. Follow this a few hundred yards to a trailhead parking lot.

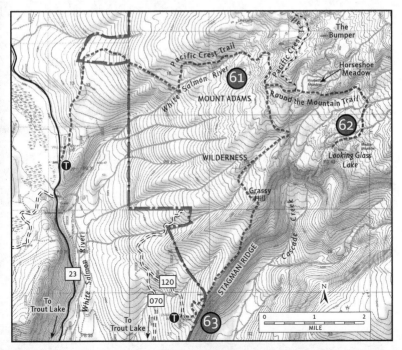

ON THE TRAIL

From the Pacific Crest Trail (PCT) trailhead, you'll climb gradually through thin stands of young timber for the first 0.5 mile or so. The trail then steepens as it climbs north along the ridge above the White Salmon River. As you cross into the Mount Adams Wilderness at about 1.75 miles in, the forest transitions into old-growth pine. Great horned owls, woodpeckers, Clark's nutcrackers, and many other bird species are found in these woods, along with black-tailed deer.

Once on the ridge, the trail levels out briefly and angles southeast for about a mile to cross the headwaters of the White Salmon River before climbing the steep southwestern slope of Mount Adams. You'll find your first good views of the mountain at about 5.5 miles, as the trail nears Horseshoe Meadow.

Here, the PCT bears sharply north as it skirts through heather meadows, staying just inside the vegetation zone. Just above the trail, the vegetation gives way to the world of barren rock and ice making up the higher slopes of the mountain.

Explore the meadows and stroll along the PCT at your leisure before heading back the way you came.

Backpackers wishing to spend more time in these sloping alpine meadows will find fine campsites throughout the Horseshoe Meadow area. Water can be found in the small streams and seeps scattered around the meadows.

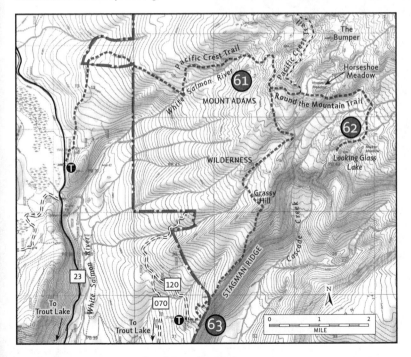

Opposite: Two equestrians pass through Horseshoe Meadow.

62 Looking Glass Lake

RATING/ DIFFICULTY	ROUND-TRIP	ELEV GAIN/ HIGH POINT	SEASON
****/5	15 miles	2400 feet/ 6000 feet	late June– October

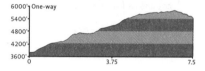

Map: Green Trails No. 367S Mount Adams; **Contact/Permits:** USFS Mount Adams Ranger District, (509) 395-3400 / Northwest Forest Pass; **GPS:** N46 5.593, W121 28.799

Pine forests give way to basalt lava beds as you climb east along the Pacific Crest Trail to the timberline on graceful Mount Adams. This wonderfully formed mountain is one of the youngest of the big volcanoes, and as such, hasn't yet lost its smooth cone shape to the forces of erosion. The only thing that could make the mountain more attractive is to see it reflected in the cold waters of a wilderness lake. Looking Glass can't truthfully be called a lake—it's far too small for that—but when the winds are calm and the air is clear, the tiny tarn does reflect the face of Adams as well as any looking glass.

GETTING THERE

From Trout Lake, drive north on Forest Road 23 for about 13.5 miles and turn right onto a small dirt road marked PCT–North Trailhead. Follow this a few hundred yards to a trailhead parking lot.

ON THE TRAIL

Follow the Pacific Crest Trail northeast into the pine forest above the road. The trail rolls gently uphill for the first 0.5 mile or so before steepening for a long climb north and east along the ridge above the White Salmon River. As you cross into the Mount Adams Wilderness at about 1.75 miles in, the forest transitions into old-growth pine. Views in the first couple miles are limited to the surrounding forest, with its dark pines and firs. Great horned owls, woodpeckers, and Clark's nutcrackers, among a host of other bird species, are found in these woods, as are black-tailed deer.

Once on the ridge, the trail levels out briefly and angles southeast about a mile to cross the headwaters of the White Salmon River before starting a grueling climb up the steep southwestern slope of Mount Adams.

You always know when you're on the Pacific Crest Trail.

Few switchbacks exist as the trail pushes up, up, up.

At 5 miles, the trail forks. Stay left to enter a world of sloping alpine meadows. In just under 0.5 mile from the junction, the trail is in the heart of Horseshoe Meadow with views of Mount Adams looming to the east.

Leave the PCT at the meadows and follow the Round the Mountain Trail (Trail No. 9) southeast about 1 mile to a small trail junction on the right. This spur leads you 1 mile south to the little pond at trail's end that is Looking Glass Lake.

63 Stagman Ridge–The Bumper

RATING/ DIFFICULTY	ROUND-TRIP	ELEV GAIN/ HIGH POINT	SEASON
****/5	12 miles	1900 feet/ 6100 feet	late June– October

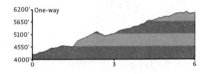

Map: Green Trails No. 367S Mount Adams;
Contact/Permits: USFS Mount Adams Ranger District, (509) 395-3400 / Northwest Forest Pass; **GPS:** N46 8.428, W121 35.864

*This route offers a wonderful intro-
duction to the diversity of the Pacific
Crest Trail in a relatively short hike. Do it as
a long hike, a simple overnight backpacking
trip, or set up a base camp at one of the fine
campsites along the way and enjoy a few
days exploring the flank of the big volcano.*

*The trail begins high on a ridge covered
with old-growth pine and climbs steeply to
the rock and ice of the alpine world. Along
the way, it offers views of rushing rivers and
hanging glaciers, cool forests and sun-filled
flower meadows, fields of berries and herds
of deer and elk.*

GETTING THERE
From Trout Lake, drive north on Forest Road 23 for about 8.5 miles and turn right (east) onto FR 8031. In about 0.25 mile, bear left onto Spur Road 8031-070 and drive about 3 miles to another road junction. Turn right onto FR 120 and follow it to the trailhead at the road's end, less than a mile farther.

ON THE TRAIL
The trail leaves the clear-cuts near the road's end and climbs to the wilderness boundary in the first quarter mile. From there, the path rides the sharp spine of Stagman Ridge. The ridge crest is shaded by ancient pine forests, but the sheer drop to the south is apparent, even in the cool shadows of the forest. The ridge slopes gently away to the north, but its southern face drops almost vertically more than 1000 feet to the bottom of the Cascade Creek valley.

This precipitous ridge walk continues for just about 1.5 miles before the trail angles north away from the cliff top and into deeper forest. At 2 miles, the way crosses a thundering (in early summer, anyway) creek at 5100 feet and begins a gentle 2-mile climb to Horseshoe Meadow at 5800 feet.

The Stagman Ridge Trail joins the PCT about 0.5 mile west of Horseshoe Meadow amid splendid views of Mount Adams. From the broad, flower-filled meadows, the White Salmon Glacier, Avalanche Glacier, and the mountain's true summit are all seen from the clearings here.

Leaving Horseshoe Meadow (5900 feet), the PCT climbs gradually for another 2 miles through alpine meadow and open stands of timber. At 6100 feet, the trail is at timberline on the western edge of The Bumper—a knob of basalt at the edge of the trees.

It's possible to scramble to the top of the 6490-foot rock, but be warned that the lava rock is sharp and brittle. Hands, clothing, and

Mount Adams from a large meadow on Stagman Ridge

even boot leather are all at risk. The jagged rock will slice and dice faster than any machine sold by Ron Popeil.

View The Bumper and its adjacent lava fields at the foot of Mount Adams before heading back down the trail. Backpackers will find fine campsites throughout the Horseshoe Meadow area. Water can be found in the small streams and seeps scattered around the meadows.

64 Crofton Butte

RATING/ DIFFICULTY	ROUND-TRIP	ELEV GAIN/ HIGH POINT	SEASON
**/3	4 miles	600 feet/ 4800 feet	late May– November

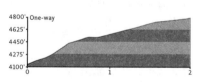

Maps: Green Trails No. 366 Mount Lone Butte, No. 367 Mount Adams West; **Contact/Permits:** USFS Mount Adams Ranger District, (509) 395-3400 / Northwest Forest Pass; **GPS:** N46 7.296, W121 33.673

Rolling along the lower slope of Mount Adams, this trail offers mountain views and, during the early season, a forest floor carpeted with lush clumps of beargrass with bulbous white flowers. Though much of the trail is under the old fir and pine forest canopy, there are enough breaks and clearings to keep Mount Adams frequently in view. The best panoramas of the peak are found from the saddle between 5272-foot Crofton Butte and its little sibling to the south, Lower Butte (4870 feet).

GETTING THERE

From Trout Lake, drive about 8.5 miles north on Forest Road 23 and turn right (east) onto FR 8031. Continue 1.4 miles on FR 8031 to Spur Road 8031-050. Turn left and drive about 2 miles to the trailhead on the left (at 4200 feet).

ON THE TRAIL

The trail heads north from Spur Road 8031-050 for 0.5 mile, crossing over into the Mount Adams Wilderness before curving east to climb gradually toward Crofton Butte. The trail climbs to 4800 feet as it squeezes between the dual cones of Crofton and Lower Buttes.

As you skirt out along the southern flank of Crofton, the trail moves out onto the bluff overlooking Crofton Creek at 2 miles. Stop and enjoy the views here, looking up at Adams, down onto the Crofton Creek valley, and out across the expanse of the lava beds littering the southern flank of Mount Adams. Turn around here after you've had your fill.

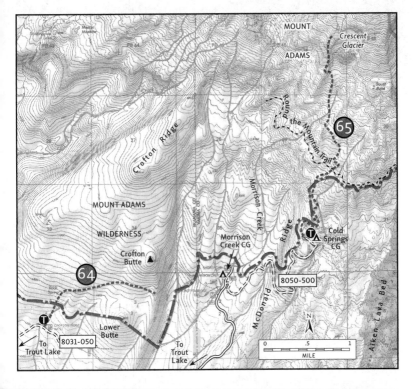

Beargrass-lined trail below Crofton Butte

65 Crescent Glacier

RATING/ DIFFICULTY	ROUND-TRIP	ELEV GAIN/ HIGH POINT	SEASON
****/5	7 miles	3800 feet/ 8500 feet	late June– October

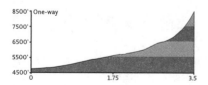

Map: Green Trails No. 367S Mount Adams;
Contact/Permits: USFS Mount Adams Ranger
District, (509) 395-3400 / Northwest Forest
Pass; **GPS:** N46 8.191, W121 29.880; **Status:**
Threatened

Anyone who has climbed Mount
Adams knows the mountain isn't
a cakewalk. This is a big rock with lots of
snow and ice, and it requires a serious com-
mitment to get even halfway up. That said,
there was a time when men not only climbed
the peak to mine sulfur from the summit
vents, they led mules to the summit. Yes,
mules. There remain a few traces of that old
mule trail visible on the upper mountain—
when the snowpack is light and nearly
melted off, you can still see the trail pounded
into the pumice of the upper mountains.

This route doesn't get us to the upper
mountain, though. It does, however, take
us into the glacier zone. Like rivers of ice all
over the world, Crescent Glacier is getting
smaller every year, so we wanted to lead

hikers up this mountain while there are still glaciers to see.

GETTING THERE

From Trout Lake, drive north on Forest Road 23 and turn right (east) onto FR 80, signed South Climb. In 12 miles, turn left again onto FR 8040, signed Morrison Creek. Past Morrison Creek, turn right onto Spur 8040-500 and follow it to the road-end parking lot. **Note:** This last section of road is rough dirt. Higher-clearance vehicles are recommended.

ON THE TRAIL

The trail follows what used to be an old miners' road as far upward as timberline—the road was actually still in use until as late as 1976. The trail intercepts the Round the Mountain Trail (No. 9) at timberline, about 1.4 miles out from the trailhead.

Continue north, climbing out from under the trees and into the world of rock and ice. The trail is sometimes easily found; sometimes it requires careful attention to cairns and other markers.

Depending on the time of year and the past winter's snowpack, you might have snow to traverse anywhere above timberline, but generally, visit after mid-July, and you won't hit ice until you reach Crescent Glacier, elevation 8500 feet, at 3.5 miles out from the trailhead. Beyond this point, there is no real established trail.

Caution: Climbing onto the upper mountain (i.e., above timberline) requires you to be skilled in navigation (map and compass

"Sooty" blue grouse, common to the trails around Mount Adams

use) and come prepared to use all of the Ten Essentials.

66 Aiken Lava Bed West–Cold Springs

RATING/ DIFFICULTY	ROUND-TRIP	ELEV GAIN/ HIGH POINT	SEASON
****/5	9 miles	2400 feet/ 6000 feet	late June– October

6000' — One-way
5400'
4800'
4200'
3600'
0   2.25   4.5

Map: Green Trails No. 367S Mount Adams; **Contact/Permits:** USFS Mount Adams Ranger District, (509) 395-3400 / Northwest Forest Pass; **GPS:** N46 5.191, W121 29.496

Mount Adams towers over the South Cascades. The big stratovolcano rises out of a jumble of lava beds, which make cross-country travel difficult along the flanks of the big mountain. But those same lava flows add a wonderful scenic element to trail hiking. Snow-capped Mount Adams fills the horizon, but at its feet is a world of jagged black rock that slashes at the boots and hands of any adventurer careless enough to scramble off-trail.

Looking down the four-mile-long Aiken Lava Bed

GETTING THERE

From Trout Lake, drive north 1.25 miles on Forest Road 23. Turn left (east) onto FR 82 and in less than a mile, stay right onto FR 80. Continue north on FR 80 until you reach a junction with FR 8020. Turn right onto FR 8020 and follow it to the trailhead on the left, just before reaching the junction with FR 8225 (if you hit this four-way junction, turn around and go back about 0.25 mile). Park at the trailhead area alongside the road.

ON THE TRAIL

Start up the trail (No. 40) in the forest and, in just 0.7 mile, turn right onto the Cold Springs Trail (No. 72). This path climbs northeast to the flank of the Aiken Lava Bed—a 4-mile-long, 0.5-mile-wide swatch of jagged black basalt. You'll enjoy good views of the basalt finger that extends south from Mount Adams before the trail angles west a bit and you stroll up into open forests and, finally, wide meadows.

At 4.5 miles, you'll reach Cold Springs Campground, the gateway to the summit of Mount Adams. The majority of climbers who scale the big volcano start at this campground. Turn around at the campground and return the way you came.

Map: Green Trails No. 367S Mount Adams; **Contact/Permits:** USFS Mount Adams Ranger District, (509) 395-3400 / Northwest Forest Pass; **GPS:** N46 5.593, W121 28.799

The east side of Mount Adams is a world unto itself. Though all of Adams is in the dry zone of the Cascades, the eastern side of the big volcano, especially along the black-rock scar of the Aiken Lava Bed, is dry as a bone. This route explores the sparse pine forests flanking the edge of that massive ancient river of molten rock that is the Aiken Lava Bed. Though the magma no longer flows, hike here in August and you'll get a sense of the heat that must have been thrown off by the molten flow—the hot August sun bakes that black basalt rock until the ambient air around the lava bed can easily climb 10 to 20 degrees hotter than that of the surrounding forestlands. That means a 90-degree summer day can be 110 degrees Fahrenheit on the rocks!

GETTING THERE

From Trout Lake, drive north on Forest Road 23 and turn right (east) onto FR 82. In about 2.5 miles, turn left onto FR 8225 and follow this to its end at a four-way junction. Continue straight ahead, now on Spur Road 8225-150, and in about 0.7 mile park at the trailhead area alongside the road.

ON THE TRAIL

Hike north from the trailhead along Gotchen Creek Trail (No. 11), hugging the eastern edge of the tall, jagged ridge of black basalt that is the Aiken Lava Bed. The trail stays well under the forest canopy most of the way, but during the heat of summer the black rocks of the lava bed throw a lot of heat back down into the forest, so pack plenty of water, though you'll

67 Gotchen Creek– Aiken Lava Bed East

RATING/ DIFFICULTY	ROUND-TRIP	ELEV GAIN/ HIGH POINT	SEASON
****/5	11 miles (longer option 15 miles)	2600 feet/ 6300 feet	late June– October

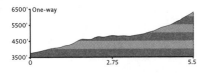

have access to Gotchen Creek, too.

As you skirt the lava bed, you'll be tempted to scramble up the lava walls. Be careful if you do—the rock is loose, sharp, and brittle. It can roll, break, and slash with little encouragement.

The trail climbs steadily from the get-go, cutting first through thick, cool forest and then into increasingly open, airy pine forests. Great fields of vanilla leaf bound the trail during the first 3 miles, and beargrass becomes common after that.

At 3 miles (4800 feet) the trail passes a side

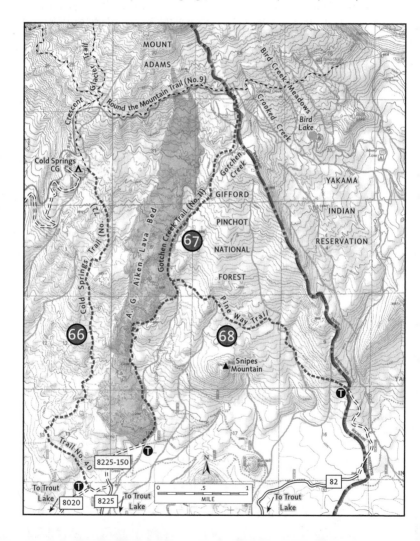

View of Mount Adams through western larch trees, from the Aiken Lava Bed

trail leading east toward Snipes Mountain (see Hike 68). From this point on, the forest becomes far more sparse, and meadows and forest clearings become common occurrences. These provide great views up onto the lava bed.

About 5 miles in, the trail parallels the national forest boundary with the Yakama Indian Reservation to the east, and at 5.5 miles intersects the Round the Mountain Trail (No. 9) at 6300 feet. This is a great place to turn around and retrace your route.

EXTENDING YOUR TRIP

For a longer hike, you can make a 15-mile circuit of the lava bed, returning on the Cold Springs Trail (see Hike 66). Turn left below the open wildflower fields of the western edge of Bird Creek Meadows, and follow the Round the Mountain Trail west across the upper reaches of the lava bed. You'll traverse Mount Adams's south slope for 2.6 miles before reaching the Crescent Glacier Trail (Hike 65) leading to the south climbing route.

Turn left here off the Round the Mountain Trail to descend the Crescent Glacier Trail for about 1 mile to the climbers' trailhead parking area at Cold Springs Campground (9.3 miles from the start). Walk through the parking area, and find the Cold Springs Trail on its eastern edge. Head south on this trail (No. 72) as it rolls down the western edge of the lava bed. The trail drops 3.7 miles to a junction with Trail No. 40. Turn left and in 0.7 mile, step out onto a small dirt road. Turn left, and in about 0.25 mile you'll come to the four-way junction at the end of Forest Road 8225. Turn left to hike the 0.75 mile up Spur Road 8225-150 to your waiting car, completing the 15-mile loop.

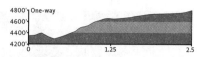

68 Snipes Mountain–Pine Way

RATING/ DIFFICULTY	ROUND-TRIP	ELEV GAIN/ HIGH POINT	SEASON
**/3	5 miles	500 feet/ 4800 feet	late May– November

Maps: Green Trails No. 367S Mount Adams West; **Contact/Permits:** USFS Mount Adams Ranger District, (509) 395-3400 / Northwest Forest Pass; **GPS:** N46 6.173, W121 26.077

Located in the eastern part of the Mount Adams Ranger District, this trail is adjacent to the Yakama Indian Reservation. Climbing along an old sheep trail, this route climbs gently through a forest that has seen selective timber harvesting. The logging scars are faint.

GETTING THERE

From Trout Lake, drive north on Forest Road 23 and turn right (east) onto FR 82. Follow this road to the boundary of the Yakama Indian Reservation. Continue another mile as the road winds north along the boundary between the reservation and the national forest property. Find the trailhead at 4300 feet just inside the national forest boundary.

ON THE TRAIL

Head west along the Pine Way Trail as it climbs alongside an old dirt track. This trail angles northwest between Snipes Mountain and Mount Adams. The first mile is frequented by cattle that graze on the tribal lands.

At about 1 mile out from the trailhead, the path leaves the forest and enters a wonderful network of meadows and woodland groves. For the next mile, the trail wanders under trees and across wildflower fields. Push on another 0.5 mile, and you'll find yourself facing the black wall of the Aiken Lava Bed, on a junction with the Gotchen Creek Trail (see Hike 67). Turn around here.

Black-backed woodpecker on a diseased tree

Opposite: Rocks dot shallow Lake Umtux in the heart of the Indian Heaven Wilderness.

indian heaven /
trapper creek region

The forestlands nestled between Mount Adams and the Lewis River are perhaps the most overlooked wildlands in the Cascades, despite being some of the most spectacular country you'll find to explore. The protected lands of the Indian Heaven Wilderness and Trapper Creek Wilderness offer hikers fantastic mountains, meadows, and lakes to visit. Between these small wilderness areas, though, is equally stunning country. The trails throughout the region are generally seldom visited, gently sloped, and remarkably wild.

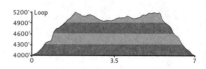

Map: Green Trails No. 365 Mount Lone Butte; **Contact/Permits:** USFS Mount Adams Ranger District, (509) 395-3400 / Northwest Forest Pass; **GPS:** N46 2.826, W121 45.369

Indian Heaven Wilderness is a wonderland of sparkling lakes, jagged peaks, open forests, and, most notably, expansive meadows filled with flowers and an array of wildlife. A pair of loops around Bird Mountain—the highest peak in the wilderness—allow hikers to experience the best of each of those offerings. The short loop stays close to the flank of Bird Mountain,

69 Bird Mountain

RATING/ DIFFICULTY	LOOP	ELEV GAIN/ HIGH POINT	SEASON
****/5	7 miles	1200 feet/ 5200 feet	late May– November

View east of Mount Adams and north of Mount Rainier from below Bird Mountain

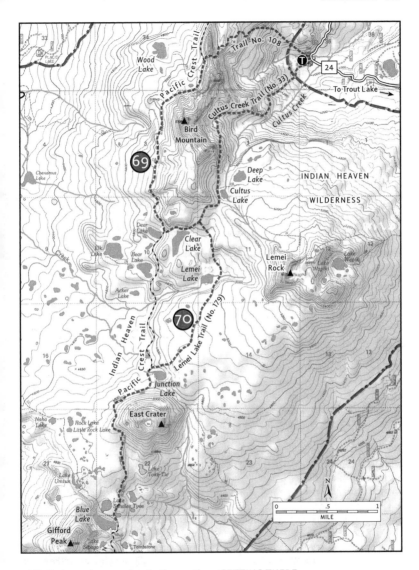

while the longer loop wanders farther south into bigger meadowlands before turning back to skirt around the mountain.

GETTING THERE

From Trout Lake, head west on State Route 141 for about 8 miles to Peterson Prairie

Campground and a junction with Forest Road 24. Turn right onto FR 24 and drive 8 miles to the Cultus Creek Campground on the left. The starting trailhead is found near the back of the campground loop.

ON THE TRAIL

This loop is best done clockwise, so begin on the Cultus Creek Trail (No. 33) and start a long, steep climb to the east flank of Bird Mountain. The first 1.5 miles gain nearly 1200 feet in elevation as the trail ruthlessly ascends the Cultus Creek valley. About a mile into the hike, the trail breaks out onto a small ridge. Look east from this rocky point, and Mount Adams dominates the horizon. Below the viewpoint, the slope drops steeply away and rolls into a long blanket of green between the base of Bird Mountain and the flank of Adams. Face north on clear days, and Mount Rainier can be seen.

From here the trail turns sharply south as it draws near the cliff faces of Bird Mountain. Pine forests enclose the trail, with occasional meadow breaks and views of the towering cliffs, until the trail passes the crystal clear waters of Cultus Lake at 2.5 miles.

A side trail leaves to the left just a few hundred feet beyond the lake. This path leads to Lemei Rock and beyond. Stay right on the main trail, and in another 0.25 mile you'll reach a second trail junction. Go right again, and you'll pass pretty Clear Lake before reaching the Pacific Crest Trail in just over 0.5 mile from that last trail fork.

Turn north onto the PCT and follow it as it angles east toward the rocky upper slopes of Bird Mountain. Just beyond Wood Lake Trail junction, leave the PCT by bearing right onto Trail No. 108, which leads back to Cultus Creek Campground in another 1.5 miles.

Before heading for the trailhead, though, stop at the ridge crest just after leaving the PCT and enjoy the views. Or, for markedly better views, climb south on a boot track along

the ridge until you see the whole of the South Cascades spread out in all their splendor. Mount St. Helens, Mount Rainier, the Goat Rocks peaks, and Mount Adams can be seen on clear days from this vantage point, less than a quarter mile off the trail. Don't bother risking the scramble to the summit of Bird, as the views are no better from that higher, more dangerous perch.

From the ridge, the final stretch on Trail No. 108 is a steep descent through trees, ending at the Cultus Creek Campground entrance.

70 Blue Lake

RATING/ DIFFICULTY	ROUND-TRIP	ELEV GAIN/ HIGH POINT	SEASON
****/3	13 miles	700 feet/ 5200 feet	late May– November

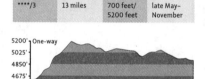

Maps: Green Trails No. 365 Mount Lone Butte, No. 397 Wind River; **Contact/Permits:** USFS Mount Adams Ranger District, (509) 395-3400 / Northwest Forest Pass; **GPS:** N46 2.826, W121 45.369

Indian Heaven Wilderness abounds in forest lakes, expansive meadows, craggy peaks, and majestic wilderness. Native Americans took advantage of all those offerings, and this trail lets you do the same. The lakes you'll pass along the route still hold hardy populations of trout. The meadows you'll cross offer a bounty of berries, and, for those who really want to feast at the wilderness buffet, camas root (a starchy staple of the local tribal diet for centuries). Deer and elk browse through the forest/meadow interface, using the timberlands for cover and

Early summer at Cultus Lake

the meadows for forage. This trail, in short, takes you on a virtual trip through time, leading you back into the wild country that provided so much to the locals that lived here for millennia.

GETTING THERE

From Trout Lake, head west on State Route 141 for about 8 miles to Peterson Prairie Campground and a junction with Forest Road 24. Turn right onto FR 24 and drive 8 miles to the Cultus Creek Campground on the left. The starting trailhead is found near the back of the campground loop.

ON THE TRAIL

The first 1.5 miles gain nearly 700 feet in elevation as the trail ascends the Cultus Creek valley along the south flank of Bird Mountain. About a mile into the hike, the trail breaks out onto a small ridge. Look east from this rocky point, and Mount Adams dominates the horizon. Below the viewpoint, the slope drops steeply away to a broad expanse of blue-green forest between you and Mount Adams.

From here the trail turns sharply south as it draws near the cliff faces of Bird Mountain. Pine forests enclose the trail, with occasional meadow breaks and views of the towering cliffs, until the trail passes Cultus Lake at 2 miles. Just a few hundred feet past the lake, a side trail leads off to the left to Lemei Rock and beyond. Stay right on the main trail, and in another 0.25 mile you'll reach a second trail junction. This is the Lemei Lake Trail (No. 179). Here, you'll take the left-hand trail and hike south to Lemei Lake. More like a vast puddle, Lemei Lake is a shallow, somewhat dirty lake.

Continuing south through the broken forest (stands of pine and fir intermingled with open meadows and clearings), you'll find Junction Lake at 5 miles from the trailhead. Junction Lake, so named because two side-trails merge into the Pacific Crest Trail at the lakeshore, is a muddy, frog-filled pond at the base of East Crater. Junction Lake is shallow and therefore warm, proving the perfect place to breed a healthy population of mosquitoes, so move on by quickly.

From Junction Lake, continue south on the PCT, following it around the west flank of the East Crater, before starting a long, gentle descent to Blue Lake, about 1.5 miles from the junction. The lake offers excellent views of the various small volcanic cones that dot this part of the South Cascades. Blue Lake supports a strong population of rainbow trout. The area is also rich with huckleberry brambles. The lush purple fruit typically ripens in early August, and the berries tend to bring out a variety of pickers, including the natives—black bears!—so take care while enjoying the sweet treats.

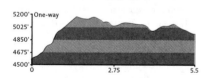

71 Gifford Peak

RATING/ DIFFICULTY	ROUND-TRIP	ELEV GAIN/ HIGH POINT	SEASON
****/3	11 miles	700 feet/ 5200 feet	late May– November

Elevation profile: One-way, from 0 to 5.5, ranging 4500' to 5200'.

Maps: Green Trails No. 365 Mount Lone Butte, No. 397 Wind River; **Contact/Permits:** USFS Mount Adams Ranger District, (509) 395-3400 / Northwest Forest Pass; **GPS:** N46 56.243, W121 49.202

🏠 *The Indian Heaven Wilderness is tiny compared to some of the wilderness preserves in Washington, but don't let its size fool you. This is a rare gem with its multitude of sparkling lakes, acres of flower-filled meadows, fields of rich berries, and herds of deer and elk. There are many ways to enter the tiny wilderness area, but from the south the most scenic access is from the top of Red Mountain, a cinder cone volcano.*

The trail starts high, and the elevation doesn't change much along the route's length as the trail follows ridges north. The route leads past a historic gathering place of Northwest tribes—the Indian Racetrack—and traverses a long ridge before ending in the shadow of another volcano, Gifford Peak.

GETTING THERE

From Carson, drive north on the Wind River Road (County Road 30) 5.6 miles and turn right (east) onto the Panther Creek Road (Forest Road 65). Continue on the Panther Creek Road 11.3 miles to a junction with FR 60. Turn right (east) onto FR 60 and drive 1.6 miles to the junction with FR 6048. Turn left onto FR 6048 and drive 4 miles to the end of the road. **Note:** This is a one-lane dirt road. High-clearance vehicles are required, and when conditions are wet, four-wheel drive is recommended. The trailhead is about a hundred yards below the summit, at the last hairpin turn in the road.

ON THE TRAIL

The trail heads due north for just a mile to reach a junction with the Indian Racetrack Trail (see Hike 72). The area was a popular gathering ground for a number of native peoples because of its rich abundance of fish, berries, big game, and a variety of roots and tubers.

Opposite: Gifford Peak overlooks Blue Lake.

At the junction with the Racetrack Trail, go right (east) on Trail No. 171A, and in 0.5 mile you'll reach the PCT. Turn north on the PCT and begin a gradual climb to the crest of Berry Mountain, a long, jagged ridge. Berry Mountain is a volcanic formation. It is what remains of vast lava vents that spewed molten basalt onto the land surface. The trail rides the crest of this mountain north.

About 4 miles from the trailhead, the trail crosses the true summit of Berry Mountain—5000 feet—and starts a gentle descent to Blue Lake at the foot of Gifford Peak, 5.5 miles out from the trailhead. There is fine camping available at the lake, and good huckleberry thickets all along the trail. Blue Lake can also be approached from the north (see Hike 69).

72 Indian Racetrack

RATING/ DIFFICULTY	ROUND-TRIP	ELEV GAIN/ HIGH POINT	SEASON
***/3	5 miles	700 feet/ 5200 feet	late May–November

Maps: Green Trails No. 365 Mount Lone Butte, No. 397 Wind River; **Contact/Permits:** USFS Mount Adams Ranger District, (509) 395-3400 / Northwest Forest Pass; **GPS:** N46 56.243, W121 49.202

The Indian Heaven Wilderness may be the most underrated wilderness area in Washington. This oft-forgotten gem is one of the most beautiful places in the Cascades, and it has been a popular gathering place for wilderness-loving humans for centuries. Part of the reason for that, of course, is the abundance of berries along the trail—starting with a vast field on the south flank of Red Mountain, just below the lookout tower—which gives a strong hint as to how the wilderness area earned its name. For centuries, local native tribes would gather here each summer to partake of the lands' bounty throughout what is now Indian Heaven Wilderness. They would harvest roots from the broad meadows that cover the areas, hunt the resident deer and elk, fish in the hundreds of small lakes that dot the landscape, and pick bushels of berries. Heaven, indeed.

The local tribes gathered in such numbers that after harvesting food all day, the young men needed some way to challenge each other. So they raced. They raced so frequently and with such vigor that the track their thundering horses drummed into the dirt still exists today. This is the Indian Racetrack.

GETTING THERE

From Carson, drive north on the Wind River Road (County Road 30) 5.6 miles and turn right (east) onto the Panther Creek Road (Forest Road 65). Continue on the Panther Creek Road 11.3 miles to a junction with FR 60. Turn right (east) onto FR 60 and drive 1.6 miles to the junction with FR 6048. Turn left onto FR 6048 and drive 4 miles to the end of the road. **Note:** This is a one-lane dirt road. High-clearance vehicles are required, and when conditions are wet, four-wheel drive is recommended.

ON THE TRAIL

A still-active lookout tower sits atop Red Mountain, and it is worth a few minutes' delay to hike up to the lookout cabin before beginning the hike. Astounding views of the volcanic landscape of the South Cascades are found from the cabin. Mount St. Helens,

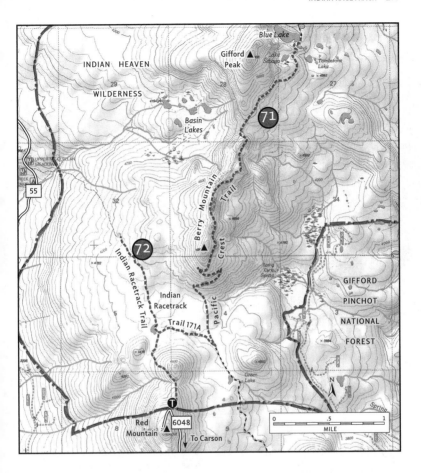

Mount Hood, and Mount Adams line the horizons. The giant scab of the Big Lava Bed sprawls at your feet to the southeast, and a host of little cinder cones dot the countryside all around—most notably, The Wart to the south, and the crater cone in the center of the Lava Bed to the east.

The trailhead is about a hundred yards below the summit, at the last hairpin turn in the road. The trail heads due north for just a

mile to reach a junction with the Indian Racetrack Trail at the racetrack itself. This first leg of the hike is a gradual descent along a ridgeline, mostly in scrub pine and open meadow. As the trail nears the racetrack, the forest closes in and the trail levels out.

The racetrack itself is a meadow area slightly to the west. Go left at a small pond, and you'll be led out into the broad, linking meadows. There wander out away from the

The famous Indian Racetrack, crossing the meadow

trail, and you'll find deep grooves in several areas around the flat meadows, proving that the races were too popular to have just a single "racetrack." This route should be renamed "Indian Racetracks."

Maps: Green Trails No. 365 Mount Lone Butte, No. 366 Mount Adams West; **Contact/Permits:** USFS Mount Adams Ranger District, (509) 395-3400 / Northwest Forest Pass; **GPS:** N46 5.109, W121 39.455

73 Sleeping Beauty Peak

RATING/ DIFFICULTY	ROUND-TRIP	ELEV GAIN/ HIGH POINT	SEASON
***/3	3 miles	800 feet/ 4900 feet	late May–November

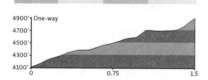

This trail may have a storybook name, but it offers real-life views and scenic wonders. Climbing steeply through a modest series of switchbacks, the trail tops out on the summit of Sleeping Beauty Peak, with views worthy of inclusion in any fairy tale. The former lookout site provides great vistas of Mount Adams and the emerald ridges and valleys of the Indian Heaven Wilderness to the southwest.

Opposite: Mount Adams from the summit of Sleeping Beauty Peak

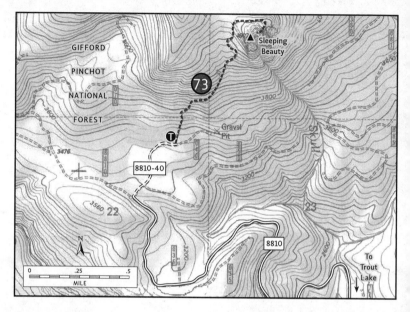

GETTING THERE

From Trout Lake, drive west on Highway 141 and turn right (north) on Forest Road 88 just outside of town. Continue about 4.5 miles before turning right onto FR 8810. Continue 6.1 miles and turn right onto FR 8810-40. Continue .25 mile to reach the trailhead on the left.

ON THE TRAIL

This short trail starts out climbing from the get-go. Initially it ascends dense second-growth forest, but that young forest ages rapidly and by the time you reach the halfway point, you'll find yourself walking in ancient forests of massive Douglas-fir and western hemlock.

At 1 mile, the trail levels considerably as it stretches out on the ridge top. Another half mile puts you at the site of the old, long-gone lookout tower. The fire watch station that once stood on this 4907-foot mountain was built in 1929 but was destroyed in the mid-1970s as technology began to phase out human watchers. Today, the top of Sleeping Beauty sits empty, expect for the occasional hiker looking for the amazing views that can only be found at these old lookout sites.

Opposite: Wildflower-lined trail up Silver Star Mountain

siouxon / silver star area

The Siouxon Roadless Area and nearby Silver Star basin include some of the most pristine old-growth stands remaining in Washington's South Cascades. The deep valley of Siouxon Creek provides wonderful hiking in both woodland and riparian wonderlands. Above the river valleys stand steep-walled ridges and high peaks, offering grand views of the southwestern section of the Cascades, from Mount St. Helens to The Gorge. The trails atop these ridges and mountains cross long fields of wildflowers inhabited by a host of birds and beasts. Look to the skies to see red-tailed hawks, turkey vultures, bald eagles, and even ospreys when salmon are running in the rivers. In the forests and meadows, keep a watchful eye out for plump grouse, bounding deer, and majestic elk. Black bears, cougars, bobcats, and various small predators— including martens and weasels—also call this wild country home.

74 Huffman Peak

RATING/ DIFFICULTY	ROUND-TRIP	ELEV GAIN/ HIGH POINT	SEASON
****/5	12 miles	2400 feet/ 4106 feet	late May– November

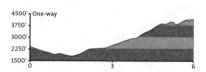

Map: Green Trails No. 396 Lookout Mountain; **Contact/Permits:** USFS Mount Adams Ranger District, (509) 395-3400 / Northwest Forest Pass; **GPS:** N45 56.428; W122 13.751

A word of warning: Bring lots of water. This trail challenges hikers right from the start as it begins with a descent and ends with a climb. The route climbs steadily and steeply for the first two-thirds of its length before moderating into a gentle roll along the ridge. But for all the sweat you pump out, all the calories you burn, you'll earn great rewards. Fabulous wildflower fields, stunning scenery, glorious views await you, as you cross one old fire lookout site.

GETTING THERE
From Interstate 5, turn east at Woodland onto State Route 503 and drive about 23 miles, heading south on SR 503 to Chelatchie. Turn left (east) at the country store onto NE Healy Road, which soon becomes Forest Road 54. Drive 9 miles on the road and turn left onto FR 57, then in 1.25 miles, turn left onto FR 5701. In less than 1 mile, the road switches back sharply to the right. As you drive out of this corner, look for the trailhead on the left (north) side of the road.

ON THE TRAIL
Head out onto the trail as it descends gradually through old, dense forest. At about 1.1 miles, turn left at the trail junction to drop to the banks of Siouxon Creek at 1.3 miles. The trail crosses the creek on a rustic old bridge and starts a long, steep climb along Huffman Ridge. The trail is the one used by the attendants of the old fire lookout station atop Huffman Peak, and as such, it heads straight for the top (the thinking being, the fire watchers should be getting to their posts as quickly and in as direct a manner as possible).

The trail climbs for nearly 4.5 miles from the river, ascending through forest with only occasional views out over the South Cascades, before rolling up to the high, windswept summit of Huffman Peak, elevation 4106 feet. Enjoy sweeping views in all directions here, and if you have pushed yourself too hard, take plenty of time to rest and soak in the views before you turn around for home.

Oxalis growing up through sword ferns along the trail

75 Lower Siouxon Creek

RATING/ DIFFICULTY	ROUND-TRIP	ELEV GAIN/ HIGH POINT	SEASON
***/2	6.5 miles (3.25 miles one-way with shuttle)	500 feet/ 1700 feet	late May– November

One-way

1700'
1575'
1450'
1325'
1200'
0   1.375   3.25

Map: Green Trails No. 396 Lookout Mountain; **Contact/Permits:** USFS Mount Adams Ranger District, (509) 395-3400 / Northwest Forest Pass; **GPS:** N45 56.428, W122 13.751

The history of the area is exemplified by mossy little Hickmans Cabin. It was built in the early 1930s by the firefighters who moved into the area to suppress and battle the fires that frequently plagued the area. The cabin was used as an advance supply hut, and firefighters stored and sharpened their tools and cooked their meals here. The scars of the fires they fought are still visible. Many of the fallen trees rotting along the route were killed by the fires and later toppled over.

At the end of the trail is the second Siouxon trailhead. Either arrange for a shuttle vehicle to pick you up here, or simply turn around and retrace your steps to the lower trailhead.

GETTING THERE

From Interstate 5, turn east at Woodland onto State Route 503 and drive about 23 miles, heading south on SR 503 to Chelatchie. Turn left (east) at the country store onto NE Healy Road, which soon becomes Forest Road 54. Drive 9 miles on the road and turn left onto FR 57, then in 1.25 miles turn left onto FR 5701. In less than 1 mile, the road switches back sharply to the right. As you drive out of this corner, look for the first Siouxon trailhead on the left (north) side of the road.

ON THE TRAIL

The Lower Siouxon Trail is the first section of the Siouxon Creek Trail; it makes a great day hike and is often ignored by those planning to hike the length of the main trail. This short route parallels the access road and links the upper and lower trailheads.

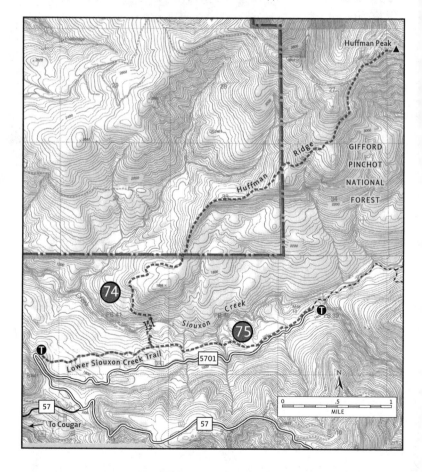

Lower Siouxon Creek

The route makes a gradual descent for nearly a mile, but doesn't drop all the way down to river level. For the next 2 miles, the trail stays above the south bank of the trail. You may be able to see and hear the river occasionally, but the Lower Siouxon isn't really a river trail. It is, instead, a beautiful forest hike that offers a history lesson. Enjoy the forest for the scenery, the river for the music.

[Elevation profile: One-way, from 900' to 1400', distance 0 to 2.25 miles]

Map: Green Trails No. 396 Lookout Mountain; **Contact/Permits:** USFS Mount Adams Ranger District, (509) 395-3400 / Northwest Forest Pass; **GPS:** N45 56.798, W122 10.638

76 Upper Siouxon–Horseshoe Falls

RATING/ DIFFICULTY	ROUND-TRIP	ELEV GAIN/ HIGH POINT	SEASON
****/3	4.5 miles	500 feet/ 1400 feet	late May–November

Everyone loves a waterfall. Put that falls on a pretty wild river, push it back into a remote forest environment, and make it accessible only by trail, and it becomes magical. That's what you'll find on the Upper Siouxon Trail, where Horseshoe Creek meets Siouxon Creek.

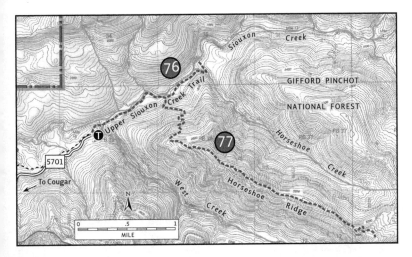

GETTING THERE

From Interstate 5, turn east at Woodland onto State Route 503 and drive about 23 miles, heading south on SR 503 to Chelatchie. Turn left (east) at the country store onto NE Healy Road, which soon becomes Forest Road 54. Drive 9 miles on the road and turn left onto FR 57, then in 1.25 miles turn left onto FR 5701. In less than 1 mile, the road switches back sharply to the right. As you drive out of this corner, look for the trailhead on the left (north) side of the road (see Hikes 74 and 75). Continue another 3 miles past this trailhead to the second Siouxon trailhead at the road's end.

ON THE TRAIL

Hop onto the Upper Siouxon Creek Trail as it angles east into the Siouxon Creek valley, descending gradually toward the river. In 0.25 mile, you'll hear what sounds like a muffled waterfall. Right you are! But not *the* waterfall. This one is a pretty little cascade on West Creek, a tributary to the Siouxon on the opposite side of the valley from you.

Press on up the river trail. You'll find a trail junction at about a mile out. The track that takes off to the right is the Horseshoe Ridge Trail (Hike 77). Ignore it for now, and walk another 0.5 mile through the rich forests filled with ferns, flowers (in season, of course), and fauna of all shapes and sizes—from tiny juncos flitting around, to big black-tailed deer browsing along the river.

At about 1.5 miles in, a small bridge leads across Horseshoe Creek—look down from the bridge, and you'll see the pretty falls. There is a scramble track that leads to the base of the falls. Hike about a quarter mile past the bridge to find a faint path on the left. Turn and descend along this rough path for about 0.5 mile to get below the falls.

77 Horseshoe Ridge

RATING/ DIFFICULTY	ROUND-TRIP	ELEV GAIN/ HIGH POINT	SEASON
*****/5	8 miles	2300 feet/ 3495 feet	late May– November

Opposite: Horseshoe Falls and the footbridge over Horseshoe Creek

Vanilla leaf in bloom

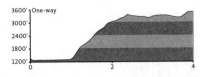

Map: Green Trails No. 396 Lookout Mountain; **Contact/Permits:** USFS Mount Adams Ranger District, (509) 395-3400 / Northwest Forest Pass; **GPS:** N45 56.798, W122 10.638

Horseshoe Ridge offers a bit of what you'd find in the larger Dark Divide Roadless Area to the east. The Siouxon area lacks the attention and the grandeur of the Dark Divide, but has its own graceful charm, and Horseshoe Ridge represents the best this region has to offer. The ridge is a long forested finger, covered with open meadows and wildflower fields. Deer and elk range through the meadows and forests, while birds soar effortlessly overhead.

GETTING THERE

From Interstate 5, turn east at Woodland onto State Route 503 and drive about 23 miles, heading south on SR 503 to Chelatchie. Turn left (east) at the country store onto NE Healy Road, which soon becomes Forest Road 54. Drive 9 miles on the road and turn left onto FR 57, then in 1.25 miles turn left onto FR 5701. In less than 1 mile, the road switches back sharply to the right. As you drive out of this corner, look for the trailhead on the left (north) side of the road (see Hikes 74 and 75). Continue another 3 miles past this trailhead to the second Siouxon trailhead at the road's end.

ON THE TRAIL

Start out as you would on Hike 76, descending gradually into the Siouxon Creek valley. Wander up the river trail for 1 mile, enjoying the cool riparian world before turning right after that first mile and starting a long, sweaty

climb up the snout of Horseshoe Ridge.

The trail runs through switchbacks for the next 0.5 mile, then crests the ridge at 2 miles from the trailhead. From this point on, the trail continues to climb, but gradually, easily. The dense forest gives way to open forest glades, and finally broad ridgetop meadows.

The trail ends at an old roadway, 4 miles from the start of the hike. Turn back before hitting the road and return the way you came.

78 Zig Zag Lake

RATING/ DIFFICULTY	ROUND-TRIP	ELEV GAIN/ HIGH POINT	SEASON
***/2	1 mile	600 feet/ 4000 feet	late May– November

Map: Green Trails No. 396 Lookout Mountain; **Contact/Permits:** USFS Mount Adams Ranger District, (509) 395-3400 / Northwest Forest Pass; **GPS:** N45 50.786, W122 6.670

Old-growth forest, a deep, green lake stocked with big, toothy brook trout, and a lush aquatic environment are the highlights of this trail. The short but steep path penetrates a cool, lush, ancient forest before bursting out of the trees on the lakeshore. If you aren't interested in angling for brookies, study the water anyway—you may see six-inch lizards darting around the shallows or lounging on the submerged logs.

GETTING THERE

From Carson, drive 8.4 miles north on Wind River Road (County Road 30) to the town of Stabler and the junction with Hemlock Road. Turn left (west) onto Hemlock Road, cross the river, and bear right (north) onto Forest Road

A family of common goldeneye gliding across Zig Zag Lake

54. Continue for 6 miles and then turn left onto FR 42. Drive 7 miles west to the trailhead on the right.

ON THE TRAIL

Dropping steeply from the trailhead, the 0.5-mile path loses 600 feet—that's a knee-crunching 1200 feet per mile. Fortunately, the short trail prevents too much descent agony. Rather, by the time you could even start to feel discomfort, the trail levels off alongside the fantastically pretty lake.

Map: Green Trails No. 396 Lookout Mountain; **Contact/Permits:** USFS Mount Adams Ranger District, (509) 395-3400 / Northwest Forest Pass; **GPS:** N45 52.707; W122 4.976

Considering the skyscraping volcanoes that surround the South Cascades, it should be no surprise that the entire area was formed by repeated eruptions and volcanic activity, and not always from the big cinder cones that decorate the horizons. This trail loops around the east side of a large volcanic crater, on the edge of one of its last massive lava flows.

79 West Crater

RATING/ DIFFICULTY	ROUND-TRIP	ELEV GAIN/ HIGH POINT	SEASON
***/2	1.6 miles	400 feet/ 4000 feet	late May– November

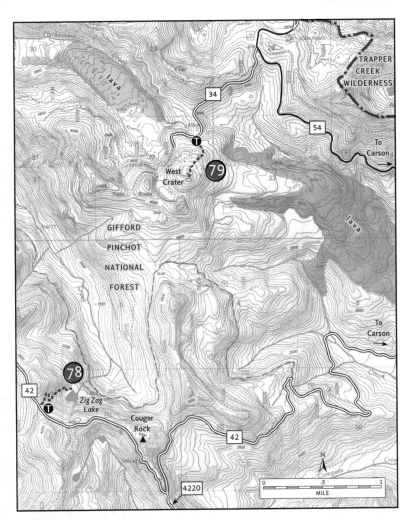

GETTING THERE

From Carson, drive 8.4 miles north on Wind River Road (County Road 30) to the town of Stabler and the junction with Hemlock Road. Turn left (west) onto Hemlock Road, cross the river, and bear right (north) onto Forest Road 54. Continue 12 miles and then turn left onto FR 34. Drive 1 mile to the trailhead.

ON THE TRAIL

From the trailhead, the path wanders gradually up through fragrant pine forests. Visit

Beargrass and tiger lily along the trail to the West Crater

in June and early July, and you'll find beargrass gracing the trail. For a bit over a half mile, the trail climbs mostly southwest, with a few gentle turns here and there. As you near the top of the peak, the trail swings around the southern face of the mountain before running northward up the last pitch to the top.

The route tops out on the West Crater's south rim, offering good southern views over the lava beds created by this crater's eruptions. The views of the big volcanoes aren't nearly as good—you can barely make out the top of Mount Adams and Mount St. Helens if you find the right spot on the crater rim.

If you are really adventurous and a skilled

scrambler, you can work your way down into the brushy crater. Be warned: the rocks are rough and very abrasive—they have a tendency to wear holes in boots, pants, and hands.

80 Observation Peak

RATING/ DIFFICULTY	ROUND-TRIP	ELEV GAIN/ HIGH POINT	SEASON
***/2	5 miles	600 feet/ 4207 feet	late May– November

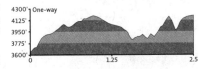

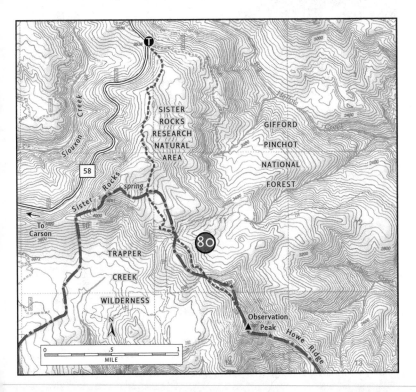

Mittens admires an old-growth fir tree . . . or the squirrel up the tree!

Map: Green Trails No. 396 Lookout Mountain; **Contact/Permits:** USFS Mount Adams Ranger District, (509) 395-3400 / Northwest Forest Pass; **GPS:** N45 52.707, W122 4.976

Wild is the keyword here. Wildflowers, wild berries, and wildlife thrive throughout this area. The trail climbs past Sister Rocks, through a natural resources research area, and onto the summit of Observation Peak.

GETTING THERE

From Carson, drive 8.4 miles north on Wind River Road (County Road 30) to the town of Stabler and the junction with Hemlock Road. Turn left (west) onto Hemlock Road, cross the river, and bear right (north) onto Forest Road 54. Continue 12 miles and then turn right onto FR 58. Drive about 7 miles north to the Sister Rocks Research Natural Area trailhead on the right.

ON THE TRAIL

From the trailhead, head south into the Sister Rocks Research Natural Area. For more than 1 mile, you'll wander through this wild research area where foresters focus on studying our native Northwestern woodlands.

At 1.5 miles, the trail skirts under the Sister Rocks, pretty geologic knobs on the ridge above Siouxon Creek. From the rocks, the trail continues south another mile to the summit of Observation Peak. Enjoy the outstanding views here before heading back down the trail you just came up.

81 Silver Star Mountain

RATING/ DIFFICULTY	ROUND-TRIP	ELEV GAIN/ HIGH POINT	SEASON
***/2	4 miles	1000 feet/ 4390 feet	late May– November

Hikers pass through wildflowers heading up Silver Star.

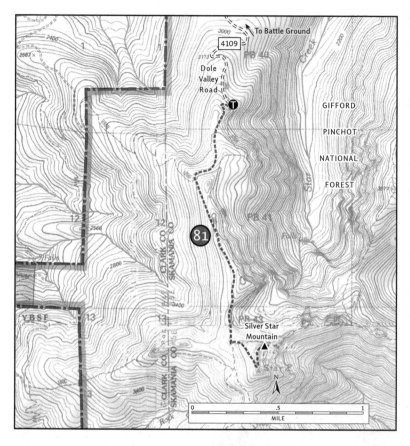

Map: Green Trails No. 396 Lookout Mountain; **Contact/Permits:** USFS Mount Adams Ranger District, (509) 395-3400 / Northwest Forest Pass; **GPS:** N45 46.091, W122 14.570

Silver Star has been a crown jewel in the Chinook Trail System—a trail system that links east and west sides of the Columbia River Gorge. The Silver Star Trail has captured the attention of many local hikers for very good reasons: it offers a high, meadow-lined ridge and lots of pretty foliage for autumn colors. It's a beautiful little trail, well worth anyone's time to visit.

GETTING THERE

From Battle Ground, drive north on State Route 503 and turn right onto Rock Creek Road. Continue nearly 9 miles to the Moulton Falls

County Park. Just past that park, turn right on Sunset Falls Road and continue 7 miles to the Sunset Falls Campground. Turn right into the campground, cross the East Fork Lewis River on FR 41 (also known as Dole Valley Road), and drive 3.5 miles. Turn right onto FR 4109 by way of a sharp hairpin turn. Continue 4 miles on FR 4109 to the road end and trailhead.

ON THE TRAIL

The trail—an old, gated road, actually—leaves the well-marked trailhead to climb the face of the long finger of Silver Star Mountain. The mountain is virtually all ridge—the prominent summit knob stands at the end of the long meadow-covered ridgeline.

Head up the old roadbed, now turned to trail, as it climbs along the valley wall below the Silver Star summit. The path leads south for more than a mile before turning east and ascending to the crest of the ridge, and finally onto the summit plateau of the big mountain. The 4300-foot peak provides enough altitude that hikers can look out over the expanse of the southwestern Cascades and even into the urban cores of Portland, Oregon, and Vancouver, Washington.

mount st. helens area

On May 18, 1980, Mount St. Helens earned global name recognition. This once perfect volcanic cone was well known to locals, but mostly unheard of outside of southwestern Washington and northwestern Oregon. But on that fateful spring day in 1980, the mountain literally exploded in a cataclysmic eruption. The top third of the mountain was vaporized into a blast of superheated ash that shot laterally out of the northern side of the mountain. Ash rained down for days across a swath that stretched more than 300 miles to the east. The ash cloud rose into the upper atmosphere and circled the globe several times before finally dissipating into the clouds. The landscape surrounding Mount St. Helens was forever changed, but it is no less beautiful than it ever was. Today, the scars of that 1980 eruption are starting to heal, but the power and devastation wrought by the big blast are still as evident now as they were more than twenty-five years ago.

82 Silver Lake–Seaquest

RATING/ DIFFICULTY	ROUND-TRIP	ELEV GAIN/ HIGH POINT	SEASON
***/2	6+ miles (including 1-mile barrier-free trail)	100 feet/ 4390 feet	late May– November

Map: Seaquest State Park map; **Contact/ Permits:** Washington State Parks and Recreation, (360) 902-8844; **GPS:** N45 46.091, W122 14.570

Boardwalks lead across areas of Silver Lake.

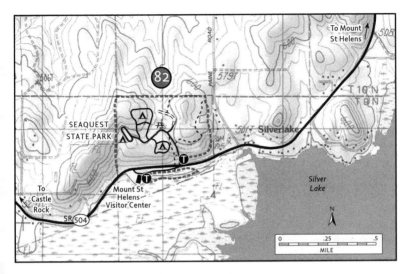

A forest walk and a wetlands walk—two trails for the price of one! Deep, old Douglas-fir and hemlock forest lines the woodland perimeter trail. Despite the number of visitors that hike the trail, expect to see deer, owls, assorted squirrels, a couple of jay varieties, and maybe even cougar or black bear tracks.

On the other side of the highway is a fully accessible shoreline trail along Silver Lake. Big, beautiful Silver Lake is entering old age. Like all living things, the lake is changing, and it will die someday. Death, for a lake, is disappearance. The shoreline of Silver Lake is extending out into the water, the water is getting shallower, and lush meadows flourish where fish once swam. The wide, paved trail loops through meadows and shoreline.

GETTING THERE

From Castle Rock, drive 5 miles east on Highway 504 to Seaquest State Park on the left (north) side of the highway. The trail can be accessed from the visitor/day-use parking area. The barrier-free shoreline trail begins at the Mount St. Helens Silver Lake Visitor Center on the right (south) side of the road. The trailhead is on the left side of the parking area.

ON THE TRAIL

Park at the Seaquest visitor lot, and head east to find the trail in the woods. The trail network weaves all around the perimeter of the park, staying in the dark forest for the length of the path. The trail is level and weaves through the trees with no particular destination. Hike as long as you like before turning back and returning to the day-use part of the park.

The Silver Lake Barrier-Free Trail starts behind the Mount St. Helens Visitor Center on the shores of Silver Lake. The mile-long fully accessible trail includes boardwalks over wetlands where a variety of birds, include an array of migratory waterfowl, may be viewed at different times of the year. Mount St. Helens dominates the eastern view from nearly everywhere on the lake, and the trail managers have positioned an accessible telescope along the route for the public to use to view the big volcano.

83 Boundary West

RATING/ DIFFICULTY	ROUND-TRIP	ELEV GAIN/ HIGH POINT	SEASON
****/4	4 miles (2 miles one-way with shuttle)	1800 feet/ 4390 feet	late June– November

4400' One-way

Map: Green Trails No. 332 Spirit Lake; **Contact/Permits:** USFS Mount St. Helens National Volcanic Monument, (360) 247-3900

/ Northwest Forest Pass; **GPS:** N46 17.211, W122 16.302

The May 18, 1980, eruption of Mount St. Helens rebuilt this entire area. New lakes were formed, old hills and valleys disappeared. Forests were flattened and rivers were obliterated. An entire landscape was altered, and though it has been nearly three decades since the big boom, recovery is occurring on geologic time, not human time. That means we still have time to get out and experience the devastation. The best way to experience the majesty of the volcanic power is to get out and just hike the landscape.

The Boundary Trail extends across vast

Western stretch of the Boundary Trail

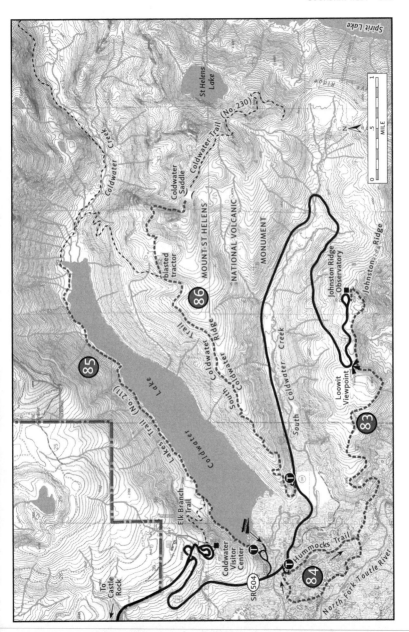

sections of the landscape, but sometimes a little goes a long way, so we're offering bits and pieces. This western segment is a good introduction to the blast.

GETTING THERE

From Castle Rock, drive about 43 miles east on Highway 504 to the Coldwater Visitor Center and continue 2.2 miles south toward Johnston Ridge. At the bottom of the hill, turn right into the Hummocks trailhead parking area. If two cars are available, you can drive one to the Johnston Ridge Observatory to do this as a one-way trek.

ON THE TRAIL

Head east on the Hummocks Trail (Hike 84), and in 0.5 mile you'll reach a trail junction. Go left to climb the ash-laden ridge snout of Johnston Ridge. Grasses, bushes, and trees are filling in the devastation, and that has brought an array of wildlife. You can commonly see elk tracks—and often elk themselves—on the flank of Johnston Ridge.

After leaving the Hummocks Trail and the convoluted valley floor, the trail crawls up the end of Johnston Ridge, climbing steeply through long, lazy switchbacks to gain a respectable 1000 feet in the first mile of serious climbing. The next 1.5 miles climb an additional 800 feet, putting you at the Loowit Viewpoint at the west end of Johnston Ridge, near a long hairpin turn in the highway. This makes a fine place to stop for a rest, a bit of reflection on the scenery, and a return to the starting point.

Of course, if you had the foresight to arrange a ride back from the Johnston Ridge Observatory, you should press on along the ridge trail. You'll reach the observatory in just 0.8 mile with another couple hundred feet of elevation gain. (See Hike 87 for additional hiking options.)

84 Hummocks Trail

RATING/ DIFFICULTY	LOOP	ELEV GAIN/ HIGH POINT	SEASON
***/3	2.3 miles	+/- 100 feet/ 2500 feet	late June– November

Map: Green Trails No. 332 Spirit Lake; **Contact/Permits:** USFS Mount St. Helens National Volcanic Monument, (360) 247-3900 / Northwest Forest Pass; **GPS:** N46 17.211, W122 16.302

The Hummocks are massive mounds of rock, ash, and mud that were piled unceremoniously around the floor of the new Coldwater Lake valley by the mighty blow. But these aren't just piles of rubble. Some of the hummocks tower 500 feet into the air and cover a once-grand ancient forest.

GETTING THERE

From Castle Rock, drive about 43 miles east on Highway 504 to the Coldwater Visitor Center and continue 2.2 miles south toward Johnston Ridge. At the bottom of the hill, turn right into the Hummocks trailhead parking area.

ON THE TRAIL

The loop trail weaves among the hummocks and the small catch-basin ponds that dot the landscape around the mounds. The Hummocks Trail features a lot of rolling up and down, but no serious, committed elevation changes.

Doing the route clockwise puts you on the pool side of the loop right off the bat. Most of the small ponds are on the northern side, near the trailhead, so you'll skirt a handful of them, with St. Helens herself looming on the horizon straight ahead.

After about 0.75 mile, you'll swing west toward the North Fork Toutle River, and then

A high-point view across the "hummocks"

loosely follow the river's course for another mile or so, weaving through a mixed bag of obstacles. Besides the hulks of the hummocks near the river, there are marshy bogs to avoid, and interwoven stream channels to be aware of.

This section of the hummocks shows great vitality. Life is booming here, as birds and bees fill the air, elk can frequently be found browsing on the lush grasses, and birds of prey overhead give testament to the fact that small land mammals are thriving, too (if there were no rodents to eat, the big raptors wouldn't waste their time here).

Closing this clockwise loop, you come out facing Coldwater Lake (just around the highway from this loop trail).

85 Lakes Trail

RATING/ DIFFICULTY	ROUND-TRIP	ELEV GAIN/ HIGH POINT	SEASON
***/3	6 miles	500 feet/ 3000 feet	late June– November

Map: Green Trails No. 332 Spirit Lake; **Contact/Permits:** USFS Mount St. Helens National Volcanic Monument, (360) 247-3900 /

The Lakes Trail passing along the shore of Coldwater Lake

Northwest Forest Pass; **GPS:** N46 17.490, W122 16.027

Before May 18, 1980, this was a forest, not a lake. The volcanic eruption that day, however, swept away the forest, and the massive mudflows in the Toutle River Basin created a huge earthen dam that trapped the waters of Coldwater Creek and formed the new lake. This area is still very fragile, and hikers must stay on the established trail—indeed, anywhere you find blast destruction, it's a good idea to stay on the trail as much as possible. The ash-soil is very light and easily disturbed.

GETTING THERE
From Castle Rock, drive about 43 miles east on Highway 504 to the Coldwater Visitor Center and continue 2.2 miles south toward Johnston Ridge. At the bottom of the hill, turn left into the Coldwater Lake boat launch and parking area. The trail starts at the east end of the parking lot.

ON THE TRAIL
Start up the Lakes Trail as it skirts the developed amenities. The path stays well above the high-water mark of the lake, but not so high you can't enjoy the aquatic nature of the trail. Birds flit through the air around the trail, nesting and feeding among the bushes along the shoreline, and feasting on the fish and aquatic insects in the lake.

As you stroll east, you'll pass a trail junction at around 0.75 mile out. The left fork—the Elk Branch Trail—leads up to the Coldwater Visitor Center. You might want to consider this trail on your return, if you still have the energy to climb. For now, though, keep moving east along the shoreline. As you walk, break out your binoculars—you did bring them, right? Pause now and then to scan the opposite shoreline and the slope above it. Elk routinely graze that ridgeline.

The trail reaches the end of the lake at about 3 miles out. Although the trail does continue on up the Coldwater Creek valley, the end of the lake makes a great place to turn around.

EXTENDING YOUR TRIP

If you want more miles, you can reach Bear Pass in another 10 miles, making for a 26-mile round trip. This option leads you deeper into the blast zone, providing in-depth observations of the devastation and restoration of this volcanic world.

86 South Coldwater Trail

RATING/ DIFFICULTY	ROUND-TRIP	ELEV GAIN/ HIGH POINT	SEASON
*****/4	10 miles	2100 feet/ 4600 feet	late June– November

Map: Green Trails No. 332 Spirit Lake; **Contact/Permits:** USFS Mount St. Helens National Volcanic Monument, (360) 247-3900 / Northwest Forest Pass; **GPS:** N46 17.490, W122 16.027

Bulldozer remains on South Coldwater Ridge

If you only have time to do one of the trails framing Coldwater Lake, my money would go on the South Coldwater Trail. The Lakes Trail on the north shore (Hike 85) is a beautiful hike, but this hike is just the complete package. You've got the human history in the shape of volcano-mangled machinery. You have wildlife, in the form of frequently present elk (and small critters are always underfoot if the big wapiti are being bashful). You've got the volcanic landscape, and of course, you have a respectable elevation gain to get your blood flowing, letting you know you are hiking in the Cascades, after all.

GETTING THERE

From Castle Rock, drive about 43 miles east on Highway 504 to the Coldwater Visitor Center and continue 2.2 miles south toward Johnston Ridge. At the bottom of the hill, continue past the Coldwater Lake boat launch area for another mile to find the South Coldwater trailhead parking area on the left.

ON THE TRAIL

The trail leaves the trailhead with a brief downhill swing then rockets upward, climbing the long, tapered nose of the Coldwater Ridge. The trail builders made a half-hearted attempt to add a few switchbacks, but mostly the trail just swings to and fro, climbing steadily but not too steeply all the while. As you ascend, you'll be amazed at the different things going on in the recovery. Grasses, wildflowers, and bushes are well entrenched now, and with that greenery in place, the elk have thundered back into the region. They seem to love this ridge, too, so keep your voices low, and you might enjoy some four-legged companionship on the route. If not, don't worry; you won't be bored.

At about 3 miles out from the trailhead,

you'll come across a rustic hulk of metal. This is an old steel-tracked logging tractor that got caught in the eruption—it was actually thrown to this location from somewhere farther up toward the main body of Mount St. Helens.

Climbing past the tractor, you'll swing around to the south, climbing up to a broad saddle on the flank of Coldwater Mountain. This is our destination. Coldwater Saddle sits at the 5-mile mark, the perfect place to enjoy the views, and then turn around for the walk home.

87 Harrys Ridge

RATING/ DIFFICULTY	ROUND-TRIP	ELEV GAIN/ HIGH POINT	SEASON
*****/3	8 miles	200 feet/ 4400 feet	late June– November

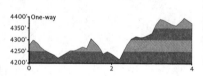

Map: Green Trails No. 332 Spirit Lake; **Contact/Permits:** USFS Mount St. Helens National Volcanic Monument, (360) 247-3900 / Northwest Forest Pass; **GPS:** N46 16.684, W122 12.971

Everyone knows about Harry Truman— not to be confused with the former U.S. president, but the sweet old curmudgeon with the just-as-old cats. Harry and his cats refused to evacuate from his beloved Spirit Lake home when the volcano started to awaken. He's still there somewhere, as much a part of the mountain as he ever was. This short trail on the ridge above Spirit Lake is one of the most picturesque routes in the monument.

Harrys Ridge near Spirit Lake

GETTING THERE

From Castle Rock, drive about 43 miles east on Highway 504 to the Coldwater Visitor Center and continue on to the road's end at Johnston Ridge Observatory. The trailhead is on the east end of the parking lot.

ON THE TRAIL

Head east along the Boundary Trail. For 2 miles, you'll be able to stroll along the narrow ridge, staring across the broad blast plain in front of the gaping maw of the mountain's breach. Utter devastation—but beautiful! The trail loops around one steeply sloped ridge spine just past the 2-mile mark before reaching a junction with the Truman Trail. Stay left at the junction to head north.

At 3.3 miles out, another trail junction awaits. Turn right onto this path, the Harrys Ridge Trail. It crosses over the ridge between you and Spirit Lake, then rolls south again, this time on the slope above Spirit. For a mile you can walk and gawk. Look down on Spirit Lake. Note the raft of logs that still jams the lake surface, twenty-six years after the blast—the remains of the once great forest that surrounded the lake.

Once you've had your fill of fantastic scenery, or (more likely) you just run out of time, turn back and return the way you came.

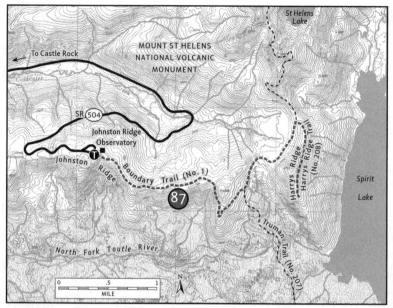

88 Goat Creek

RATING/ DIFFICULTY	ROUND-TRIP	ELEV GAIN/ HIGH POINT	SEASON
***/3	5 miles	400 feet/ 2400 feet	late May– November

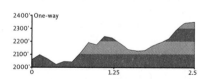

Map: Green Trails No. 332 Spirit Lake; **Contact/Permits:** USFS Mount St. Helens National Volcanic Monument, (360) 247-3900 / Northwest Forest Pass; **GPS:** N46 25.860, W122 9.157

The northernmost section of the Mount St. Helens National Volcanic Monument sees far fewer visitors than any other part of the monument, or so it seems to us. There's no real reason for this, as far as I know, other than it's a bit more remote. But it's certainly no less scenic. The Green River–Vanson Peak section of the monument offers some great hiking scenery to explore, and the Goat Creek Trail provides a great introduction to the region.

GETTING THERE

From Randle, drive west on U.S. Highway 12 for just over 11 miles, and turn left (south) onto Kosmos Road. Take a left at the T intersection at the bottom of the hill, and follow this road past Riffe Lake toward Taidnapam Park and Campground. Go past the campground, over the bridge, and then right onto Forest Road 2600. After about 0.75 mile, turn left onto FR 2750. Follow this to the road's end and trailhead.

ON THE TRAIL

The trail leaves the end of the road and starts a long traverse along the valley wall above Goat Creek. This slope is home to a stunning stand of ancient timber, protected from the 1980 eruption by the very hill on which the trees stand—living on the leeward side of things can be a very good thing!

For most of the way in, you climb across the hillside forest as the creek in the valley bottom slowly comes up toward you. At 2 miles the trail brings you alongside the creek at a junction. Go straight ahead here, and you'll find a creek crossing in another 0.5 mile. Stop here to dip your feet in the cool water and to enjoy the wonderful woodland experience before heading for home.

89 Vanson Peak

RATING/ DIFFICULTY	LOOP	ELEV GAIN/ HIGH POINT	SEASON
****/2	5 miles	600 feet/ 4948 feet	late May– November

Hiker admiring a waterfall along the Goat Creek Trail

Map: Green Trails No. 332 Spirit Lake;
Contact/Permits: USFS Mount St. Helens
National Volcanic Monument, (360) 247-3900
/ Northwest Forest Pass; **GPS:** N46 24.906,
W122 10.573

*There's an awful lot to see here, although
the trail mileage may look low to some.
You'll find expansive meadows full of wildflowers, berries, and possibly big black-
tailed deer. You'll be able to visit a beautiful
mountain lake, and climb a stunning peak
to panoramic views. And you'll explore
some glorious ancient forests. All within a
couple miles' radius.*

GETTING THERE

From Randle, drive west on U.S. Highway 12
for just over 11 miles, and turn left (south) onto
Kosmos Road. Take a left at the T intersection
at the bottom of the hill, and follow this road
past Riffe Lake toward Taidnapam Park and
Campground. Go past the campground, over
the bridge, and then right onto Forest Road
2600. Follow this for several miles, staying
on the primary road at each fork. The road
weaves around several drainages and valleys.

About 14 miles from the Taidnapam Park,
you'll find a trailhead on the right, just as
you are entering the national forest. **Note:**
The roads you've followed to get here are all

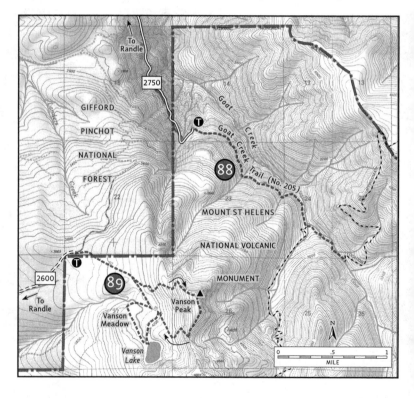

Mountain huckleberries ready for the picking

owned by Champion Timber and, as private timberland, the roads and the forests are subject to rapid change. Check with the ranger station before you head out, as they'll have the latest maps and road information from the landowner.

ON THE TRAIL

From the trailhead, head southeast across the gentle slope that leads you into the public land. The trail runs for about 0.75 mile before it splits. Here, you have a choice to make: lake first, then peak; or peak first, then lake. I'd suggest the peak first.

Go left at the trail fork and climb the moderate slope of Vanson Peak. Most of the forest is still intact here, though parts of the upper mountain have been seared clean. The trail doesn't run to the true summit, but you can scramble up to the 4948-foot summit to find the awesome 360-degree views. Look over the Goat Creek valley, Goat Mountain, Mount Whittier, Mount St. Helens, and the deep cut of the Green River Valley.

From the summit, drop down the east flank of the peak to a trail junction at about the 1.8-mile mark. Turn right and begin looping back toward the trailhead. However, in about 0.1 mile take a detour, dropping down a side trail to Vanson Lake. Enjoy the refreshing waters of this mountain tarn, then angle west up into Vanson Meadow before working your way back to the northwest on faint trails to rejoin the main path. The final 0.5 mile of walking is the trail that got you started.

90 Goat Mountain

RATING/ DIFFICULTY	ROUND-TRIP	ELEV GAIN/ HIGH POINT	SEASON
*****/4	6 miles	1600 feet/ 5025 feet	late May– November

Map: Green Trails No. 332 Spirit Lake; **Contact/Permits:** USFS Mount St. Helens National Volcanic Monument, (360) 247-3900 / Northwest Forest Pass; **GPS:** N46 24.906, W122 10.573

Traversing a high ridge due north of Mount St. Helens, this trail offers some of the best views of the volcano's massive crater and huge blast area. Goat Mountain hikers can see the yawning crater and the piled rubble of the new lava dome, as well as the incredible changes to the land in front of the blast. You can look out over vast hillsides that used to be covered in thick, green forest; in a mat-

ter of minutes in 1980, they were reduced to stark gray wastelands. Vegetation has only begun to come back in the last few years, and the new greenery is especially vivid against the sterile ash backdrop. Even the ridge along which the trail runs was scarred by the blast, and streaks of ash are evident everywhere.

GETTING THERE

From Randle, drive about 8 miles south on Forest Road 25 and cross the Cispus River. Just beyond the river turn right (west) onto FR 26. Continue 12 miles to FR 2612. Turn right onto FR 2612 and continue 0.4 mile to the trailhead parking area.

ON THE TRAIL

The trail takes off and immediately climbs steeply from the trailhead near Ryan Lake for about 2 miles (a 1500-foot elevation gain)

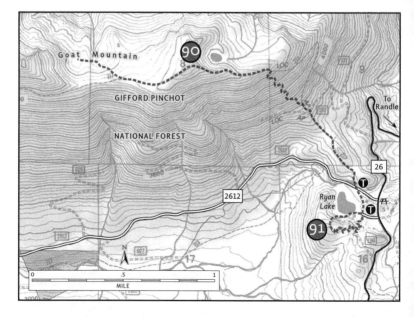

View of the Green River Valley from Goat Mountain

to the long ridge of Goat Mountain and then heads west along its southern flank.

The remnants of Mount St. Helens are put in proper context when you turn north from the summit of Goat Mountain and view noble, towering Mount Rainier. The low, gray hulk of St. Helens used to be white-capped and, some say, even more majestic in appearance than Rainier, the King of the Cascades. Even kings can be laid low—Mount Rainier is considered active and expected to erupt in the next 100 years.

Enjoy your ramble along the summit ridge before turning back the way you came.

91 Ryan Lake

RATING/ DIFFICULTY	ROUND-TRIP	ELEV GAIN/ HIGH POINT	SEASON
**/1	1 mile	100 feet/ 3300 feet	late May– November

Map: Green Trails No. 332 Spirit Lake; **Contact/Permits:** USFS Mount St. Helens National Volcanic Monument, (360) 247-3900 / Northwest Forest Pass; **GPS:** N46 24.906, W122 10.573

This interpretive trail loops around a broad clearing just south of Ryan Lake. It includes several steep sections, but none is longer than a few dozen yards. Generally speaking, this is an easy, relaxing trail on which to explore a small segment of the Mount St. Helens blast area—the trailhead is just 12 miles from the volcano's crater.

GETTING THERE

From Randle, drive about 8 miles south on Forest Road 25 and cross the Cispus River. Just beyond the river turn right (west) onto FR

Ryan Lake

26. Continue to a junction with FR 2612 and turn right into the trailhead parking area at Ryan Lake.

ON THE TRAIL
Set out onto the broad path as it rolls away to the south from the parking area. In just a few dozen yards, you'll reach the loop section. Stay left to hike the loop clockwise. This will present you with the best views of Mount St. Helens, and when you have to turn your back on those views, you'll find yourself facing Ryan Lake.

Note that this is a great route for families, as kids will love the scenery, and what kid can pass up a chance to play on the shores (and in the water) of a mountain lake?

Interpretive signs are found throughout the length of the trail. These informative signs help explain the nature of the Mount St. Helens eruption and how the force of that blast shaped the landscape here to the north of the volcano. The signs also help point out the natural recovery of the local flora and fauna.

The last half of the loop brings you back to the northeast, taking you briefly along the shoreline of Ryan Lake. This is the place were kids can get wet if they want. From the water's edge, it's just a quarter mile back to the car.

RATING/ DIFFICULTY	ROUND-TRIP	ELEV GAIN/ HIGH POINT	SEASON
*****/5	14.2 miles	2000 feet/ 5883 feet	late May– November

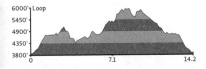

Map: Green Trails No. 332 Spirit Lake;
Contact/Permits: USFS Mount St. Helens
National Volcanic Monument, (360) 247-3900
/ Northwest Forest Pass; **GPS:** N46 18.267,
W122 4.914

You won't find a more difficult trail in this book—nor a more scenic hike. This trail was carved out of cliff faces and mountaintops. The route is long, sun-baked, and incredibly scenic, while the trail itself is rough, steep and very exposed. One section on the flank of Whittier was blasted from a sheer rock face—anyone with acrophobia should be prepared for a case of the jitters, as the trail on this section features a sheer drop. Indeed, given the rough-hewn nature of much of the Mount Whittier section of the route, we join the national monument officials in recommending that only experienced hikers comfortable on scramble routes attempt this trail. Those who don't want to deal with the vertigo-inducing exposure and rock-strewn trail can still enjoy this route—just make it

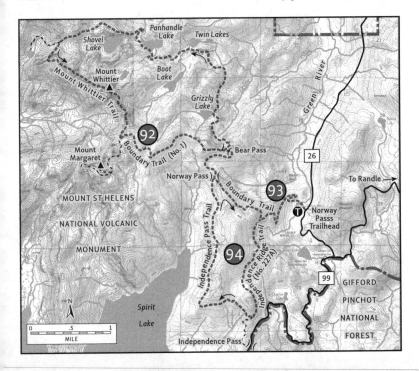

an out-and-back trek on the northern (lakes region) section of the loop component, skipping Whittier's rugged slope altogether.

GETTING THERE

From Randle, drive south on Forest Road 25 to its junction with FR 99 (found just past Iron Creek Falls). Turn right (west) onto FR 99 and drive 9.2 miles before turning right (north) onto FR 26. Continue about 1 mile on FR 26 to the Norway Pass trailhead.

ON THE TRAIL

From the trailhead, hike west along the Boundary Trail, climbing steadily through blown-down forests as the trail angles southwest to a ridge crest (4600 feet). The way then turns northward, following the ridgeline to reach Norway Pass (4500 feet) at 2.2 miles. From the pass, enjoy great views down the ash-laden valley to Spirit Lake; note the huge cluster of logs that cover the lake surface, the remains of the once great forest that surrounded the beautiful lake.

Continue north 1 mile from Norway to Bear Pass (5000 feet) and the start of the loop section. For best views, stay right to do the lakes portion of the loop first. The trail rolls north, weaving through acres of timber stacked like toothpicks in a box. In the next 5 miles, you'll pass several small lakes, set in the blast-scoured landscape like fine gems in a tarnished ring. You'll skirt the eastern edge of Grizzly Lake, travel between Twin Lakes and Boot Lake, and swing around the southern shore of Panhandle Lake to reach the north side of Shovel Lake.

At 8 miles, the trail splits. Stay left to climb the Mount Whittier Trail southeast, and in just a mile you'll be on the summit ridge, oohing and ahhing over the scenery laid before you. To the south resides the still-steaming mass

of Mount St. Helens—you can peer directly into the breach of the northeastern face of the once-great mountain to see the building lava dome in the crater. Between you and the crater stand Coldwater Peak and The Dome. To the north are the many pretty lakes you just hiked past, and far to the east stands Mount Adams.

Continue along the summit ridge another mile to a trail junction at 5600 feet on the flank of Mount Margaret. Turn left to traverse along a mile-long ridge back to Bear Pass, 11 miles from the start. Turn right and hike the 3.2 miles back to the trailhead.

93 Norway Pass

RATING/ DIFFICULTY	ROUND-TRIP	ELEV GAIN/ HIGH POINT	SEASON
*****/3	4.5 miles	300 feet/ 4500 feet	late May– November

Map: Green Trails No. 332 Spirit Lake; **Contact/Permits:** USFS Mount St. Helens National Volcanic Monument, (360) 247-3900 / Northwest Forest Pass; **GPS:** N46 18.267, W122 4.914

Hike just over 2 miles west from Norway Pass, and you hit . . . Norway Pass. No, it's not some magical bending of the fabric of the universe, merely a quirk of the cartographer. The Norway Pass at the trailhead is one of those road features named for nearby places, whereas the true Norway Pass is found on the ridge above Spirit Lake and below Mount Margaret. To get from the wannabe pass to the really-is pass, you'll stroll along

Opposite: Volcano view from the climb toward Whittier Ridge

Close-up view of Mount St. Helens from Norway Pass

a stunning trail through the blown-down woods up onto a high windswept ridge with incredible views of the mighty Mount St. Helens and the expanse of the Mount Margaret backcountry area.

GETTING THERE

From Randle, drive south on Forest Road 25 to its junction with FR 99 (found just past Iron Creek Falls). Turn right (west) onto FR 99 and drive 9.2 miles before turning right (north) onto FR 26. Continue about 1 mile on FR 26 to the Norway Pass trailhead.

ON THE TRAIL

Savvy hikers will get to the trailhead early—not to avoid crowds of hikers (well, there will be these as well on a nice summer weekend), but rather to be hiking in the coolness of early morning with the sunrise hitting the open slopes around you!

Hike west on the Boundary Trail about a mile through the dusty ash-laden landscape to the junction with the Independence Ridge Trail (No. 227A). The scenery around the trail is total devastation, with a few strong signs of returning life—flowers and shrubs are coming back to this scorched zone. At the trail junction, turn right (north) to stay on the Boundary Trail.

About 0.25 mile past the trail fork, you'll come around a bend in the trail and be able to look forward, seeing the next mile of trail laid out before you, all the way to Norway Pass. As you stride along this exposed trail, you'll enjoy views north down in the upper Green River valley.

At 2.2 miles from the trailhead you'll crest Norway Pass proper. You'll suddenly be basking in the stunning views of Spirit Lake, and Mount St. Helens' gaping breach beyond. To increase your viewing pleasure, walk about 0.1 mile south on the Independence Pass Trail, which joins the Boundary Trail at Norway Pass. This short side-trek opens up views southeast to Windy Ridge.

94 Independence Pass Loop

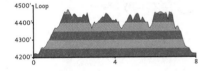

RATING/ DIFFICULTY	LOOP	ELEV GAIN/ HIGH POINT	SEASON
*****/3	8 miles	300 feet/ 4500 feet	late May– November

Map: Green Trails No. 332 Spirit Lake; **Contact/Permits:** USFS Mount St. Helens National Volcanic Monument, (360) 247-3900 / Northwest Forest Pass; **GPS:** N46 18.267, W122 4.914

Fantastic scenery notwithstanding, this route offers a great lesson in volcanic destruction and resurrection. Life has returned en masse. The recovery of this area is evident not only from the flowers, bushes, and trees that are springing up, but also by the wildlife that has returned. Most impressively, massive Rocky Mountain elk have moved back into the area, and the beasts can often be seen along this ridge.

GETTING THERE

From Randle, drive south on Forest Road 25 to its junction with FR 99 (found just past Iron Creek Falls). Turn right (west) onto FR 99 and

Mount St. Helens and Spirit Lake from Independence Ridge

drive 9.2 miles before turning right (north) onto FR 26. Continue about 1 mile on FR 26 to the Norway Pass trailhead.

ON THE TRAIL

Hike west on the Boundary Trail as if heading for Norway Pass (see Hike 93). You'll be walking through blown-down forests showing remarkable evidence of recovery. About a mile from the trailhead, you'll reach a junction with the Independence Ridge Trail (No. 227A). At the trail junction, turn left (south) on the Independence Ridge Trail and head toward Independence Pass.

After more of the same starkly beautiful landscape (marked here and there with a few large living Douglas-firs which were protected from the volcanic blast a little bit on the north side of the ridge), the trail turns westward at a junction (4500 feet) with the Independence Pass trail on the left.

Stay right and hike out around a low ridge point into moonscape of blasted forest—a forest now trying to re-establish itself—and awesome views of Spirit Lake with the backdrop of the open face of Mount St. Helens' north side.

From the knob at the end of the ridge (about 3.3 miles from the trailhead), hike north, staying at or near the same elevation (4500 feet) for another 2.5 miles to reach Norway Pass proper. All along this stretch, enjoy great views down to Spirit Lake and across to Mount Margaret.

At Norway Pass, turn right and hike the Boundary Trail 2.2 miles back to the trailhead.

95 Harmony Falls

RATING/ DIFFICULTY	ROUND-TRIP	ELEV GAIN/ HIGH POINT	SEASON
***/2	2 miles	<700 feet/ 4000 feet	late May– November

Open hiking down the Harmony Trail

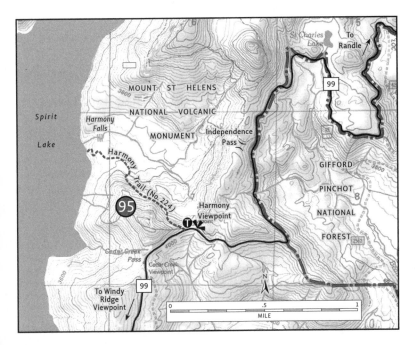

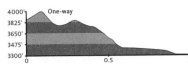

Map: Green Trails No. 332 Spirit Lake;
Contact/Permits: USFS Mount St. Helens
National Volcanic Monument, (360) 247-3900
/ Northwest Forest Pass; **GPS:** N46 18.267,
W122 4.914

Overlooking the east bay of Spirit Lake,
this trail drops from the Harmony Falls
viewpoint on gentle switchbacks. Harmony
Trail's name seems appropriate so long
after the eruption, but as you hike down
this route, you'll recognize the lack of
harmony—in fact, the ultimate chaos—
that reigned here years ago. You'll be awed
by the precise pattern of the fallen trees laid

low by the huge blast. The trees lie parallel
to each other like matches in a matchbook,
pointing away from the volcano's crater.
At the bottom of the trail are volcano-
redesigned Spirit Lake and Harmony Falls.
Once a beautiful high cascade, Harmony
Falls was reduced in height by half. The
massive mudflows that accompanied the
eruption dammed the outlet of Spirit Lake,
raising its water level by 200 feet. The
shoreline is rough and treacherous, lined
with gritty ash and loose rock.

GETTING THERE
From Randle, drive south on Forest Road 25
to its junction with FR 99 (found just past Iron
Creek Falls). Turn right (west) onto FR 99 and
drive about 12 miles to the trailhead on the
right (3 miles past the junction with FR 26).

ON THE TRAIL

The trail descends gradually from the trailhead, dropping through the blasted forest to the shores of Spirit Lake. The path parallels Harmony Creek, though staying well clear of the tumbling water. The trail initially hugs the wall of a steep headwall basin of the creek, before traversing down the valley. Halfway down, you'll be able to look down into the narrow gorge that holds the creek and its crashing falls.

The trail forgoes switchbacks as it drops, but they really aren't needed. You'll weave through a few looping turns, each providing a different angle from which to admire the grand views: Look northwest over the wild and rugged Mount Margaret area before turning a corner to look southwest over the expanse of Spirit Lake and the long spine of Harrys Ridge beyond (see Hike 87).

The trail hits the shores of Spirit Lake after

a mile. Enjoy a refreshing rest on the silver-gray logs that line the shoreline before heading back up the path.

96 Meta Lake

RATING/ DIFFICULTY	ROUND-TRIP	ELEV GAIN/ HIGH POINT	SEASON
***/1	1.3 miles	50 feet/ 4090 feet	late May– November

Map: Green Trails No. 332 Spirit Lake; **Contact/Permits:** USFS Mount St. Helens National Volcanic Monument, (360) 247-3900 / Northwest Forest Pass; **GPS:** N46 17.742, W122 4.690

The Meta Lake Trail celebrates life that miraculously escaped devastation during the 1980 eruption of Mount St. Helens. This broad, paved trail weaves through a lush forest of alpine and noble firs; these trees survived the

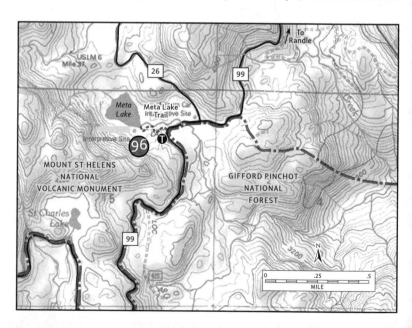

Meta Lake

fiery blast because of their youth and diminutive size. The early-spring eruption leveled tall, mature trees in the area, but, because there was still more than 10 feet of snow on the ground at the time of the blast, the younger, smaller trees along this trail were shielded by a deep snow blanket.

GETTING THERE

From Randle, drive south on Forest Road 25 to its junction with FR 99 (found just past Iron Creek Falls Turn right (west) onto FR 99 and drive about 10 miles to the Meta Lake trailhead on the right.

ON THE TRAIL

The trail rolls past the rusty hulk of a mangled car caught by the blast. This route also visits the lakeshore and cuts through the thick new grass growing in the meadows.

Other plants and animals are moving back into the region, including a family of beavers at Meta Lake. Listen, and you might hear the solid ker-splash of a big dam-builder slapping his tail on the water, alerting his friends to your presence.

97 Plains of Abraham Loop

RATING/ DIFFICULTY	LOOP	ELEV GAIN/ HIGH POINT	SEASON
*****/5	8 miles	700 feet/ 4885 feet	late May– November

Map: Green Trails No. 364S Mount St. Helens NW; **Contact/Permits:** USFS Mount St. Helens

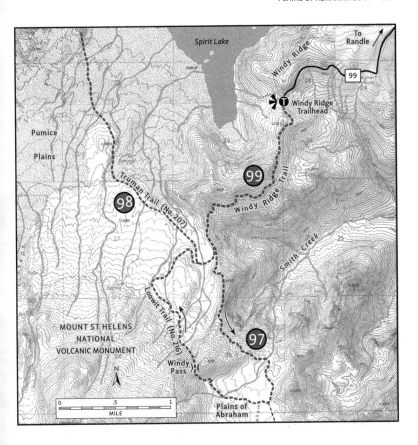

National Volcanic Monument, (360) 247-3900 / Northwest Forest Pass; **GPS:** N46 14.997, W122 8.169

The trail begins with spectacular views from the trailhead; Windy Ridge is the best road-accessible vantage point in the national monument. From there it travels up and down ridges and pumice slopes onto the Plains of Abraham—broad, barren, ash-strewn meadows that are *just beginning to recover from the devastation wrought by the eruption, allowing you to experience the power of an active volcano.*

GETTING THERE

From Randle, drive south on Forest Road 25 to its junction with FR 99 (found just past Iron Creek Falls). Turn right (west) onto FR 99 and drive to the road-end viewpoint and the Windy Ridge trailhead.

Opposite: Dan Jordan hiking the Plains of Abraham Trail

ON THE TRAIL

The hike starts on the Windy Ridge Trail, as an old road leading away from the southern end of the trailhead. The old logging road makes for easy walking as you enter the scorched-earth region of the blast zone. At 1.7 miles, leave the road by taking a single-track trail on the left, which continues to traverse the long ridgeline.

From the ridgeline above Smith Creek, enjoy views east to Mount Adams and, of course, southwest to Mount St. Helens. The trail descends a pumice slope at the end of the ridge to Smith Creek, then ascends straight back up the ridge on the other side before running you up onto the expanse of the Plains of Abraham.

The trail skirts the east side of the broad plain to a trail junction 4 miles from the trailhead. Go right here onto the Loowit Trail as it crosses the Plains of Abraham and climbs the slope on the west side. From the Plains, the trail climbs up and through Windy Pass at 5 miles before dropping back down to a short spur trail at 6 miles. Turn right and follow this connector about a mile back to the old roadbed down which you came, leaving you just 2 miles of hiking to get back to your trailhead on Windy Ridge.

98 Truman Trail–Pumice Plains

RATING/ DIFFICULTY	ROUND-TRIP	ELEV GAIN/ HIGH POINT	SEASON
****/3	10 miles	200 feet/ 4000 feet	late May– November

Butterfly in one of the many sunny, open flower fields along the Truman Trail

Maps: Green Trails No. 364S Mount St. Helens NW, No. 332 Spirit Lake; **Contact/Permits:** USFS Mount St. Helens National Volcanic Monument, (360) 247-3900 / Northwest Forest Pass; **GPS:** N46 14.997, W122 8.169

The eruption of Mount St. Helens in 1980 is held up as an example of the destructive power of nature, yet today, the Mount St. Helens National Volcanic Monument is the perfect classroom in which to learn about nature's strong ability to recover and rebuild.

It's been nearly three decades, after all, and this broad valley proves that life does return. This area was inundated with up to 600 feet of mud from the initial landslide, but today birds and animals fill the area. Elk roam the basin, browsing on the lush plant life around the small pothole lakes and ponds. During one visit, we identified the burrow of a snowshoe hare on the gentle western slope at the base of Windy Ridge, and we heard the yipping cries of a family of coyotes as we started down the trail earlier that morning. The plain above Spirit Lake rang with the relentless "ribbet" of frogs seeking mates along the wetland shores, and the scraggly bushes nearby rustled as flycatchers and flickers flew from branch to branch.

GETTING THERE

From Randle, drive south on Forest Road 25 to its junction with FR 99 (just past Iron Creek Falls). Turn right (west) onto FR 99 and drive to the road-end viewpoint and Windy Ridge trailhead.

ON THE TRAIL

Descending the old logging road from the Windy Ridge trailhead leads you directly into the blast zone. This area is a stark reminder of the volcano's power, but also of the recuperative power of nature.

At about 2 miles the road ends and becomes instead a single-track trail leading north onto the sloping field of scoured rock and ash directly in front of Mount St. Helens' crater breach.

From here, you continue to descend along the Truman Trail into a marvelous world of eroded mud and ash that resembles the slick-rock country of Utah more than the southern Cascades. After 2 miles or so of wandering north along the trail that pierces the water-beaten bare rock and mud, you'll find yourself deep into the Pumice Plains near the southern shore of Spirit Lake. Rest here above the shores of the lake and enjoy the views before returning the way you came.

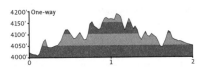

99 Windy Ridge Trail

RATING/ DIFFICULTY	ROUND-TRIP	ELEV GAIN/ HIGH POINT	SEASON
*****/5	4 miles	200 feet/ 4200 feet	late May– November

Map: Green Trails No. 364S Mount St. Helens NW; **Contact/Permits:** USFS Mount St. Helens National Volcanic Monument, (360) 247-3900 / Northwest Forest Pass; **GPS:** N46 14.997, W122 8.169

Sometimes, less is more. There are wonderful trails beyond the end of Windy Ridge, but the 4-mile ramble from the end of the drivable road to the end of the old ash-blasted logging road offers some of the finest views you'll find in the entire Mount St.

Dust devil spinning about on the crater rim

Helens National Volcanic Monument. This makes a fabulous late-afternoon hike, as you can enjoy the setting sun behind the jagged crown of the big volcano.

GETTING THERE

From Randle, drive south on Forest Road 25 to its junction with FR 99 (just past Iron Creek Falls). Turn right (west) onto FR 99 and drive to the road-end viewpoint and Windy Ridge trailhead.

ON THE TRAIL

From the Windy Ridge trailhead parking area, walk south to the gate that marks the southern end of the parking lot, and walk down the old logging road. This road was used by people fleeing the eruption, and prior to 1980 it was used by loggers who pulled the massive old trees from the once-rich forest that filled this region. Today, many of those same trees can be found along the old road-turned-trail—no longer as towering cathedral forests, but instead as massive matchsticks. The explosive superheated winds that came out of the eruption laid all the mighty trees down neatly and perfectly arranged, all side-by-side. All point the same direction (directly away from the source of the blast), and most were instantly stripped of all limbs and even bark, leaving a forest of silver logs stacked along the ridgeline.

Beyond this horizontal forest, the Windy Ridge Trail provides unmatched views across the blast plain and right into the gaping maw of the Mount St. Helens crater. As you walk the ridge, you can look right into the mountain's heart. At the end of the road, where the single-track trail takes over, turn back for the trailhead.

100 Lava Canyon

RATING/ DIFFICULTY	ROUND-TRIP	ELEV GAIN/ HIGH POINT	SEASON
****/5	5 miles (including 0.5-mile barrier-free loop)	1600 feet/ 2800 feet	late May–November

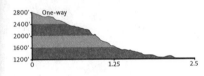

Map: Green Trails No. 364 Mount St. Helens; **Contact/Permits:** USFS Mount St. Helens National Volcanic Monument, (360) 247-3900 / Northwest Forest Pass; **GPS:** N46 9.924, W122 5.337

This hike begins with the wide, paved Lava Canyon Interpretive Trail, which leads to a viewing platform overlooking a stunning canyon—a deep, jagged cut through a thick layer of ancient lava. From the viewing area, the trail loops down to the canyon rim in a long series of steep (for wheelchair users) switchback turns offering excellent views. The Muddy River cuts through the heart of this basalt canyon, which was scoured clean by the rushing mudflows during the 1980 eruption. The main Lava Canyon Trail continues east along the wild gorge of the Muddy River. You won't find grand vistas or sweeping panoramas here. You will find a remarkable lesson in geological change—this valley was carved in part by a massive lahar, or volcano-induced mudflow of massive proportions.

GETTING THERE

From Cougar, drive east on Forest Road 90 just 1 mile beyond the Swift Dam, and turn left (north) onto FR 83. Drive about 12 miles to the road end and trailhead.

ON THE TRAIL

Start off your hike with a warm-up along the 0.5-mile-long Lava Canyon Interpretive Trail. This barrier-free trail is designed to be accessible to wheelchairs and anyone with mobility issues. The interpretive trail offers an excellent lesson in the awesome power of nature. Numerous benches line the route, offering welcome rest stops on the climb up the 8-percent grade back to the trailhead.

From the end of the paved route, head out along the main trail. The trail starts on a few metal stairs through the fields of broken lava, then leads across a springy suspension bridge. From the far end of the bridge, descend a steep 0.5 mile to the very edge of the heart of the Lava Canyon Gorge. A long ladder leads down about 30 feet to the gorge floor.

Walk the bottom of the gorge as the trail winds through clumps of fern and bracken and alongside the small creek. The trail soon loops back out of the inner gorge and continues down the valley, staying up the canyon wall above the inner gorge.

A bit over a mile past the suspension bridge, you'll find a small side trail marked "The Ship," referring to a tall fin of lava. A stand of trees atop the fin appear to be masts rising from a ship of rock. The spur trail leads to the crest of this formation, offering views of a series of small waterfalls in the lower Muddy River canyon.

The main trail continues down the canyon, weaving through dense forest growth along

the steep canyon wall. The exposure here is extreme at times, as the path runs along the edge of the gorge now and then. Use extreme caution. The trail leaves the forest and bursts out on a broad plain of rock and flood debris. This is the junction of Smith Creek and Muddy Creek. Turn back here.

101 Ape Canyon

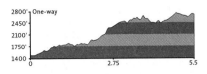

RATING/ DIFFICULTY	ROUND-TRIP	ELEV GAIN/ HIGH POINT	SEASON
***/4	11 miles	1300 feet/ 2800 feet	late May– November

Map: Green Trails No. 364 Mount St. Helens; **Contact/Permits:** USFS Mount St. Helens National Volcanic Monument, (360) 247-3900 / Northwest Forest Pass; **GPS:** N46 9.880, W122 5.527

A mile-wide lahar (see Hike 100) scoured portions of the Muddy River valley, while

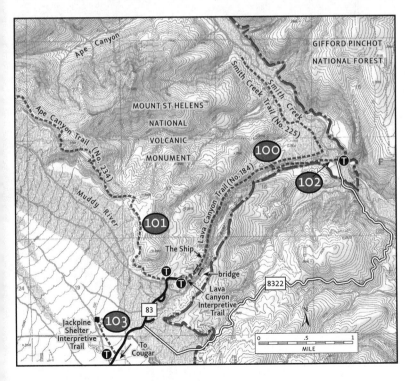

Opposite: Muddy River flowing through Lava Canyon

other parts of the canyon offer you features created by eons of erosion from floods and long-forgotten mudflows. The trail takes you in and out of several small side basins, each providing a unique thrill. Some are filled with wildflowers and ferns. Others are rich woodlands. All are alive with birdsong and critter activity.

GETTING THERE

From Cougar, drive east on Forest Road 90 just 1 mile beyond the Swift Dam, and turn left

An ash-swollen creek tumbles into Ape Canyon.

(north) onto FR 83. Drive about 11.8 miles to the trailhead on the left, found approximately 0.25 mile before reaching the road's end at the Lava Canyon Trailhead.

ON THE TRAIL

From the trailhead, the route starts out fairly level, moving up alongside the massive mud-flow that swept the Muddy River. You'll find lots of greenery and wildflowers along the first mile, before coming to a nice viewpoint looking out over the lahar basin to the volcano that spawned it.

From here, the trail climbs slowly but steadily into a lush stand of ancient forest. For nearly 2 miles, you'll climb through this rich woodland, marveling at the massive old Douglas-firs that line the trail.

At more than 3 miles out, the trail breaks out onto the ridgetop, providing long, open views down into Ape Canyon and up onto East Dome on the flank of Mount St. Helens. These views continue for the remainder of the climb up the ridgeline.

At 5.5 miles, the trail intercepts the Loowit Trail just below East Dome. Turn around here.

View down the Smith Creek Trail

102 Smith Creek

RATING/ DIFFICULTY	ROUND-TRIP	ELEV GAIN/ HIGH POINT	SEASON
***/4	6 miles	200 feet/ 1800 feet	late May– November

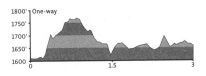

Map: Green Trails No. 364 Mount St. Helens; **Contact/Permits:** USFS Mount St. Helens National Volcanic Monument, (360) 247-3900 / Northwest Forest Pass; **GPS:** N46 10.956, W122 3.274

This is a stark river valley walk, providing an in-depth examination of a mudflow valley and the forest it pierces. Smith Creek isn't as well known, nor perhaps as scenic, as its two nearby neighbors, Lava Canyon (Hike 100) and Ape Canyon (Hike 101). But Smith has something those don't: solitude. Few folks venture up this trail, so chances are good you'll have it to yourself.

GETTING THERE

From Cougar, drive east on Forest Road 90 just 1 mile beyond the Swift Dam, and turn left (north) onto FR 83. Drive about 11 miles, then turn right onto FR 8322 and follow this about 4 miles to the road-end trailhead.

ON THE TRAIL

The trail starts west, rolling up the Muddy River valley toward the Lava Canyon Trail. About a mile up this forested trail, you'll meet that trail and turn right to descend back down the valley, now on the north side. Another mile of hiking down through the rocky debris in the floodplain at the confluence of the Muddy River and Smith Creek gets you just across the river from where you started. The trail now turns north and rolls up the creek valley.

The trail stays in the valley bottom. In about a mile, you'll discover an old ghost forest—a stand of trees that, though killed in the big blast of 1980, still refuses to fall. Turn back at this silent forest.

103 Jackpine Shelter

RATING/DIFFICULTY	ROUND-TRIP	ELEV GAIN/HIGH POINT	SEASON
***/1	1 mile	200 feet/1800 feet	late May–November

Map: Green Trails No. 364 Mount St. Helens;
Contact/Permits: USFS Mount St. Helens National Volcanic Monument, (360) 247-3900 / Northwest Forest Pass; **GPS:** N46 9.264, W122 6.210

The Jackpine Shelter Interpretive Trail explores an old forest and its in- teraction with the surrounding volcanic environment. Despite the Mount St. Helens catastrophe of May 18, 1980, this beautiful, ancient forest grove remains wonderfully intact. The trees, primarily Douglas- and noble firs, were sheltered from the blast—its heat was most severely felt to the north of this area.

The trees and forest ecosystem here survived the eruption, but some damage did occur. This trail explores the Pine Creek Basin, which was gouged deeply by massive mudflows that followed the blast. Farther on, the south flank of Mount St. Helens is visible with all its scars and mantle of gray ash. The route also passes historic Jackpine Shelter, a shack that was built in 1932 to keep backcountry visitors (primarily rangers and hunters) warm and dry.

GETTING THERE

From Cougar, drive east on Forest Road 90 for 1 mile beyond Swift Dam. Turn left onto FR 83 and drive 10.5 miles to the trailhead on the left.

ON THE TRAIL

The trail starts out in ancient forests, and in less than 0.1 mile the old-growth stand gives way to young second-growth, providing visitors with a great chance to compare the native, untouched forest with clear-cut renewal forest.

The old, rustic shelter is one of the standard three-sided buildings that were erected to help keep forest visitors dry but not necessarily warm—the three sides basically exist to hold up the roof, rain protection being the primary purpose of these old structures. This shelter was restored in 1991, and today hikers can rest here and enjoy the peace of the quiet forest—there are log benches to sit on while you relax in the forest setting.

The rustic Jackpine Shelter

104 Trail of Two Forests

RATING/ DIFFICULTY	LOOP	ELEV GAIN/ HIGH POINT	SEASON
***/1	0.5 mile	50 feet/ 1885 feet	late May– November

Map: Green Trails No. 364 Mount St. Helens; **Contact/Permits:** USFS Mount St. Helens National Volcanic Monument, (360) 247-3900 / Northwest Forest Pass; **GPS:** N46 5.959, W122 12.818

The two forests in question are separated in age by 2000 years, but they stand side by side. One forest is a lush, old-growth Douglas-fir and western red-cedar ecosystem that surrounds this boardwalk trail. The other is a young forest that was originally engulfed and consumed by the lava flows from an eruption of Mount St. Helens more than two millennia ago. The trees from that ancient forest are gone, and all that remains are the imprints left by their burning hulks in the cooling lava. The lava solidified faster than the trees burned, and as a result there are hollow impressions of trees engulfed by the river of rock. These three-dimensional imprints of trees are called lava casts—three-dimensional impressions in the rock—and this scenic loop trip offers plenty of opportunity to study them.

GETTING THERE

From Cougar, drive east on Forest Road 90 just 1 mile beyond the Swift Dam, and turn left (north) onto FR 83. Drive 2 miles and turn left onto FR 8303. Continue for 0.5 mile to the trailhead on the left.

Lava tube along the Trail of Two Forests

ON THE TRAIL

The trail loops through the two forests, passing some remarkably beautiful lava beds along the way. The old-tree molds in this lava show that the forest that was gobbled up by the liquid rock was truly impressive—some of the hollowed-out tree casts are more than 5 feet wide. Kids will love the trail, especially two connecting tree hollows about halfway around the loop. Kids can crawl about 50 feet through the heart of these "trees."

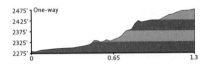

105 Ape Caves

RATING/ DIFFICULTY	ROUND-TRIP	ELEV GAIN/ HIGH POINT	SEASON
***/1	2.6 miles	200 feet/ 2475 feet	late May– November

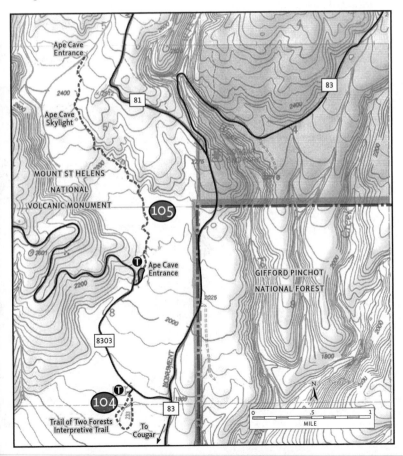

Map: Green Trails No. 364 Mount St. Helens;
Contact/Permits: USFS Mount St. Helens
National Volcanic Monument, (360) 247-3900
/ Northwest Forest Pass; **GPS:** N46 6.499,
W122 12.687

The primates that gave their name to two
lava tubes found along this trail weren't
monkeys—they were members of a 1950s
outdoor club who found and explored the
tubes. They called themselves the Mount
St. Helens Apes, and the lava tubes became
known as their caves. The tubes are long tun-
nels in the thick lava beds; they run roughly
parallel to the surface of the land.

Interpretive signs line both the trail
through the forest and the tubes' mouths.
The lower tube is the easiest (but still requires
a certain amount of care) and the upper
tube is larger. It is not possible to hike in the
caves the entire length between the two
entrances. Descending into the tubes requires a jacket—it's a constant, cool 42
degrees under the earth, regardless of what
happens on the surface—and a powerful
flashlight or lantern. The tube beds are
rough and uneven.

Note: Powerful flashlights with well-
charged batteries or a strong lantern are
required for walking in the caves. Do not
try to explore these spots without a good
light.

Interior view of the Ape Cave entrance

GETTING THERE

From Cougar, drive east on Forest Road 90 just 1 mile beyond the Swift Dam, and turn left (north) onto FR 83. Drive 2 miles on FR 83 and turn left onto FR 8303. Continue for 1 mile on FR 8303 to the trailhead on the right.

ON THE TRAIL

A pleasant, flat 1.3-mile trail through the old forest links the two lava tubes and leads from the trailhead to these underworld entrances. This trail leads through wonderful old forests. About 1 mile out, the trail passes a small crack in the ground. This "skylight" allows hikers to peer into the caves and allows cave explorers to see a bit of sunlight. The trail ends at the upper cave entrance.

106 June Lake

RATING/ DIFFICULTY	ROUND-TRIP	ELEV GAIN/ HIGH POINT	SEASON
***/1	2.8 miles (longer option 5.8 miles)	200 feet/ 2480 feet	late May– November

Map: Green Trails No. 364 Mount St. Helens; **Contact/Permits:** USFS Mount St. Helens National Volcanic Monument, (360) 247-3900 / Northwest Forest Pass; **GPS:** N46 8.141, W122 9.497

This scenic trail climbs gently to the shore of June Lake, a small, shallow pool near the timberline on the southern flank of Mount St. Helens. The surrounding wildflowers are examples of the resiliency of nature, the meadows are once again lush and green, and the lake seems to host a healthy population of frogs and salamanders. The south bank of the lake is a gorgeous tapered beach of gray sand. While the cinder cone summit is hidden behind a ridge, there are good views of the south end of the Worm Flows, an interesting network of mud and lava flows.

GETTING THERE

From Cougar, drive east on Forest Road 90 just 1 mile beyond the Swift Dam, and turn left (north) onto FR 83. Drive 10 miles on FR 83 to the June Lake trailhead on the left.

ON THE TRAIL

From the trailhead, the popular June Lake Trail angles up the small creek valley flowing out of the lake basin. The trail dips near the creek bed in the first few hundred yards, then climbs up onto the slope above the valley bottom and rolls north through forests for the next mile.

As you near the lake basin, the trail leaves the woods and enters a small rugged lava flow along the southern edge of the lake. The trail sweeps around the west side of the small lake.

Stop at the lake to rest and return the way you came, or press on another 0.3 mile, climbing to the Loowit Trail on the edge of the lava fields at 3400 feet.

EXTENDING YOUR TRIP

For more adventures, turn right (east) onto the Loowit Trail—the long trail that encircles St. Helens—and follow it as it skirts along the flank of Mount St. Helens, exploring the meadows and woodlands of the southeastern slope of the big mountain. Just 0.5 mile after jumping onto the Loowit, you'll find yourself walking along an old lava bed, and for the next mile you'll be strolling through long ribbons of hardened lava flows. These rolling mounds of lava are known as the Worm Flows. Turn around about 1.5 miles past the junction to add a 3-mile jaunt to your June Lake hike.

Reflections in June Lake

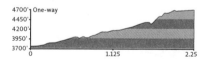

107 Ptarmigan Trail

RATING/ DIFFICULTY	ROUND-TRIP	ELEV GAIN/ HIGH POINT	SEASON
*****/4	4.5 miles	1000 feet/ 4700 feet	late May– November

Map: Green Trails No. 364 Mount St. Helens; **Contact/Permits:** USFS Mount St. Helens National Volcanic Monument, (360) 247-3900 / Northwest Forest Pass; **GPS:** N46 8.748, W122 11.004

Folks looking to bag the summit start here. The Ptarmigan Trail is the only route remaining to get to the summit of Mount St. Helens since the eruption of May 18, 1980. Hikers who don't plan to summit will also enjoy this route, as far as the Loowit Trail junction. The trail weaves through wonderful open forests, runs along nice ridgelines, and offers incredible views over the Yale Reservoir Basin all the way to Mount Hood in Oregon and Mount Adams to the east.

GETTING THERE

From Cougar, drive east on Forest Road 90 just 1 mile beyond the Swift Dam, and turn left (north) onto FR 83. Continue north on FR 83 to the junction with FR 81. Turn left onto FR 81

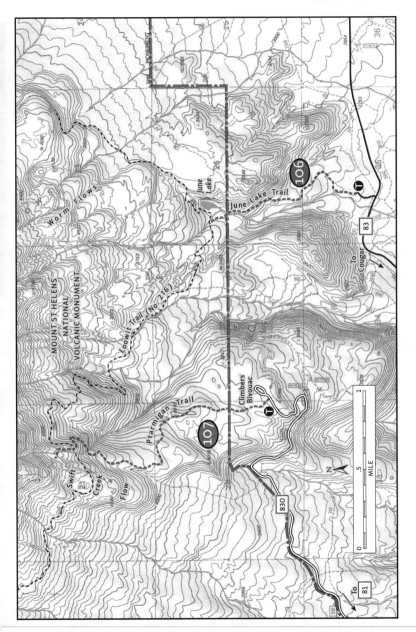

Calypso orchid

views, the forests begin to open a bit. As you near 2 miles, you'll enjoy views both up the southern face of Mount St. Helens and south to the expanse of forests between St. Helens and Oregon's Mount Hood.

At 2.1 miles, the Ptarmigan Trail crosses the round-the-mountain Loowit Trail. Here, you have a few options. You can go east on the Loowit a short distance (about 0.1 mile) to a broad hillside meadow. This is a nice, cool place to sit and enjoy lunch while marveling at the sweeping views spread out before you.

You could also go west on the Loowit about the same distance (0.1 mile) to a stark lava flow, where you'll revel in the experience of seeing the result of an old magma eruption of this big volcano. Or, you can ignore the Loowit and push on up the Ptarmigan Trail another 0.2 mile to a grand viewpoint on the flank of Monitor Ridge. Note that at this point, non-climbers *must* turn back. To go above the 4800-foot level requires a climbers' permit.

108 Blue Lake–South Fork Toutle

RATING/ DIFFICULTY	ROUND-TRIP	ELEV GAIN/ HIGH POINT	SEASON
*****/4	4.5 miles	1000 feet/ 4700 feet	late May– November

and drive 1.6 miles before turning right onto FR 830. Follow this to the large trailhead parking lot. The trailhead, known as the Climbers' Bivouac since it is the starting point for every group headed for the crater rim, offers composting toilets and plenty of parking.

ON THE TRAIL

The trail climbs right from the get-go, ascending steeply at times through rich forest environments. You'll find the forests filled with blooming beargrass early in the summer, and ripe huckleberries later in the summer.

After more than 1.5 miles of very limited

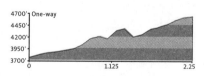

Map: Green Trails No. 364 Mount St. Helens; **Contact/Permits:** USFS Mount St. Helens National Volcanic Monument, (360) 247-3900 / Northwest Forest Pass; **GPS:** N46 8.748, W122 11.004

The Mount St. Helens National Volcanic Monument is all about the raw destructive power of a big volcano, right? Wrong, as this trail proves. Here you find not destruction, but a celebration of life. Wildflowers flourish in gaudy displays of color along this route, and wildlife abounds. Deer and elk are commonly seen browsing on those rich wildflowers. Deer mice and ground squirrels also feast on those plants and their seeds. And red-tailed hawks and falcons feast on those seed-fattened rodents.

GETTING THERE

From Cougar, drive east on Forest Road 90 just 1 mile beyond the Swift Dam, and turn left (north) onto FR 83. Continue 3 miles on this road and then turn left onto FR 81. Continue to its junction with FR 8123. Turn right (north) and drive to the trailhead near the junction with Spur Road 8123-170.

ON THE TRAIL

As you climb from the Blue Lake basin along Coldspring Creek, you find a forest of old

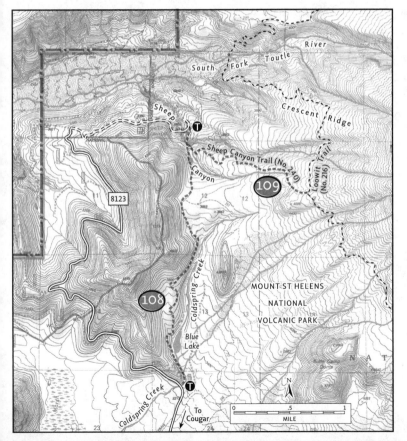

noble firs; these deep-green, soft-needled conifers seem to live up to their regal name. The trail leaves the creek and runs up and over a low ridge before dropping into the Toutle River Valley.

From the ridge top you'll find great views of Mount St. Helens, and as you near the Toutle River, you'll see evidence of the vast destruction that took place on May 18, 1980. On that day the normally placid, clear South Fork Toutle River turned into a massive raging torrent of mud—more than 100 feet deep—that scoured the valley clean and left new land formations throughout the basin.

Explore the area near the Toutle before retracing your steps to Blue Lake.

109 Sheep Canyon

RATING/ DIFFICULTY	ROUND-TRIP	ELEV GAIN/ HIGH POINT	SEASON
****/3	4.5 miles	1200 feet/ 4600 feet	late May– November

Map: Green Trails No. 364 Mount St. Helens; **Contact/Permits:** USFS Mount St. Helens National Volcanic Monument, (360) 247-3900 / Northwest Forest Pass; **GPS:** N46 12.135, W122 16.059

Offering great views down the mud-filled Toutle River Valley, this trail explores areas of destruction as well as healthy old forests that miraculously escaped the ravages of

the 1980 eruption. The route also offers a much shorter option for those who want to enjoy the very best views but don't have the time and/or energy to do the full out-and-back route. The best views of the entire route—and arguably the best views found on the western side of the monument—are found just a quarter mile into the walk. This makes a great half-mile hike if you want to cut short your walking adventure and just focus on the views.

GETTING THERE

From Cougar, drive east on Forest Road 90 just 1 mile beyond the Swift Dam, and turn left (north) onto FR 83. Continue 3 miles on this road and then turn left onto FR 81. Continue to the road's junction with FR 8123. Take a right (north) turn onto FR 8123 and drive to the road's end and the trailhead.

ON THE TRAIL

From a viewing platform less than 0.25 mile into the hike, you can see the upper Toutle River basin with its deep mudflows and new contours. The trail then winds into the deep shadows of an old fir and hemlock forest, where it stays during a sometimes-steep climb to the west flank of Mount St. Helens. At about 2.25 miles, the trail meets the Loowit Trail. A short walk in either direction on this trail leads to great views of the mountain. Remember that a permit is needed to go above 4800 feet (the trail junction is at 4600 feet), so don't go off-trail to find views.

Retracing your steps from the junction, take advantage of the periodic breaks in the forest to look down on Sheep Canyon and the Toutle River.

Opposite: Blue Lake

Bridge over Sheep Creek in Sheep Canyon

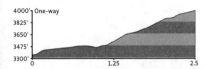

110 Butte Camp

RATING/ DIFFICULTY	ROUND-TRIP	ELEV GAIN/ HIGH POINT	SEASON
***/3	5 miles	700 feet/ 4000 feet	late May– November

Map: Green Trails No. 364 Mount St. Helens;
Contact/Permits: USFS Mount St. Helens National Volcanic Monument, (360) 247-3900

/ Northwest Forest Pass; **GPS:** N46 8.610, W122 13.932

Butte Camp offers a great destination for those wanting an easy outing, or even a short overnight backpacking trip. The trail starts with grand vistas and runs through fields of wildflowers along the way. You'll experience the majesty of a native Northwest forest and the awesome power of the volcanic landscape.

GETTING THERE

From Cougar, drive east on Forest Road 90 just 1 mile beyond the Swift Dam, and turn left (north) onto FR 83. Continue 3 miles on

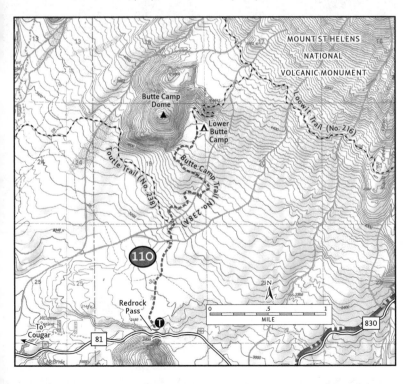

A chirping sparrow pausing on a dead branch

this road and then turn left onto FR 81. Continue about 3 miles to Redrock Pass and the trailhead.

ON THE TRAIL

The trail runs north from the trailhead, climbing a low ridge where you can enjoy dramatic views of the mountain's south face. From this ridge the trail runs up a small lava bed and then into meadows. Wildflowers fill these meadows, making a glorious foreground from which to view the mountain.

At 1.2 miles, the trail splits. Stay right to climb up the east side of Butte Camp Dome. For the next mile, the trail climbs through open forests, made up of hemlock and pine. The fragrant woods frequently resound with the thundering noise of woodpeckers in search of insects.

Lower Butte Camp, a pretty campsite at 4000 feet elevation on the flank of Butte Camp Dome, is reached at 2.5 miles. This makes a fine turnaround point. Or you can push on another mile upward to the Loowit Trail.

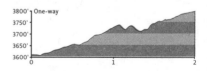

111 Kalama River

RATING/ DIFFICULTY	ROUND-TRIP	ELEV GAIN/ HIGH POINT	SEASON
***/3	4 miles	200 feet/ 3800 feet	late May– November

Map: Green Trails No. 364 Mount St. Helens;
Contact/Permits: USFS Mount St. Helens National Volcanic Monument, (360) 247-3900 /

Log-littered Kalama River

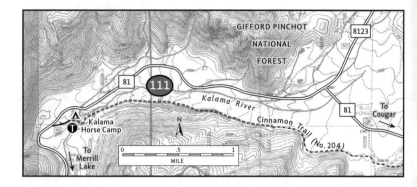

Northwest Forest Pass; **GPS:** N46 8.572, W122 19.486

Following the beautiful Kalama River, this trail presents a stunning and unique riparian forest environment to explore. The river is lined with dark basalt lava beds, while this black rock terrain is lined with emerald moss and vibrant fern clusters. It's a remarkable forest and river valley, well worth the long drive.

GETTING THERE

From Cougar, drive east on Forest Road 90 just 1 mile beyond the Swift Dam, and turn left (north) onto FR 83. Continue 3 miles on this road and then turn left onto FR 81. Continue to the trailhead at the Kalama Horse Camp on the Kalama River.

ON THE TRAIL

Hike east along the Kalama River on the Cinnamon Trail, following the spring-fed river upstream into the lush moss-laden forest. The trail parallels the river for its length, sometimes running well back from the water, and sometimes dipping right down to the creek's banks.

Look for water ouzels when you get close to the creek—these small birds like to dive off small rocks, dipping underwater to snag tiny aquatic bugs (thus earning them the name "water dippers").

The trail crosses an old logging road at 2 miles. This is a good place to turn around. If you want to extend the mileage, the trail continues another 2 miles to McBride Lake. From there, it angles north to Redrock Pass.

Opposite: Views of Wind Mountain greet hikers on the Dog Mountain Trail.

the columbia river gorge area

The Columbia River Gorge—known to locals simply as "The Gorge"—was carved not by the slow grind of the Columbia River but by the massive wall of water known as the Missoula Floods. Toward the end of the last great ice age, a wall of ice in northern Montana and southern Canada blocked the meltwaters, creating a vast lake behind it. When the ice dam broke, the waters rushed across eastern Washington, carving out the great coulees of that desert country before pounding into the narrow riverbed that wound through the Cascades near what is now the Washington–Oregon border. That wall of water cut fast and deep, creating what we see today—the deep slash of the Columbia River Gorge. Many wonderful trails explore the steep walls and side canyons of The Gorge, but there's more to the Columbia River Gorge Area than just the majestic Gorge itself. A great number of trails explore the rivers (and

the mountains they drain) that feed down to the Gorge.

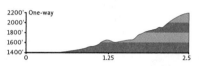

112 Lower Falls Creek Trail

RATING/ DIFFICULTY	ROUND-TRIP	ELEV GAIN/ HIGH POINT	SEASON
***/3	5 miles	800 feet/ 2200 feet	late May– November

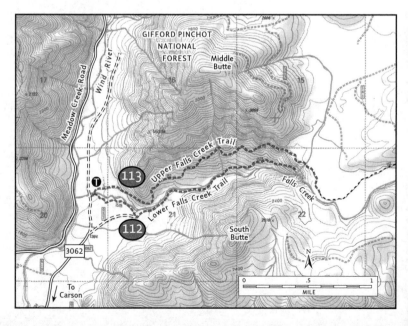

Map: Green Trails No. 397 Wind River; **Contact/Permits:** USFS Mount Adams Ranger District, (509) 395-3400 / Northwest Forest Pass; **GPS:** N45 54.480, W121 56.847

One-hundred-foot Upper Falls may be this hike's key attraction, but it's by no means

Beautiful patterns in Falls Creek

the only one. The thick forest along the lower half of the trail shelters plump huckleberries in the autumn and clumps of beargrass in the early summer.

The waterfall comes into view about 2 miles into the hike, and you find a wide, deep pool of crystal-clear water just above the falls. Local populations of white-tailed deer and elk frequent this 50-foot-wide pool, and there is a beaver den along the shore—don't be surprised if the big wood eaters make themselves scarce, but you might hear them slipping into the water and signaling their family with a loud ker-splashing slap of the tail. Lounge around the pool, admire the thundering falls, and explore the surrounding area before returning the way you came.

GETTING THERE

From Carson, drive 15 miles north on Wind River Road (County Road 30) to its junction with Forest Road 3062. Turn right (east), and drive 1.8 miles to the trailhead.

ON THE TRAIL

Stay right to follow the Lower Falls Creek Trail to the south as it rolls gently along a previously logged slope—the logging scars are well covered by regrowth. The trail stays to the south side of the creek, reaching a second trailhead in about 0.5 mile. Keep moving up this trail, and in a mile or so you'll cross the creek and then keep moving up the north bank of the creek.

The falls at trail's end are well worth the 4 miles (round trip) of modest forest walking.

113 Upper Falls Creek Trail

RATING/ DIFFICULTY	ROUND-TRIP	ELEV GAIN/ HIGH POINT	SEASON
***/3	5 miles	1100 feet/ 2400 feet	late May– November

Vine maple trees seem to be embracing old-growth firs.

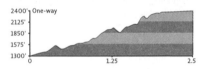

Map: Green Trails No. 397 Wind River;
Contact/Permits: USFS Mount Adams
Ranger District, (509) 395-3400 / Northwest
Forest Pass; **GPS:** N45 54.480, W121 56.847

*This more upland route along Falls Creek
rides the ridge above the creek, so the Upper
Falls Creek Trail is a poorly named trail: You
don't get falls, and you don't get a creek—at
least, not much of either.*

*But you do get a splendid forest experience
and a chance to meet some of the locals: Mr.
Grouse and Ms. Blacktail Deer are frequently
found at home here, and the Pileated Woodpecker family frequently can be heard knock-*
ing their heads against the many trees in this
old second-growth forest.

GETTING THERE

From Carson, drive 15 miles north on Wind
River Road (County Road 30) to its junction
with Forest Road 3062. Turn right (east), and
drive 1.8 miles to the trailhead.

ON THE TRAIL

The trail goes left up the ridgeline above
Falls Creek. The climbing is very easy, and
the forest is wonderfully cool. Indeed, you
might consider this as a summer refresher
hike—stretch your legs in the cool forest,
then dip your feet in Falls Creek when you
return to the trailhead.

The route runs a full 4 miles (8 miles round
trip), but the best bet is to stride out about 2.5
miles to a point where the trail levels off with

views down into the Falls Creek Falls Gorge from above.

114 Lava Butte

RATING/DIFFICULTY	ROUND-TRIP	ELEV GAIN/HIGH POINT	SEASON
***/3	2.5 miles	1100 feet/2400 feet	late May–November

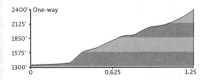

Map: Green Trails No. 397 Wind River; **Contact/Permits:** USFS Mount Adams Ranger District, (509) 395-3400 / Northwest Forest Pass; **GPS:** N45 56.921, W121 56.116

With trails like this, it is nearly impossible to forget that this entire region was shaped and built by volcanic activity. This little cinder cone is a wonderful place to explore and to enjoy some beautiful views from the top of the butte.

GETTING THERE

From Carson, drive 21 miles north on Wind River Road (County Road 30) to the Paradise Creek Campground. The trailhead is in the campground at site 30D. The Lava Butte Trail is convenient for people staying at the campground.

ON THE TRAIL

The hike begins at a short valley meadow, fords a stream, and climbs steeply through a dense second-growth forest. The forest ends abruptly

Ford of the Wind River below Lava Butte

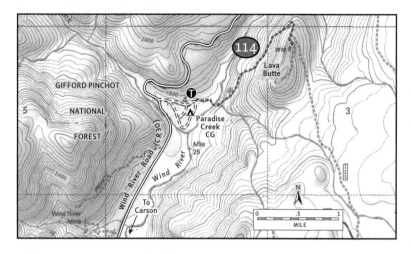

near the summit in a broad clear-cut. Cross the clear-cut to the top of the butte to obtain fine views of the surrounding countryside.

The trail ends at an old logging road atop the butte. Forget about driving a shuttle car up here, though—it's quicker and easier to return on the trail.

115 Bunker Hill

RATING/ DIFFICULTY	ROUND-TRIP	ELEV GAIN/ HIGH POINT	SEASON
***/3	4 miles	1300 feet/ 2400 feet	late May– November

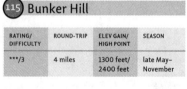

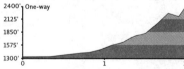

Map: Green Trails No. 397 Wind River;
Contact/Permits: USFS Mount Adams Ranger District, (509) 395-3400 / Northwest Forest Pass; **GPS:** N45 48.437, W121 56.436

After following the Pacific Crest Trail east for a mile, this trail turns north and climbs steeply for another mile to the top of lonesome Bunker Hill. This peak stands apart from other mountains in the area and therefore offers great unobstructed views in all directions. The Forest Service used to maintain a fire lookout station at the summit, and it's easy to see why. The views of the Wind River valley and the southern Washington Cascades are fantastic.

The summit is a maze of rocky outcroppings, which (while fun to scramble over) are potentially dangerous; they end abruptly at tall cliffs that drop hundreds of feet to jagged rocky slopes. Enjoy the views, but stay away from the edges.

GETTING THERE

From Carson, drive 8.4 miles north on Wind River Road (County Road 30) to the town of Stabler and the junction with Hemlock Road. Turn left (west) onto Hemlock Road, cross the river, and continue 1.2 miles to Forest Road 43. Turn right and drive 0.6 mile to the junction

Bunker Hill rises above the Pacific Crest Trail.

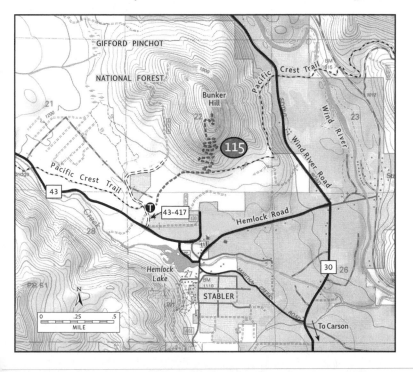

with Spur Road 43-417. Drive 0.25 mile to the trailhead on the right, which is marked as the Pacific Crest Trail.

ON THE TRAIL

Start north and east on the Pacific Crest Trail (PCT), and in about 0.5 mile turn left off the PCT and start climbing. From here, it's 1.5 miles of switchbacks through the forest to get you to the top. This gains all of the 1300 feet of vertical you'll have to cover on the route, so pace yourself.

As you huff up onto the top of Bunker, find a good place to sit and relax. Just make sure you don't lose all track of time as you sit and enjoy the scenery from atop this pretty peak.

116 Big Lava Bed

RATING/ DIFFICULTY	ROUND-TRIP	ELEV GAIN/ HIGH POINT	SEASON
****/4	13 miles	600 feet/ 4000 feet	late May– November

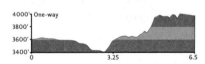

Map: Green Trails No. 397 Wind River;
Contact/Permits: USFS Mount Adams Ranger District, (509) 395-3400 / Northwest Forest Pass; **GPS:** N45 54.478, W121 48.142

The Big Lava Bed is the home of an old lava flow—magma oozed out of fissures and cracks in the heart of the Lava Bed (as well as along the lower flanks of Mount Adams, in the southern Indian Heaven area, and of course, around Mount St. Helens). The flows began some 9000 years ago and, as Mount St. Helens showed, volcanic activity in the area is still occurring. The Big Lava Bed is a volcanic formation, but it's not the classic conical volcano. Rather, it is a 20-square-mile flow of basalt that flowed out of a source vent found in the north-central part of the bed, just south of Goose Lake.

GETTING THERE

From Carson, drive north on the Wind River Road (County Road 30) 5.6 miles and turn right (east) onto the Panther Creek Road (Forest Road 65). Continue on the Panther Creek Road 11.3 miles to a junction with FR 60. Turn right (east) onto FR 60 and drive 2.4 miles to the Crest Horse Camp on the right. The PCT crosses FR 60 here. Find the start of the trail to the south just behind the outhouses on the south side of the horse camp.

ON THE TRAIL

Spindly pines cover much of the Big Lava Bed, giving it the appearance of a gentle, young forest from a distance. Get near the lava, though, and the truth comes out: There is nothing gentle about this landscape.

The PCT skirts the west side of the basalt field, and almost immediately after starting the hike, the harsh nature of the lava bed is nakedly evident. Step off the trail, and the landscape is nearly impassable. The lava is abrasive, brittle, and very unstable. Try to scramble to the top of one of the short lava knobs scattered around the area, and you'll find your leather boots not just scuffed but slashed and cut to ribbons. Better to enjoy the rugged beauty of the lava flow from the relative safety of the trail.

The trail leaves the horse camp and within the first 0.25 mile meets the lava flows. The trail then rolls with the flow, as it were, skirting the rough lava on its western flank. To the west of the trail is an open pine forest scarred with clear-cuts, but the buffer of trees along the trail block most of that logging damage from view. Besides, the lava beds will keep your eyes turned away from the other side of the trail.

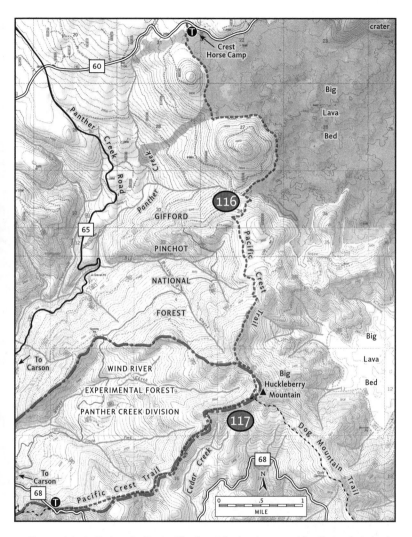

The terrain in the Big Lava Bed is a jumble of rock. Huge blocks of lava, towering up like black cotton-candy tufts, dot the landscape. Many of these are pahoehoe formations—wrinkled masses of rock formed by fast-moving lava.

Pahoehoe is easy to identify: just look for the rocks that remind you of shar-pei dogs, a solid mass of ropey folds and wrinkles. Between the great tufts of lava are fissures, crevices, pressure ridges, and fields of sharp, jagged black basalt.

Western edge of the Big Lava Bed

The trail follows alongside this world of volcanic turmoil for nearly 3 miles before edging away from the lava into a calmer world of pine forests. The trail rolls gently through the forest for another 3.5 miles to the southeast flank of Big Huckleberry Mountain.

For a full day of hiking, turn around where the trail leaves the lava for a short outing over to Big Huckleberry Mountain. Take note that the mountain is aptly named—in late summer the area around the mountain is flush with marble-sized purple fruit. There is no path to the mountain's forested top, so stick to the sun-dappled clearings along the trail.

117 Panther Creek Experimental Forest

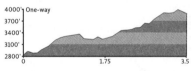

Map: Green Trails No. 397 Wind River; **Contact/Permits:** USFS Mount Adams Ranger District, (509) 395-3400 / Northwest Forest Pass; **GPS:** N45 49.692, W121 50.134

The Panther Creek Experimental Forest is a protected area of old, open pine and fir forest. The PCT rolls along the south and east sides of the forest preserve. The woods are teeming with wildlife, but remarkably lacking in human visitors, making it a wonderful place in which to find solitude and an opportunity to see a variety of birds and animals. During a visit in late September, I counted no less than a dozen species of birds, including downy woodpeckers, ravens, siskins, a mountain bluebird, an oriole, and

RATING/ DIFFICULTY	ROUND-TRIP	ELEV GAIN/ HIGH POINT	SEASON
****/4	7 miles	1200 feet/ 4000 feet	late May– November

a Cooper's hawk. Among the animals I saw were deer, rabbits, and squirrels. I also noted the tracks of a big coyote and, on my return, found the tracks of a cougar overlying my earlier tracks. I didn't see these critters but was certainly seen by them.

GETTING THERE

From Carson, drive north on the Wind River Road (County Road 30) 5.6 miles and turn right (east) onto the Panther Creek Road (Forest Road 65). Continue on the Panther Creek Road about 4 miles to a junction with FR 68. Make a sharp right turn and begin a steep ascent of FR 68. In 2 miles, at the crown of the hill, pull off into the PCT trailhead parking area on the right.

ON THE TRAIL

The Pacific Crest Trail (PCT) comes in from the south along an old jeep track, crosses FR 68, and enters the Panther Creek Experimental Forest as a narrow, little-used path. The trail climbs through a pair of switchbacks in the first 0.5 mile, then rolls into a long, climbing traverse along a wooded ridge.

In 2.6 miles, you'll reach a junction with a small side trail (Cedar Creek Trail). Stay left on the PCT for another mile or so to reach the southeast flank of Big Huckleberry Mountain and the junction with the Dog Mountain Trail (not the same Dog as described in Hike 121). There is no path to the forested top of Big Huckleberry Mountain. Rather, stick to the huge sun-dappled clearings in the forest along the trail to enjoy the bright sunshine, colorful flowers, and—in later summer and early autumn—the abundant huckleberries.

The forest is somewhat sparse, with huge openings in the canopy allowing great beams of sunlight to illuminate the forest floor. Beargrass

View of Mount Hood looking south from the Pacific Crest Trail

blooms along the trail in early spring, while Oregon grape and huckleberries color the hillside in the autumn. The route is dry, so pack plenty of water.

118 Little Huckleberry Mountain

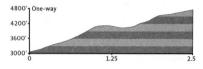

RATING/ DIFFICULTY	ROUND-TRIP	ELEV GAIN/ HIGH POINT	SEASON
***/3	5 miles	1800 feet/ 4781 feet	May– November

Map: Green Trails No. 398 Willard; **Contact/ Permits:** USFS Mount Adams Ranger District, (509) 395-3400 / Northwest Forest Pass; **GPS:** N45 54.323, W121 42.263

Steep, hot, and dusty is an accurate description of this hike up the western edge of the Monte Cristo Range, but the views from the summit of Little Huckleberry Mountain are astoundingly beautiful. And don't be fooled by the name—there is nothing little about the big, juicy huckleberries you gobble down while plodding along the ridge trail.

From the trail, you'll enjoy views east to Mount Adams, and south to Oregon's Mount Hood. The 9-mile long black scar of the Big Lava Bed can also be viewed to the west. The trail starts in cool forests where you'll find the berry bushes thick and heavy with fruit, but the best picking is near the top of the trail, where more sun reaches the berries,

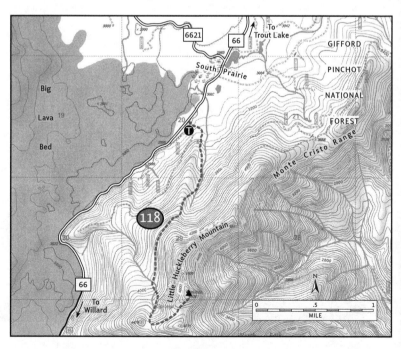

Mount Adams through clearing clouds from Little Huckleberry Mountain

creating sweeter, juicier delights for you and the resident birds and bears.

GETTING THERE

From Trout Lake, drive about 14 miles west on State Route 141 (which becomes Forest Road 24 at the forest boundary) to its junction with FR 60. Go left onto FR 60 and follow it to FR 66. Turn left onto FR 66 and drive 3 miles to South Prairie where you'll find a small lake and adjacent broad meadow. Continue another mile past South Prairie to the trailhead on the left.

ON THE TRAIL

The route leads up through a thick stand of timber along a ridge on the north face of the mountain. Near the top the trees fall away to reveal a broad, open meadow on the summit. Enjoy the views west over the scarred landscape of the Big Lava Bed and beyond to Goose Lake. Beyond those big lava scars you'll see the lava producers: Mount Adams and Mount Hood punctuate the horizons east and south.

Little Huckleberry's 4781-foot peak was home to a fire lookout cabin from 1924 to 1970 when it was destroyed as new technology replaced the need for human fire-watchers.

119 Monte Cristo

RATING/ DIFFICULTY	ROUND-TRIP	ELEV GAIN/ HIGH POINT	SEASON
***/3	5 miles	400 feet/ 3000 feet	May– November

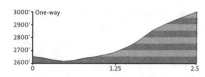

Map: Green Trails No. 398 Willard; **Contact/ Permits:** USFS Mount Adams Ranger District, (509) 395-3400 / Northwest Forest Pass; **GPS:** N45 53.513, W121 34.445

This is an easy hike—a gentle climb with just under 1000 feet elevation gain in a mile and a half to an old fire lookout site where you find great views of the surrounding region. From here you can look south to the Columbia River and into the dry lands of eastern Washington. You don't find any water near this trail, so pack plenty.

GETTING THERE

From Carson, head east on State Route 14 along the Columbia River and turn north onto U.S. Highway 18, heading north along the Little White Salmon River. Just a few miles past Willard, turn left onto Forest Road 1840. Drive FR 1840 to its junction with Spur Road 1840-100. Turn left onto the spur road and drive a few hundred yards to the road-end trailhead.

ON THE TRAIL

From the trailhead, you begin a moderate climb through open forests and clearings,

Monte Cristo Trail

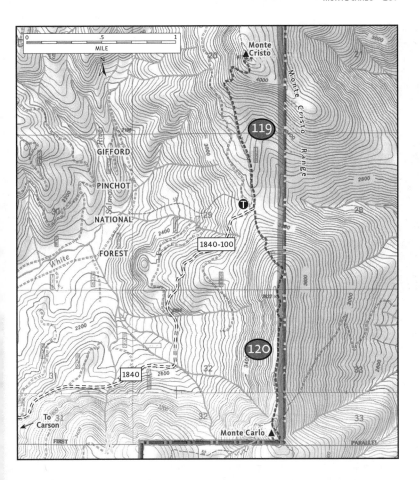

weaving upward on a somewhat rough trail. The trail rolls past wonderful huckleberry patches that provide glorious fruit in late August and early September. If you visit early in the summer, you'll miss the berries but should be able to enjoy the bulbous blooms of beargrass that dot the forest around you.

As you near the top of the ridgeline, the trail turns steeply up the south flank of Monte Cristo at 2 miles to reach the summit at 2.5 miles. Enjoy the views from the summit, including peeks at the Columbia River and Big Lava Bed.

120 Monte Carlo

RATING/ DIFFICULTY	ROUND-TRIP	ELEV GAIN/ HIGH POINT	SEASON
***/3	4 miles	800 feet/ 4078 feet	May– November

Flower-filled view from Monte Carlo

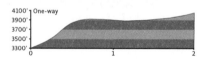

Map: Green Trails No. 398 Willard; **Contact/ Permits:** USFS Mount Adams Ranger District, (509) 395-3400 / Northwest Forest Pass; **GPS:** N45 53.513, W121 34.445

Thick second-growth forest lines this route, with occasional old-growth trees poking through the low, thick canopy. Those infrequent big trees are the survivors of several old logging operations as well as some more recent cuts. The trail follows along the boundary of the Gifford Pinchot National Forest, with private forestlands to the east.

GETTING THERE

From Carson, head east on State Route 14 along the Columbia River and turn north onto U.S. Highway 18, heading north along the Little White Salmon River. Just a few miles past Willard, turn left onto Forest Road 1840. Drive FR 1840 to its junction with Spur Road 1840-100. Turn left onto the spur road and drive a few hundred yards to the road-end trailhead.

ON THE TRAIL

Leaving the trailhead, hike south along the ridgeline trail as it climbs gradually through a few small clear-cuts and selective-cut harvest areas. These small man-made "meadows" and forest glades cross the trail, providing sunlight and some views.

After the first 0.75 mile of hiking, the

trail mostly levels off and rides the long ridgeline up the north flank of Monte Carlo. Enjoy the views from the summit, which include peeks at the Columbia River and the Big Lava Bed.

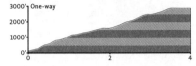 121 Dog Mountain

RATING/ DIFFICULTY	ROUND-TRIP	ELEV GAIN/ HIGH POINT	SEASON
*****/4	8 miles	2800 feet/ 2948 feet	March–November

Map: Green Trails No. 430 Hood River; **Contact/Permits:** USFS Mount Adams Ranger District, (509) 395-3400 / Northwest Forest Pass; **GPS:** N45 41.956, W121 42.395

 With a trailhead in the Columbia River Gorge, this mountain offers wonderful views of the deep cut of the Columbia as it slices through the Cascades. This is a popular trail that offers great views and a pleasant trail experience—wildflowers grace the forest meadows and clearings, and wildlife roams the area.

GETTING THERE
From Carson, drive approximately 9 miles east on State Route 14 to the trailhead, just beyond milepost 53. The parking area and trailhead are on the left (north) side of the highway.

ON THE TRAIL
From the large parking area, the trail begins with a steep, 0.5-mile climb to a junction. Both trails before you lead to the top. My recommendation is to go right, since the left fork climbs steeply up the northern flank of the mountain. Use the longer, more gradual route on the right as it loops around to the east and climbs through broken forest that offers periodic views across the gorge. You can descend by the

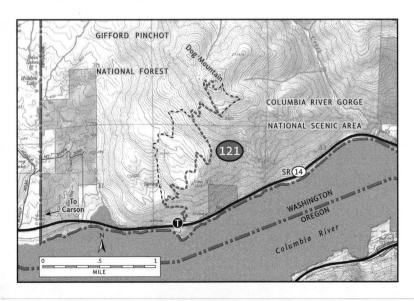

Young northern Pacific rattlesnake on the lower Dog Mountain Trail

steeper northern route, or retrace your steps.

The trails climb steeply, reconvening near the 3-mile mark, before the combined path crosses a little knoll known as Puppy Lookout. You're only 500 feet below the top at this point, so keep pushing and soon you'll be striding through the broad meadows of balsamroot blooms into the fabulous views south and west into the Columbia River Gorge.

Map: Green Trails No. 430 Hood River; **Contact/Permits:** Washington State Parks and Recreation, (360) 902-8844; **GPS:** N45 39.416, W121 5.182

Horsethief Lake State Park, also known as Dalles Mountain Ranch State Park, offers great experiences in the desert country east of the Columbia River Gorge. Unique views of the eastern gate of the Columbia

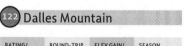

122 Dalles Mountain

RATING/ DIFFICULTY	ROUND-TRIP	ELEV GAIN/ HIGH POINT	SEASON
****/3	8 miles	2500 feet/ 2825 feet	February– November

River Gorge can be enjoyed here, but more importantly, you can immerse yourself into the natural desert world that Lewis and Clark encountered as they passed through along the Columbia. This route leads hikers past a picturesque waterfall, and through fields of wildflowers, including white biscuit root, yellow bells, salt-and-pepper lomatium, chokecherry and serviceberry, and mock orange.

GETTING THERE
From Yakima, drive east on I-82 to Exit 37, signed U.S. Highway 97/Goldendale. Drive this four-lane highway to Toppenish and (right-turn only) onto Highway 97. Drive south on Highway 97 through Goldendale until you reach a junction with State Route 14. Drive west on SR 14 for 13.9 miles to a gated pull-out/road on your right. Pull in by the "Road Closed" gate—do not block the gate!—and park on the shoulder of SR 14.

ON THE TRAIL
From the trailhead, hike up the gated road, immediately finding glorious views of a stunning waterfall. A short 0.5-mile hike up the road puts you right alongside the waterfall.

As you climb, the views of Horsethief Butte and the Columbia River grow increasingly impressive. The road winds up a gully along the creek, and at times the brush alongside encroaches to the point that the road becomes a faint trail.

Near the top, keep hiking as the slope levels off east of the creek gully. About 2.5 miles into

Balsamroot by the Dalles Mountain Ranch wagon

the hike, you'll hit the Dalles Mountain Road. Cross the road and find a steep trail leading the final 1.5 miles to the summit.

123 Hamilton Mountain

RATING/ DIFFICULTY	LOOP	ELEV GAIN/ HIGH POINT	SEASON
***/3	9 miles	2000 feet/ 2438 feet	February– November

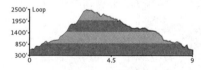

Map: Green Trails No. 429 Bonneville Dam; **Contact/Permits:** Washington State Parks and Recreation, (360) 902-8844; **GPS:** N45 37.950, W122 1.200

This is a steep, rocky trail leading up past a pair of pretty waterfalls, to a high peak on the western end of the Columbia River Gorge. The views are unmatched: Mount Hood is so close it could almost be touched. The array of waterfalls that crash down the steep walls of the Oregon side of the Gorge present themselves as silver ribbons on the dark-green background of the forested slopes. There's also a slight chance hikers will get to see humans take flight from this peak: Paraglider pilots launch from this high butte, soaring out over the gorge and landing near the river.

GETTING THERE

From I-205 in Vancouver, Washington, drive east on State Highway 14 for 30 miles to Beacon Rock State Park. Turn left (north) and drive up into the day-use parking area.

ON THE TRAIL

The trail leaves the day-use area of the park, cuts under a cluster of powerlines, and then angles out around a ridge face to dip back into a deep river canyon. Here, at about 1.3 miles, you'll pass Hardy Falls and just beyond, Rodney Falls.

Push on past the falls, though, and start climbing steeply northeast. The trail rolls up around sheer cliffs, which present spectacular views over the river. The trail switches back and forth as it nears the summit plateau, then runs straight up the last steep pitch through an expansive field of wildflowers to the true summit of Hamilton Mountain at 2438 feet.

The trail continues across the top of the mountain until, at about 4.5 miles, it turns back to the southwest to begin winding down around the northern ridgeline. You'll drop in long, sweeping switchbacks, generally following an old roadway-turned-trail, to reach upper Hardy Creek at about 5.4 miles. The tumbling creek can often be heard but seldom seen as the trail stays up on the forested valley wall above the creek itself.

As you hike south down the valley, keep an ear open. Blue grouse are frequently heard

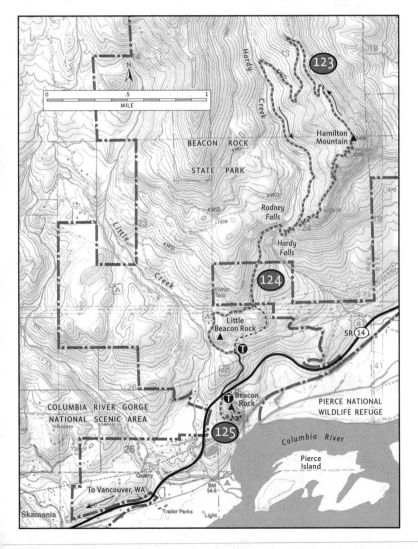

Hamilton Mountain from the upper trail vistas

here in the early summer. The big upland birds drum their wings and bellow out resonating calls of "Whomp, whomp, whomp" to attract mates. If you hear the distinctive call, stop and try to locate its source. The grouse are either stupid or fearless, and you can usually get within a yard of them for pictures.

The trail follows the Hardy Creek valley back to Rodney Falls. You'll rejoin the trail you hiked up just above Rodney Falls, about 7.3 miles into the hike. Turn right to visit Hardy and Rodney Falls before striding back to your waiting car.

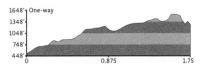

Map: Green Trails No. 429 Bonneville Dam; **Contact/Permits:** Washington State Parks and Recreation, (360) 902-8844; **GPS:** N45 37.950, W122 1.200

If the long, rocky route around the summit crown of Hamilton is too much for legs, lungs, or time schedule, don't despair. There are alternatives, and the best is this one: Hike up the trail to the twin cascades of Hardy and Rodney Falls.

124 Hardy and Rodney Falls

RATING/ DIFFICULTY	ROUND-TRIP	ELEV GAIN/ HIGH POINT	SEASON
*****/4	3.5 miles	1200 feet/ 1648 feet	late June– October

GETTING THERE

From I-205 in Vancouver, drive east on State Highway 14 for 30 miles to Beacon Rock State

A hiker pausing by Rodney Falls

Park. Turn left (north) and drive up into the day-use parking area.

ON THE TRAIL

You'll head up the trail as if you plan to top Hamilton Mountain (Hike 123), but take your time since your route is actually shorter. You'll reach the first of the pretty waterfalls at 1.3 miles. Note the small spur trail on the right at this point. Trot down this little trail to find exquisite views of the falls.

Then head up the main trail again to reach Rodney in just another 0.1 mile. Spend a little time enjoying the splash pool and the splash Rodney makes when he jumps into the pool, before heading back the way you came.

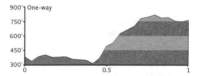

125 Beacon Rock

RATING/ DIFFICULTY	ROUND-TRIP	ELEV GAIN/ HIGH POINT	SEASON
*****/3	2 miles	550 feet/ 848 feet	February– November

Map: Green Trails No. 429 Bonneville Dam; **Contact/Permits:** Washington State Parks and Recreation, (360) 902-8844; **GPS:** N45 37.744, W122 1.312

The wild stairways of Beacon Rock

Beacon Rock earned its name when Captains Lewis and Clark camped in its shadow on their way to the Pacific Ocean in 1805. The rock is an 848-foot basalt column that formed the core of an ancient volcano. It towers over the Columbia River, and its sheer walls were unscaled until 1901—the date of the first recorded ascent of the rock. Notably, that first climb followed the route now covered by the intricate system of paths, bridges, and stairs that make up the trail today.

GETTING THERE

From I-205 in Vancouver, drive east on State Highway 14 for 30 miles to the Beacon Rock parking area on the north side of the highway. The trail is found on the south side of the highway.

ON THE TRAIL

The hike begins as a gentle walk through the forest as the trail leads hikers around to the southern face of the rock. Then the climbing begins. Traversing and climbing sheer rock walls, the trail is daunting to consider but easy to hike. The ironworks that make up the bridges and stairs are solid and well braced on the indestructible rock face. The trail was built between 1915 and 1918 by Henry Biddle, who owned the rock and all the land about it at the time.

The structures have been repaired, replaced, and reinforced in places over the years, but the trail built by Biddle is the one now used by thousands of recreationists every year. The route covers nearly a mile as it switches back and forth up the rock, but there are plenty of places folks can pause and catch their breath while enjoying the magnificent views of the Columbia River Gorge.

At the top the views are even better, and there is never any question that the climb is worth the effort, for even when the gorge is filled with rain or fog, the view is splendid, wrapped in mists and shrouded in mantles of gray.

Appendix: Conservation and Trail Organizations

Cascade Land Conservancy
615 2nd Avenue, Suite 625
Seattle, WA 98104
(206) 292-5907
info@cascadeland.org
www.cascadeland.org

Conservation Northwest
1208 Bay Street #201
Bellingham, WA 98225
(360) 671-9950
www.conservationnw.org

Issaquah Alps Trail Club
PO Box 351
Issaquah, WA 98027
www.issaquahalps.org

Mountains to Sound Greenway
911 Western Avenue, Suite 523
Seattle, WA 98104
(206) 382-5565
info@mtsgreenway.org
www.mtsgreenway.org

Sierra Club, Cascade Chapter
180 Nickerson Street, Suite 202
Seattle, WA 98109
(206) 378-0114
cascade.chapter@sierraclub.org
www.cascade.sierraclub.org

Volunteers for Outdoor Washington
8511 15th Avenue NE, Room 206
Seattle, WA 98115-3101
(206) 517-3019
info@trailvolunteers.org
www.trailvolunteers.org

Washington Trails Association
2019 3rd Avenue, Suite 100
Seattle, WA 98121
(206) 625-1367
info@wta.org
www.wta.org

Index

About the Author

Dan Nelson's personal and professional life has long focused on the great outdoors of the Pacific Northwest. After a short stint as a newspaper reporter, Dan joined the staff of the Washington Trails Association (WTA) where he worked and played for eleven years as the editor of *Washington Trails* magazine. Currently, Dan serves as the public information officer for the Olympic Region Clean Air Agency—an agency charged with ensuring the air remains clean, clear, and healthy on the beautiful Olympic Peninsula. In addition to loving to walk the wild country, Dan is an avid fly fisher, canoeist, snowshoer, telemark skier, and paraglider pilot. If he's not out enjoying the backcountry, he's indoors writing about it.

In addition to his past work at the WTA, Dan continues as a regular contributor to the *Seattle Times*, *Backpacker* magazine, and *Hooked on the Outdoors* magazine. He specializes in Northwest destinations and outdoor-equipment reviews. He is also author or editor of several outdoor guidebooks published by The Mountaineers Books. He lives in Puyallup with his partner Donna and their yellow lab, Parka (co-researcher for *Best Hikes with Dogs in Western Washington*).

About the Photographer

Alan L. Bauer is a professional freelance photographer specializing in the natural history of the Pacific Northwest and coverage of local history. He is a lifelong resident of the Pacific Northwest, having grown up on a large family farm in Oregon's Willamette Valley and now calling Washington State his home for the past 20 years. Much of his love for the outdoors can be traced back to his life outside on the farm working and playing—an experience he wouldn't trade for anything!

His work has been published in *Backpacker*, *Odyssey*, *Northwest Runner*, *Oregon Coast*, and *Northwest Travel* magazines as well as numerous publications and books across fourteen countries. He regularly provides images for projects including CD covers, textbooks, websites, presentations, research, and corporate materials. Prior to his involvement with this new book series he was co-author of *Best Desert Hikes: Washington* and *Best Dog Hikes: Inland Northwest* with The Mountaineers Books.

He resides happily in the Cascade foothills east of Seattle with his caring family and border collie. For further information and to see samples of his work, please visit www.alanbauer.com.

THE MOUNTAINEERS, founded in 1906, is a nonprofit outdoor activity and conservation club, whose mission is "to explore, study, preserve, and enjoy the natural beauty of the outdoors...." Based in Seattle, Washington, the club is now the third-largest such organization in the United States, with seven branches throughout Washington State.

The Mountaineers sponsors both classes and year-round outdoor activities in the Pacific Northwest, which include hiking, mountain climbing, ski-touring, snowshoeing, bicycling, camping, kayaking, nature study, sailing, and adventure travel. The club's conservation division supports environmental causes through educational activities, sponsoring legislation, and presenting informational programs.

All club activities are led by skilled, experienced instructors, who are dedicated to promoting safe and responsible enjoyment and preservation of the outdoors.

If you would like to participate in these organized outdoor activities or the club's programs, consider a membership in The Mountaineers. For information and an application, write or call The Mountaineers, Club Headquarters, 300 Third Avenue West, Seattle, WA 98119; 206-284-6310. You can also visit the club's website at www.mountaineers.org or contact The Mountaineers via email at clubmail@mountaineers.org.

The Mountaineers Books, an active, nonprofit publishing program of the club, produces guidebooks, instructional texts, historical works, natural history guides, and works on environmental conservation. All books produced by The Mountaineers Books fulfill the club's mission.

Send or call for our catalog of more than 500 outdoor titles:

The Mountaineers Books
1001 SW Klickitat Way, Suite 201
Seattle, WA 98134
800-553-4453
mbooks@mountaineersbooks.org
www.mountaineersbooks.org

The Mountaineers Books is proud to be a corporate sponsor of The Leave No Trace Center for Outdoor Ethics, whose mission is to promote and inspire responsible outdoor recreation through education, research, and partnerships. The Leave No Trace program is focused specifically on human-powered (nonmotorized) recreation.

Leave No Trace strives to educate visitors about the nature of their recreational impacts, as well as offer techniques to prevent and minimize such impacts. Leave No Trace is best understood as an educational and ethical program, not as a set of rules and regulations.

For more information, visit *www.LNT.org*, or call 800-332-4100.

1% for Trails & Washington Trails Association

Your favorite Washington hikes, such as those in this book, are made possible by the efforts of thousands of volunteers keeping our trails in great shape, and by hikers like you advocating for the protection of trails and wild lands. As budget cuts reduce funding for trail maintenance, Washington Trails Association's volunteer trail maintenance program fills this void and is ever more important for the future of Washington's hiking. Our mountains and forests can provide us with a lifetime of adventure and exploration—but we need trails to get us there. One percent of the sales of this guidebook goes to support WTA's efforts.

Spend a day on the trail with Washington Trails Association, and give back to the trails you love. WTA hosts over 750 work parties throughout Washington's Cascades and Olympics each year. Volunteers remove downed logs after spring snowmelt, cut away brush, retread worn stretches of trail, and build bridges and turnpikes. Find the volunteer schedule, check current conditions of the trails in this guidebook, and become a member of WTA at *www.wta.org* or (206) 625-1367.

WASHINGTON
T R A I L S
ASSOCIATION

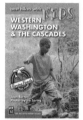